Cyberhate

Cyberhate

The Far Right in the Digital Age

Edited by
James Bacigalupo, Kevin Borgeson,
and Robin Maria Valeri

LEXINGTON BOOKS
Lanham • Boulder • New York • London

Published by Lexington Books
An imprint of The Rowman & Littlefield Publishing Group, Inc.
4501 Forbes Boulevard, Suite 200, Lanham, Maryland 20706
www.rowman.com

86-90 Paul Street, London EC2A 4NE, United Kingdom

British Library Cataloguing in Publication Information Available

Library of Congress Cataloging-in-Publication Data

Names: Bacigalupo, James, 1987– editor. | Borgeson, Kevin, editor. | Valeri, Robin
    Maria, editor.
Title: Cyberhate : the far right in the digital age / edited by James Bacigalupo, Kevin
    Borgeson, Robin Maria Valeri.
Other titles: Cyber hate
Description: Lanham : Lexington Books, 2022. | Includes index. | Summary: "Cyberhate:
    The Far-Right in the Digital Age explores the online world of right-wing political
    extremism through the propaganda, funding mechanisms, online subcultures, violent
    movements, and the ideologies that drive it"—Provided by publisher.
Identifiers: LCCN 2021045359 (print) | LCCN 2021045360 (ebook) |
    ISBN 9781793606976 (cloth) | ISBN 9781793606983 (epub)
Subjects: LCSH: Hate crimes—Law and legislation. | Cyberterrorism—Law and
    legislation. | Right-wing extremists.
Classification: LCC KZ7177.H38 C93 2022 (print) | LCC KZ7177.H38 (ebook) |
    DDC 345/.025—dc23/eng/20211013
LC record available at https://lccn.loc.gov/2021045359
LC ebook record available at https://lccn.loc.gov/2021045360

♾ ™ The paper used in this publication meets the minimum requirements of American
National Standard for Information Sciences—Permanence of Paper for Printed Library
Materials, ANSI/NISO Z39.48-1992.

Contents

Introduction

James Bacigalupo, Kevin Borgeson, and Robin Maria Valeri

Unfortunately, there is no shortage of hatred on the Internet. Technically speaking, the term "cyberhate" can be a reference to any form of hate spewed online. As the subtitle suggests, this book has a particular focus on a type of hate that has all too often transcended the World Wide Web and made its way into the physical world in the form of extremist violence. We are focusing on far-right political extremism and its relationship with the Internet. While those on the far right do not have a monopoly on Internet-based hate, they have been particularly savvy, utilizing online communications since 1984 (Berlet, 2001), and effectively putting it to use ever since. Of those who have put a definition to the concept of cyberhate, Quandt and Festl (2017) most closely describe the term as it is used throughout this book:

> various forms of online communication initiated by hate groups with the purpose of attracting new members, building and strengthening group identity, coordinating group action, distributing propagandistic messages and indoctrination, provoking counterreactions as part of propagandistic campaigns, and attacking societal groups and individuals with hateful messages. (p. 1)

We would modify this definition slightly to recognize that it is not just hate groups that initiate the communication; it may also be individuals advocating on behalf of a political ideology or movement. The necessity of this project was made clear after a series of deadly far-right attacks that had an indisputable link to the Internet. *Cyberhate: The Far Right in the Digital Age* explores how right-wing extremists operate in cyberspace by examining their propaganda, funding, subcultures, movements, offline violence, ideologies, as well as the legal and cultural responses to its presence.

The book begins with Dr. Michael Hoffman explaining what cyberspace is, and how it works. This chapter provides a basic understanding of a range of topics including threats and protective measures encountered in cyberspace. In chapter 2, Dr. Robin Valeri examines the difficulty in recognizing extremist content online, and the psychological processes that explain how this deception works. The legality of cyberhate is explored by Janine Fodor in chapter 3. She discusses the applicability and limitations of criminal and civil law in relation to various forms of cyberhate. The use of bitcoin in funding far-right content creators is thoroughly analyzed by John Bambenek in chapter 4. He includes a description of popular far-right commentators, groups, and channels that are funded via bitcoin.

The book then moves to some of the most extreme movements on the Internet, focusing on specific groups, individuals, and their acts of violence. Unlike the propaganda that Dr. Valeri covered in chapter 2, Atomwaffen Division is a neo-Nazi terrorist group that is very direct in their messaging. In chapter 5, Dr. Michael Loadenthal, Samantha Hausserman, and Matthew Thierry conduct both a visual and textual analysis of the group's propaganda, and explain "accelerationism," the strategy that Atomwaffen hopes will bring about the collapse of the U.S. government.

Relying heavily on the manifestos and other correspondence posted on the Internet by recent perpetrators of mass murder, chapter 6, authored by Dr. Kevin Borgeson and James Bacigalupo, explains how the concept of "white genocide" and the misogynist incel ideology have motivated recent deadly violence. In this chapter, relevant theories are presented to explain why these individuals may have taken the path of violence. This is followed by chapter 7, where Bacigalupo and Dr. Borgeson focus on the alt-right, an online far-right movement that was unique in its ability to break into the mainstream. This chapter includes a content analysis of alt-right preferred webpages. The book concludes with Bacigalupo discussing the response to cyberhate, focusing on issues such as censorship, law enforcement's role, and the current political climate that extremism is thriving in.

REFERENCES

Berlet, C. (2001, April). When hate went online. Paper presented at the Northeast Sociological Association Spring Conference, Fairfield, CT.

Quandt, T., & Festl, R. (2017). Cyberhate. In P. Rössler (Ed.), *The international encyclopedia of media effects*. Malden: Wiley-Blackwell.

Chapter 1

Welcome to Cyberspace

Michael Hoffman

Welcome to cyberspace! As we enter the third decade of the second millennium, the world of cyberspace is having an increasingly profound impact upon our lives. Much of this impact has undoubtedly been positive. Indeed, cyberspace has provided a medium to support beneficial research, helped connect people from around the globe, and has made information readily accessible to billions of people. There is, however, a dark side to cyberspace. Cyberspace has been used by individuals and groups to spread cyberhate (Coliandris, 2012). It has also enabled cyberbullying and has resulted in numerous breaches of individual privacy. Cyberspace is much like the real world, with both benevolent and malicious actors at work. This chapter will serve as an introduction to cyberspace, including defining what is meant by the term "cyberspace," providing a basic understanding of how cyberspace works, detailing a review of how we navigate cyberspace, examining the role social media plays in cyberspace, and finally discussing the threats and protective measures encountered in cyberspace.

CYBERSPACE—WHAT IS IT?

Before we delve more deeply into the ramifications of our increasing reliance on cyberspace, we should first define what cyberspace is, and what it is not. First, cyberspace is not the Internet. The Internet is a set of computers and other electronic devices that communicate using Internet Protocol (IP) (Moschovitis et al., 1999). Cyberspace, by contrast, can be thought of as the information contained by all of the devices connected to the Internet. Cyberspace is made possible by the Internet, but they are not synonymous. Similarly, the World Wide Web is also not the same as cyberspace. The

World Wide Web is a system that allows for the nonlinear storage, indexing, and retrieval of information using Hypertext Transfer Protocol (HTTP) and Hypertext Markup Language (HTML) (Moschovitis et al., 1999). For example, websites such as ESPN.com and CNN.com are part of the World Wide Web. As such, the World Wide Web is part of cyberspace, but cyberspace includes much more. As previously mentioned, cyberspace is inclusive of all of the information accessible via the Internet. Certainly websites on the World Wide Web are included in cyberspace but so too would information stored on mobile devices such as smartphones, wearable technology including fitness trackers, and Internet-connected appliances. Yes, your smart television is part of cyberspace!

Our video and voice calls can also be contained within cyberspace. Two of the most popular video-conferencing applications, Microsoft's Skype and Apple's FaceTime, utilize the Internet to make and receive calls between devices. These applications, and others like them, allow for high-quality, real-time video connections between users around the globe. Most only require an Internet connection and are free to use, and have thus become increasingly popular. Skype, for instance, boasted approximately 300 million unique monthly users as of May 2019 (Smith, 2019). As Skype and FaceTime utilize the Internet, they too can be thought of as part of cyberspace.

There are two other notable components of cyberspace that require discussion: the deep web and the dark web. The deep web is defined as "the part of the web that is hidden from view" (Chertoff & Simon, 2014, p. 8). While the World Wide Web is indexed and searchable, the information on the deep web is not. Examples of deep web content might include the medical records stored by a hospital, banking information, and even the contents of your email account. Think of cyberspace as an iceberg. The portion one can see contains the World Wide Web and content that is easily searched and accessed. Some refer to this as the surface web. The deep web is the portion of the iceberg below the water. The size of the deep web is difficult to estimate precisely due to its very nature of being difficult to navigate. A commonly cited, albeit antiquated, reference pins the deep web at 400 to 550 times larger than the surface web (Bergman, 2001). Again, no one knows precisely how large the deep web really is; however, most agree it is far, far larger than the surface web.

The dark web can be thought of as a subset of the deep web and is defined as "a part of the deep web that has been intentionally hidden and is inaccessible through standard Web browsers" (Chertoff & Simon, 2014, p. 7). The dark web is typically accessed through a special, encrypted browser known as Tor and provides for anonymous activity. Some utilize the anonymity of the dark web for benign purposes like challenging a corrupt regime (Chertoff & Simon, 2014). Others, however, use the dark web to obfuscate nefarious activities such as trading in illegal drugs and identity theft (Chertoff & Simon, 2014). More on this later, but for now keep in mind that cyberspace is inclusive of all of the information contained on Internet-connected devices including the World Wide Web, the deep web, and the dark web.

Cyberspace continues to grow in scope. Indeed, from 2009 to 2018 global participation in the Internet grew from 24% to 51% (Meeker, 2019). Much of this growth is being driven by Asian countries with China and India having the first and second largest number of Internet-connected users in the world, respectively (Meeker, 2019). In the United States, the number of users of wearable technology doubled from 25 million users to 52 million from 2014 to 2018 (Meeker, 2019). This explosive growth of connected people and devices has resulted in a similar growth in the information that makes up cyberspace. The 2018 International Data Corporation report predicts that cyberspace will grow from 33 zettabytes of information in 2018 to 175 in 2025 (Reinsel et al., 2018). How large is a zettabyte? One zettabyte is equivalent to one trillion gigabytes. To better put that number into perspective, a zettabyte equivalent of books would amount to 10,000 books per living person on the planet ("Infographic: Just How Big Is a Zettabyte?," 2013).

NAVIGATING CYBERSPACE AROUND THE GLOBE

With this tremendous amount of information and content the question of how to effectively navigate cyberspace becomes paramount. One component of cyberspace, the World Wide Web, was designed to be indexed and easily searched. Over the years a battle for this search traffic has been fought by companies such as Microsoft, Yahoo, and Google. In the United States, the battle for World Wide Web search traffic has largely been won by Google, with Google claiming 87% of World Wide Web search market share in 2018 (Capala, 2019). Google's success has been replicated in many other countries, including Japan with 70%, Germany with 93%, the UK with 90%, and India with 97% of search market share in 2018 (Capala, 2019). The story is far different, however, in the world's most populated Internet-connected country. Indeed, in China Google's search market share in 2018 was a paltry 1.47% (Capala, 2019). Rather the search market in China is dominated by Baidu with 70% and Shenma with 19% in 2018 (Capala, 2019). Why has Google struggled to compete in China? One chief reason may be the censorship requirements the Chinese government places on search engines. The censorship of search results in China is colloquially referred to as "the Great Firewall of China" (Simonite, 2019).

While searching and navigating the World Wide Web is relatively easy and straightforward, the same cannot be said for many of the other components of cyberspace. Indeed, the deep web is not, by its very design, indexed or searchable (Chertoff & Simon, 2014). And rightly so! I doubt any of us would appreciate our emails being indexed and searchable via Google. Similarly, patient medical and customer banking records also should not be readily accessible to the public. Navigation of the deep web is done in a purposeful way by those who know the data they are looking for and have the proper means to access said data.

The dark web is, as previously mentioned, that portion of the deep web that is intentionally hidden and is inaccessible through standard web browsers (Chertoff & Simon, 2014). A special browser known as Tor will allow users to access encrypted dark web content (Chertoff & Simon, 2014). The U.S. Naval Research Laboratory created TOR as a "tool for anonymously communicating online" (Weimann, 2016, p. 40). The Tor browser allows users to browse the dark web in near anonymity by forwarding encrypted traffic through a series of routers known as onions (Chertoff & Simon, 2014). The TOR browser "relies upon a network of volunteer computers to route users' web traffic through a series of other users' computers so that the traffic cannot be traced to the original user" (Weimann, 2016, p. 40). The dark web is not readily searchable. There have been search engines developed for use in the dark web, but they are very limited in their usefulness (Weimann, 2016). Generally speaking, however, one must know where to find a dark website in order to access it directly (Weimann, 2016).

The level on anonymity, the security afforded by encryption, and the inability for general users of the surface web to access it make the dark web an ideal tool for those trafficking in illicit or illegal activities. For example, a great deal of anti-Semitic activity takes place on the dark web (Topor, 2020). International and regional terrorist organizations have made use of the dark web to communicate among members and spread propaganda (Weimann, 2016). White nationalist groups have also used the dark web in support of their activities. For example, after being banned by Google and GoDaddy, the neo-Nazi propaganda site *The Daily Stormer* moved to the dark web (Robertson, 2017). Indeed, in a 2017 article in *The Guardian*, Hern posited that the "Anonymity network Tor has become a safe-space for white supremacists" (p. 1). While there are undoubtedly many benign uses of the dark web, particularly for those seeking to use cyberspace without fear of repression, the very nature of the dark web system will continue to draw activity from white nationalists and others seeking protection and anonymity from authorities.

SOCIAL MEDIA

Social media activity and content make up another significant portion of cyberspace. According to the report "Demographics of Social Media Users and Adoption in the United States" by the Pew Research Center (2019), social media adoption in the United States has grown from 5% of adults in 2005 to 72% by the start of 2019. Pew reported that as of February 2019 the most popular social media services in the United States were YouTube with 73% of U.S. adult users, Facebook with 69%, Instagram with 37%, Pinterest with 28%, LinkedIn with 27%, and Snapchat with 24%. Social media penetration worldwide was reported at 45% as of January 2019 (Carter, 2019).

Social media usage varies greatly around the world. For example, a study performed by Addthis (Booth, 2019) found that WhatsApp, a messaging services, was far more popular than Facebook in countries like Brazil and India. While usage rates and the popularity of various social media platforms vary from country to country, the nature of social media competition in China is radically different. The most popular social media network in China is WeChat, a messaging app that combines features found in networks like Facebook, Instagram, and Skype (DeGennaro, 2019). Indeed, none of the popular aforementioned social media networks including Facebook, Instagram, and LinkedIn crack the top ten most used social media networks in China (DeGennaro, 2019). The censorship demands placed upon Western social media companies by the Chinese government is one reason why the social media landscape in China looks much different. Even though the social media networks are different in China, usage of social media is every bit as strong in China as in other countries with the average Chinese user spending two hours per day on social media compared with 2.1 hours for U.S. users (Kemp, 2019).

In Russia and several former Eastern Bloc countries, VKontakte is the social media network of choice. VKontakte, also known as VK, is used by 83% of social media users in Russia. Facebook, by contrast, only has a 39% share in Russia (Prins, 2019). VK is very similar to Facebook in that it allows users to post pictures, videos, and manage social contacts. VK was designed to appeal to Russian and Eastern European users. In fact, VK was banned by the Ukraine in 2017 as part of economic sanctions against Russia (Oliphant, 2017). Yet as of late 2018 VK still remained in the top five most visited online services in the Ukraine (2018).

While virtually all social media networks operate on the basis of connecting people, they do have significant differences in the manner in which they connect people. YouTube, the most popular social media network in the United States, is primarily a video sharing platform. Founded in 2005, YouTube now has approximately two billion monthly users worldwide (Spangler, 2019). Facebook was founded by Mark Zuckerberg with the original purpose of connecting Harvard University students, which was then expanded to other college campuses. Facebook allows people to stay connected by adding friends to their social network, sharing pictures, and updating friends on one's activities. Facebook now has over 43,000 employees and boasts approximately 2.45 billion monthly users worldwide (Noyes, 2020). Instagram, a social network owned by Facebook, is used primarily to share pictures and other media between friend groups and with the general public. As of July 2019 over 50 billion photos had been shared via Instagram (Aslam, 2020a). Pinterest is a social network that allows users to easily curate lists of Internet resources to be shared with a network of friends or with the public. This is done by "pinning" an Internet source to one or more Pinterest boards controlled by the user. There had been a total of 200 billion "pins" as of March of 2019 (Aslam, 2020b). While each of these networks connects users in different ways, their scope and reach are undeniably impressive. This has drawn many advertisers to utilize social media networks to reach their customers. It also serves as an extremely effective means for individuals, groups, and organizations to distribute their messaging.

Social media's ability to connect people has proven enormously popular. Indeed, the very goal of social media is to enable people to be social (Rosen, 2012). Social media has given people an outlet to express themselves, connected people across great distances, and has allowed new ways for customers to interact with corporations. There have been, however, many downsides to the adoption of social media. Rosen (2012) argues that the very nature of social media encourages narcissistic behavior in its users by asking them, for example, to find the perfect profile picture, update their statuses on a regular basis, and select who one's friends should be.

While social media may encourage narcissistic behaviors, there are even darker uses that have caused significant societal issues, such as cyberbullying (Freitas, 2017). Social media can provide an extremely effective forum for cyberbullying, particularly for younger people (Freitas, 2017). In fact, the world of social media "can be soul-crushing for a child or young adult, humiliating in a way that is so severe they cannot see beyond it, so horrific they cannot find a way to survive it" (Freitas, 2017, p. 146). Many teens have committed suicide as a result of cyberbullying, and it remains a significant downside to our infatuation with social media networks (Freitas, 2017).

Another malicious use of social media is the propensity for the networks to be used to promulgate cyberhate. Hate speech can be defined as "an expression of hostility toward individuals or social groups based on their perceived group membership, which can refer to their race, ethnicity, nationality, religion, disability, gender or sexual orientation" (Bojarska, 2019, p. 2). Social media, such as Facebook, has enabled users to "contribute to dissemination of prejudice, fake news and hostility against refugees or other marginalized groups on an unprecedented scale" (Bojarska, 2019, p. 1). While social media is not responsible for cyberhate it certainly provides a technology platform that enables this type of activity.

Of particular concern to many governments and law enforcement agencies is the development and inclusion of encrypted communications tools within social media networks. Facebook, for example, plans to encrypt its Facebook Messenger chat service (Wright, 2019). This enhancement would serve to increase privacy for users of Facebook's Messenger service. Encryption would also, however, make it difficult, if not impossible, for law enforcement or other third parties to access communications between two or more parties. There is significant concern that this could make criminal activity more difficult to discover and will hamper prosecutions. For example, Musotto and Wall (2019) posit that "Facebook's push for end-to-end encryption is good news for user privacy, as well as terrorists and pedophiles" (p. 1). Encryption could potentially make illicit activity much more difficult to uncover, as the communications would be almost impossible for a third party to access. Indeed, the social media network Telegram, a social media service that supports encrypted communications, was "widely adopted by ISIS and its affiliates globally" (Shehabat et al., 2017, p. 27). Furthermore, the Islamic State (IS) terrorist organization used Telegram to encourage "lone wolf" terrorist attacks in the United States and other Western European countries (Shehabat et al., 2017). There is well-founded concern that a greater proliferation of encrypted communications tools in the most popular social media applications will make policing illicit activities such as pedophilia, cyberhate, and terrorism much more difficult. The juxtaposition is that these encryption technologies also improve privacy and increase security for law-abiding citizens.

Perhaps the most infamous use of social media was the extent to which Russia used social media networks, including Facebook, in an attempt to manipulate the 2016 U.S. presidential election. Indeed, Confessore and Wakabayashi (2017) assert that during the campaign "Russian agents harvested posts and videos from Americans and used them on social media to sow division" (p. 1). Russian agents are alleged to have created a number of Facebook pages such as the "Defend the 2nd" gun rights group and a group supporting lesbian/gay/bisexual/trans rights (Isaac & Shane, 2017). These pages, and many others, are believed by the Federal Bureau of Investigation (FBI) to have been created and used by Russian agents to spread fake news, create confusion, and stir dissent among U.S. citizens in the run-up to the 2016 presidential election (Isaac & Shane, 2017). Facebook took steps to identify and remove this type of activity and increased its efforts in an attempt to prevent similar activity from happening prior to the 2020 U.S. presidential election (Wong, 2019).

THREATS AND DEFENSES IN CYBERSPACE

Unfortunately cyberspace is replete with threats and bad actors. In the beginning, many of the most common threats in cyberspace were nuisances. Computer viruses and worms (viruses designed to self-replicate) were often designed to slow down computers or incapacitate them in other ways. While these attacks could be very disruptive and at the very least annoying, the consequences of infection were not terribly serious compared with the threat landscape faced today. Indeed, while cybercrime used to be primarily malicious, today cybercrime is big business (Zetlin, 2018). Cybercrime was estimated to cost the global economy 800 billion dollars in 2017, up from 500 billion dollars in 2014. Today's cybercriminals do not want to slow a victim's computer down or inconvenience said victim in any way unless there is money to be made from doing so.

While it is not within the scope of this chapter to provide an in-depth exploration of cybercrime, we will review some of the most common types of threats. Many cyberattacks are essentially malicious software distributed to unsuspecting users in the guise of a legitimate email or similar communication, also known as phishing. This malicious software, once unwittingly downloaded by the host, will often seek valuable information that can be stolen and sent back to the origination of the attack. This information may include banking records, medical records, or other types of personally identifiable information. This information can then be used by the attacker to gain access to secured systems or can be sold on the dark web. Credit card information and other personally identifiable information can fetch hundreds or even thousands of dollars on the dark web (Canner, 2018). This profit motive is what drives many of today's cybercriminals.

Another increasingly common threat is malicious software that will encrypt, or virtually lock, a computer system. The computer system can then be unlocked by paying a ransom to the attacker. This practice is known as ransomware (Richardson & North, 2017). It is another method cybercriminals use cyberspace to generate income. While some ransomware attacks are perpetrated against individuals, many criminals launch these attacks against business and organizations. Why has this activity shifted toward corporations and other large organizations? Similar to the quote attributed to the famous criminal Willie Sutton, "I rob banks because that's where the money is," cybercriminals target these organizations due to their capacity to pay larger ransoms (Richardson & North, 2017). As long as individuals and organizations pay these ransoms these types of attacks will continue.

Some of these types of attacks are leveraged by digital activists. The hacking, or seeking unauthorized access to a computer system, that is perpetrated for political or social objectives is what is commonly thought of as hacktivism (Jordan, 2002). Perhaps the most famous, or infamous, hacktivist group is Anonymous. Anonymous is a decentralized group of hacktivists that have engaged in high-profile cyberattacks for various political or ideological reasons. For example, Anonymous claimed to have shut down several websites used by white supremacist groups after the deadly events in Charlottesville,

Virginia, in 2017 (McGoogan & Molloy, 2017). Anonymous often employs distributed denial of service attacks, or DDoS, to shut down organizational websites (Ryan, 2011). These DDoS attacks often leverage large numbers of infected computers, also known as botnets, which can be remotely controlled to flood a website with traffic which essentially shuts the website down (Deseriis, 2017).

When we think of threats in cyberspace we have a tendency to think of targets such as computers, data, and websites. The unfortunate reality, however, is that threats in cyberspace can include targets in the real world. Indeed, as the Internet of Things expands there is a greater and greater risk that cyberattacks will target real-world infrastructure. The Internet of Things is the name given for the propensity for a wide variety of everyday objects to be connected to the Internet and, thus, act as part of cyberspace. For example, there are Internet-connected televisions, refrigerators, video-enabled door-bells, ovens, and even thermostats (Hossain et al., 2015). As more devices are connected to cyberspace the risk of an attack grows. Some attacks may be to compromise these devices to gather information and pose a risk to personal privacy (Hossain et al., 2015). Large numbers of compromised Internet of Things devices could also be used as a botnet to perpetrate an attack else-where in cyberspace.

While the prospect of having one's toaster oven succumb to a cyberat-tack may not seem particularly catastrophic, consider how other, much more critical infrastructure is connected to cyberspace. What if a cyberattack was successfully perpetrated on the U.S. electrical grid? The U.S. Department of Homeland Security's Cybersecurity and Infrastructure Security Agency (CISA) lists 16 critical infrastructure sectors of such importance that the "inca-pacitation or destruction would have a debilitating effect on security, national economic security, national public health or safety, or any combination thereof" (Cybersecurity and Infrastructure Security Agency, n.d., p. 1). These critical infrastructure sectors include communications, dams, transportation, and water systems (Cybersecurity and Infrastructure Security Agency, n.d). In 2013, a hacker associated with the Iranian government targeted a small dam in Rye Brook, New York (Kutner, 2016). The Rye Brook Dam systems happened to be in a maintenance mode during the attack, which prevented the attacker from causing damage including potentially raising or lowering the dam's flood gates (Kutner, 2016). Additionally, a report in *The New York Times*, citing FBI sources, suggests cyberattacks are being perpetrated on nuclear power facilities including an attack on the Wolf Creek Nuclear Operating Corporation, which operates a nuclear power plant in Kansas (Perlroth, 2017). The threat of cyberattacks has made cyber defense of critical national infra-structure an important issue for organizations and nations (Maglaras et al., 2019).

While the prospect of direct attacks on critical infrastructure is alarming, there have been no reports of large-scale successful attacks in this area. Cyberterrorists have, however, been successful in using other attack vectors in cyberspace. Attacks in cyberspace are being seen as an increasingly important element in the conflict between terrorist groups and nation-states (Banks, 2017). In 2015 Ardit Ferizi, a citizen of Kosovo, was arrested and charged with "providing material support to the IS, computer hacking and identity theft, all in conjunction with the theft and release of personally identifiable information belonging to 1,351 U.S. service members" (Stewart, 2015, p. 1). This information was stolen by Ferizi via a cyberattack he perpetrated on a large U.S. retail chain (Stewart, 2015). He then supplied this information directly to the IS, which then used this information to threaten the United States (Stewart, 2015). While surely governments and other organizations are boosting their defenses against cyberterrorism, efforts are hampered by a general belief that acts of terrorism are limited to actions in the physical world with physical consequences (Banks, 2017).

In the United States, the administration of President Trump has taken several steps to boost cybersecurity defenses. In 2017 an executive order was signed to strengthen the cybersecurity defenses of federal networks and other critical infrastructure (Exec. Order No. 13,800, 2017). Another executive order was signed in 2019 to strengthen the U.S. cybersecurity workforce (Vincent, 2019). This includes the creation of a "President's Cup" competition to "challenge and reward the government's top cyber personnel" (Vincent, 2019, p. 1). The recent tension with Iran also has the U.S. government bracing for potential Iranian cyberattacks (Marks, 2020). It has become apparent that cyber defenses are a critical component to a nation-state's overall defensive posture, and this is likely to become increasingly important as cyberattacks become even more sophisticated.

REFERENCES

Aslam, S. (2020a, January 13). Instagram by the numbers: Stats, demographics & fun facts. *Omnicore*. Retrieved from https://www.omnicoreagency.com/instagram-statistics/

Aslam, S. (2020b, January 6). Pinterest by the numbers: Stats, demographics & fun facts. *Omnicore*. Retrieved from https://www.omnicoreagency.com/pinterest-statistics/

Banks, W. C. (2017). Developing norms for cyber conflict. In Ohlin, J. D. Editor (Eds.), *Research Handbook on Remote Warfare*. Edward Elgar Publishing.

Banned social network VKontakte remains the fourth most popular Internet site in Ukraine (2018, September 15). Retrieved from https://blogs.elenasmodels.com/en/vk-vkontakte-ukraine/

Bergman, M. K. (2001). White paper: The deep web: Surfacing hidden value. *The Journal of Electronic Publishing, 7*(1).

Bojarska, K. (2019). The dynamics of hate speech and counter speech in the social media: Summary of scientific research. *Centre for Internet and Human Rights.* Retrieved from https://cihr.eu/wp-content/uploads/2018/10/The-dynamics-of-hate -speech-and-counter-speech-in-the-social-media_English-1.pdf

Booth, J. (2019, June 6). Most popular social media platforms around the world. *AddThis.* Retrieved from https://www.addthis.com/blog/2019/06/06/most-popular -social-media-platforms-around-the-world/

Canner, B. (2018, March 22). By the numbers: Armor's black market report looks onside the dark web. *Solutions Review.* Retrieved from https://solutionsreview .com/endpoint-security/numbers-armors-black-market-report-look-inside-dark -web/

Capala, M. (2019, February 12). Global search engine market share for 2018 in the Top 15 GDP Nations. *Alphametic.* Retrieved from https://alphametic.com/global -search-engine-market-share

Carter, J. (2019, October 25). Global social media research summary 2019. *Smart Insights.* Retrieved from https://www.smartinsights.com/social-media-marketing/ social-media-strategy/new-global-social-media-research/

Chertoff, M., & Simon, T. (2015). The impact of the dark web on internet governance and cyber security. *Global Commission on Internet Governance.* Retrieved from https://www.cigionline.org/sites/default/files/gcig_paper_no6.pdf

Coliandris, G. (2012). Hate in a cyber age. In Blakemore, B., & Awan. I. (Eds.), *Policing Cyber Hate, Cyber Threats and Cyber Terrorism* (pp. 75–94). Farnham: Ashgate.

Confessore, N., & Wakabayashi, D. (2017, October 17). How Russia harvested American rage to reshape US politics. *New York Times.* Retrieved from https:// www.nytimes.com/2017/10/09/technology/russia-election-facebook-ads-rage.html

Cybersecurity and Infrastructure Security Agency (CISA). (n.d.). Critical infrastructure sectors. *Department of Homeland Security.* Retrieved from https://www.cisa .gov/critical-infrastructure-sectors

DeGennaro, T. (2019, September 18). The 10 most popular social media sites in China (2019). *Dragon Social.* Retrieved from https://www.dragonsocial.net/blog /social-media-in-china/

Demographics of Social Media Users and Adoption in the United States (2019, June 12). *Pew Research Center.* Retrieved from https://www.pewresearch.org/internet/ fact-sheet/social-media/

Deseriis, M. (2017). Hacktivism: On the use of botnets in cyberattacks. *Theory, Culture & Society, 34*(4), 131–152.

Exec. Order No. 13800, 82 FR 22391 (May 11, 2017).

Freitas, D. (2017). *The happiness effect: How social media is driving a generation to appear perfect at any cost.* Oxford University Press.

Hern, A. (2017, August 23). The dilemma of the dark web: Protecting neo-Nazis and dissidents alike. *The Guardian.* Retrieved from https://www.theguardian.com /technology/2017/aug/23/dark-web-neo-nazis-tor-dissidents-white-supremacists -criminals-paedophile-rings

Hossain, M. M., Fotouhi, M., & Hasan, R. (2015). Towards an analysis of security issues, challenges, and open problems in the internet of things. In *IEEE World Congress on Services* (pp. 21–28).

Infographic: Just how big is a zettabyte? (2013, January 14). *Economy Watch.* Retrieved from https://www.economywatch.com/in-the-news/infographic-just -how-big-is-a-zettabyte.14-01.html

Isaac, M., & Shane, S. (2017, October 2). Facebook's Russia-linked Ads came in many disguises. *New York Times.* Retrieved from https://www.nytimes.com/2017 /10/02/technology/facebook-russia-ads-.html

Jordan, T. (2002). *Activism!: Direct action, hacktivism and the future of society.* Reaktion Books.

Kemp, S. (2019, January 30). People spend 1/7 of their waking lives on social media (and other stats). *Hootsuit.* Retrieved from https://blog.hootsuite.com/simon-kemp -social-media/

Kutner, M. (2016, March 30). Alleged dam hacking raises fears of cyber threats to infrastructure. *Newsweek.* Retrieved from https://www.newsweek.com/cyber -attack-rye-dam-iran-441940

Maglaras, L., Ferrag, M. A., Derhab, A., Mukherjee, M., Janicke, H., & Rallis, S. (2019). Threats, protection and attribution of cyber attacks on critical infrastruc- tures. arXiv preprint arXiv:1901.03899.

Marks, J. (2020, January 13). The cybersecurity 202: Get ready for serious cyberat- tacks from Iran, experts say. *The Washington Post.* Retrieved from https://www .washingtonpost.com/news/powerpost/paloma/the-cybersecurity-202/2020/01/13 /the-cybersecurity-202-get-ready-for-serious-cyberattacks-from-iran-experts-say /5e1b7ef288e0fa2262dcbc70/

McGoogan, C., & Molloy, M. (2017, August 14). Anonymous shuts down neo-Nazi and KKK websites after Charlottesville rally. *The Telegraph.* Retrieved from http://www.telegraph.co.uk/technology/2017/08/14/anonymous-shuts-neo-nazi -kkk-websites-charlottesville-rally/

Meeker, M. (2019). Internet trends 2019. *Bond.* Retrieved from https://www.bondcap .com/report/itr19/#view/1

Moschovitis, C. J., Poole, H., Schuyler, T., & Senft, T. M. (1999). *History of the internet: A chronology, 1843 to the present.* ABC-CLIO, Incorporated.

Musotto, R., & Wall, D. S. (2019, December 17). Facebook's push for end-to-end encryption is good news for user privacy, as well as terrorists and pedophiles. *The Conversation.* Retrieved from http://theconversation.com/facebooks-push-for-end -to-end-encryption-is-good-news-for-user-privacy-as-well-as-terrorists-and-pae- dophiles-128782

Noyes, D. (2020, January 6). Top 20 Facebook statistics—Updated January 2020. *Zephoria.* Retrieved from https://zephoria.com/top-15-valuable-facebook -statistics/

Oliphant, R. (2017, May 16). Ukraine bans Russian social networks in sweeping expansion of sanctions. *The Telegraph.* Retrieved from https://www.telegraph.co .uk/news/2017/05/16/ukraine-bans-russian-social-networks-sweeping-expansion -sanctions/

Perlroth, N. (2017, July 6). Hackers are targeting nuclear facilities, Homeland Security Dept. and F.B.I. Say. *The New York Times*. Retrieved from https://www.nytimes.com/2017/07/06/technology/nuclear-plant-hack-report.html

Prins, N. (2019). An analysis of the Russian social media landscape in 2019. Retrieved from https://www.linkfluence.com/blog/russian-social-media-landscape

Reinsel, D., Gantz, J., & Rydning, J. (2018). The digitization of the world: From edge to core. *International Data Corporation*. Retrieved from https://www.seagate.com/files/www-content/our-story/trends/files/idc-seagate-dataage-whitepaper.pdf

Richardson, R., & North, M. M. (2017). Ransomware: Evolution, mitigation and prevention. *International Management Review*, *13*(1), 10–21.

Robertson, A. (2017, August 15). Neo-Nazi site moves to dark web after GoDaddy and Google bans. *The Verge*. Retrieved from https://www.theverge.com/2017/8/15/16150668/daily-stormer-alt-right-dark-web-site-godaddy-google-ban

Rosen, L. D. (2012). *IDisorder: Understanding our dependency on technology and overcoming our addiction*. New York: Palgrave Macmillan.

Shehabat, A., Mitew, T., & Alzoubi, Y. (2017). Encrypted jihad: Investigating the role of telegram app in lone wolf attacks in the West. *Journal of Strategic Security*, *10*(3), 27–53.

Simonite, T. (2019, June 3). US companies help censor the internet in China, too. *Wired*. Retrieved from https://www.wired.com/story/us-companies-help-censor-internet-china/

Smith, C. (2019, September 6). 26 amazing Skype statistics and facts. *DMR*. Retrieved from https://expandedramblings.com/index.php/skype-statistics/

Spangler, T. (2019, May 3). YouTube now has 2 billion monthly users, who watch 250 million hours on tv screens daily. *Variety*. Retrieved from https://variety.com/2019/digital/news/youtube-2-billion-users-tv-screen-watch-time-hours-1203204267/

Stewart, S. (2015, October 22). The coming age of cyberterrorism. *Stratfor*. Retrieved from https://worldview.stratfor.com/article/coming-age-cyberterrorism

Topor, L. (2020). Dark hatred: Antisemitism on the dark web. *Journal of Contemporary Antisemitism*, *2*(2), 25–42.

Vincent, B. (2019, May 2). Trump signs executive order to boost federal cyber workforce. *Nextgov*. Retrieved from https://www.nextgov.com/cybersecurity/2019/05/trump-signs-executive-order-boost-federal-cyber-workforce/156709/

Weimann, G. (2016). Terrorist migration to the dark web. *Perspectives on Terrorism*, *10*(3), 40–45.

Wong, J. C. (2019, October 21). Facebook discloses operations by Russia and Iran to meddle in 2020 election. *The Guardian*. Retrieved from https://www.theguardian.com/technology/2019/oct/21/facebook-us-2020-elections-foreign-interference-russia

Wright, M. (2019, December 11). Social media encryption now "biggest challenge" to keeping children safe online, global watchdog warns. *The Telegraph*. Retrieved from https://www.telegraph.co.uk/news/2019/12/11/social-media-encryption-now-biggest-challenge-keeping-children/

Zetlin, M. (2018). Once purely malicious, cybercrime is now big business. *Oracle*. Retrieved from https://blogs.oracle.com/profit/once-purely-malicious-cybercrime-is-now-big-business

Chapter 2

Looks Can Be Deceiving

The Challenges of Recognizing Hate in Cyberspace

Robin Maria Valeri

Can you recognize hate and extremism, someone who is an extremist, or a hate website? While I am confident that most of us would answer yes to these questions and also that most of us think we can do so easily, looks can be deceiving. Take this example, from real life, about a credible organization, the American Historical Society, being deceived by a seemingly credible person.

In February 2017 *The American Historical Review*, the official scholarly journal of the American Historical Society, published a review by Raymond Wolters, PhD, of the book *Making the Unequal Metropolis: School Desegregation and Its Limits* by Ansley T. Erickson. Wolters's review concluded with the statement "Like most historians and social scientists, Erickson says nothing about sociobiology" (Wolters, 2017, p. 211). In response to the publication of Wolters's review *The American Historical Review* received many "Letters to the Editor" criticizing the organization not only for publishing Wolters's review but also, and perhaps more shockingly, for having invited Wolters to review the book. The reason for their consternation, and as stated by one letter writer, is that "Wolters is an avowed white supremacist" (Scribner, 2017, p. 637). What alerted many readers of Wolters's book review to his prejudicial attitudes was his reference to sociobiology, which as one letter writer noted meant "eugenics" (Connolly, 2017, p. 638) and another described as "this twenty-first-century version of scientific racism" (Petrzela, 2017, p. 639).

The question is, how or why did *The American Historical Review* come to invite someone with racist views to write a book review for their journal?

Robert A. Schneider (2017), who was then serving as the interim editor of *The American Historical Review*, in responding to these criticisms wrote,

> I have reviewed the process by which he [Wolters] was placed on our "pick list" of potential reviewers, and I have been reassured that we were not aware of his publicly aired and published views when he was selected. His university webpage reveals him to be a legitimate scholar with a fairly long and solid publication record; our database also confirmed his status as an academic who has published in credible scholarly venues. It is absolutely true, of course, that a little more digging would have turned up evidence that would have—and has—discredited him as a legitimate scholar. Regrettably, we did not dig further. (Schneider, 2017, p. 639)

Schneider's response highlights three salient points. First, *The American Historical Review*, like many of us (Shearer, 2021), turned to the web for information. Second, Wolters has solid academic credentials. Specifically, Wolters has a doctorate, was associated with a legitimate academic institution, and had a record of scholarship—all of which lent him an air of credibility. Third, *The American Historical Review* chose not to dig further than his university webpage and their own database. Thus they chose not to invest the time and effort to more carefully scrutinize Wolters. As noted by Schneider, had *The American Historical Review* invested the time, they would have learned of Wolters's racist views and not have made this error. Instead they relied on his credentials and dug no further. These last two points were reiterated by Alex Lichtenstein (2017), the editor of *The American Historical Review*, in response to Wolters's own defense of his book review. Lichtenstein, like Schneider, recognizes Wolters's academic credentials but also notes how his credentials and use of scholarly language can be used to hide his white supremacist views. Lichtenstein wrote,

> I can't put it more bluntly than this: in the guise of a book review, and cloaked in what he [Wolters] now claims to be the scholarly language of evolutionary biology, Wolters advanced a view more appropriate for the pages of white supremacist publications like American Renaissance—his usual outlet. . . . It is, of course, entirely within Professor Wolters's rights to air such ideas openly if he can find a place willing to publish them. . . . we would never presume to tell Wolters to stop publishing his discredited white nationalist views elsewhere; but neither does it require the AHR to help him promote them as if they were based on real scholarship. (Lichtenstein, 2017, p. 1386)

Both Schneider's and Lichtenstein's responses highlight the fact that it was Wolters's academic credentials that led *The American Historical Review* to solicit a book review from him. Based on those credentials, it was assumed that Wolters's review would be a fair and unbiased one. Unfortunately, and as noted by Lichtenstein, those same credentials, coupled with Wolters's scholarly language, make his white supremacist views sound respectable and perhaps make them more acceptable to the general public. In fact, social psychologists studying attitude change and persuasion have often noted that people are frequently influenced by a communicator's credentials when they are deciding whether to accept or reject their message. In today's world, where so much of our information and communication happens in cyberspace, the same holds true in the virtual world. We judge the credibility of information, whether it is a webpage, blog, or tweet, by cues we associate with credibility.

In Part I of this chapter I will discuss the psychology of persuasion and explore the reasons why we choose to carefully scrutinize information presented and when we choose not to. In Part II we will examine some of the shortcuts people use, including credibility, that allow us to quickly make judgments and how extremist groups have used our reliance on these shortcuts to their advantage. Finally in Part III will explore research conducted by me and my colleagues that examines our ability to recognize hate websites.

PART I: THE PSYCHOLOGY OF PERSUASION

Research on persuasion suggests that there are two routes to persuasion (Chaiken, Liberman & Eagly, 1989; Eagly & Chaiken, 1993; Petty & Cacioppo, 1986). According to the Elaboration Likelihood Model of Persuasion (ELM) these two routes are referred to as the central route and the peripheral route to persuasion (Petty & Cacioppo, 1986), while the Heuristic and Systematic Model of Persuasion (HSM) suggests that people engage in systematic or heuristic processing (Chaiken et al., 1989; Eagly & Chaiken, 1993). Because these models share several assumptions, in this chapter the terms "central route" and "systematic processing" and the terms "peripheral route" and "heuristic processing" will be viewed as synonymous and used interchangeably unless otherwise noted. People who follow the central route to persuasion carefully scrutinize a message, evaluate the quality of the arguments put forward, and consider how a message's content fits with other things they know (Eagly & Chaiken, 1993; Greenwald, 1968). As you might imagine, following the central route requires both ability and effort (Chaiken et al., 1989). Situational factors such as time and distraction can influence an individual's ability to carefully consider the information presented. Therefore, only those people who are both motivated and able to process a communication will follow the central route to persuasion.

People who lack either the motivation or ability to carefully consider the merits of a communication will follow, or be forced to follow, the peripheral route to persuasion. These individuals will make a judgment about a communication based on cognitive heuristics or shortcuts rather than by the quality of the arguments put forward. For example, and as mentioned earlier, a person following the peripheral route may rely on the heuristic "Experts' statements can be trusted" to judge the validity of a message. Consequently, the message recipients may agree more with a message delivered by an expert than with a message delivered by a nonexpert without carefully considering the message content and the merits of the arguments put forward. Examples of heuristic cues include message length, number of arguments, communicator likeability, and communicator attractiveness, to name a few. Note that the heuristics an individual relies upon are based on the individual's own past experiences and observations and can mediate or bias the resulting attitude (Eagly & Chaiken, 1993; Petty & Cacioppo, 1981; Petty, Cacioppo, & Goldman, 1981; Petty, Cacioppo, & Schumann, 1983).

Who is motivated to carefully process a communication? Typically people who will be impacted by the outcome of the message will be more likely to carefully consider the merits of a communication than people who will not be impacted by the outcome. The extent to which the outcome of a communication impacts an individual's goals is referred to as outcome-relevant involvement (Johnson & Eagly, 1989) or issue-relevant involvement (Petty & Cacioppo, 1981). Researchers have typically manipulated outcome-relevant involvement by varying the relevance of an issue to the message recipient's currently important goals or outcomes (Petty & Cacioppo, 1986; Petty, Cacioppo, & Goldman, 1981; Petty, Cacioppo, & Schumann, 1983). Research suggests that when outcome-relevant involvement is high and thus will have an impact on an individual's ability to achieve an important goal, people desire to form an accurate attitude and will therefore engage in unbiased information processing. As a result of their thoughtful, open-minded, and unbiased examination of the message, these individuals will be more persuaded by strong versus weak arguments.

In contrast to the unbiased information processing associated with outcome-relevant involvement, sometimes people are motivated to engage in biased message processing in order to defend their beliefs or another aspect of their identity. The extent to which a message is related to values an individual holds near and dear to their heart is termed value-relevant involvement (Johnson & Eagly, 1989) or ego involvement (Ostrom & Brock, 1968). Researchers have typically manipulated value-relevant involvement by varying the relevance of the issue to important values or other central aspects of the individual's self-concept. When value-relevant involvement is high, people may still engage in systematic processing but will do so in a biased fashion (Liberman & Chaiken, 1992). Specifically, these individuals will attend to and elaborate on message content that is consistent with their beliefs and also on information that opposes the non-preferred position but will do so in a manner that will help them to maintain or bolster their beliefs. For example, research by Liberman and Chaiken (1992) reveals that participants high in value relevance did carefully process message content but did so in a way that was less critical of those message parts that were consistent with their beliefs and values and more critical of those parts that threatened their beliefs and values.

Note that individuals who are motivated to defend their values but are following the peripheral route to persuasion will also be biased in their processing. For those individuals following the peripheral route to persuasion, a peripheral cue will be attended to or a heuristic invoked only if it validates the preferred attitudinal position or invalidates the non-preferred position.

In summary there are two routes to persuasion, the central route and the peripheral route. Following the central route requires that an individual have both the motivation and ability to engage in careful processing of the message. An individual who lacks either the motivation or ability to follow the central route must follow the peripheral route to persuasion. An individual following the central route to persuasion will carefully scrutinize the information presented and relate it to other information and knowledge they possess. When outcome relevance is high, individuals following the central route to persuasion will engage in unbiased message processing and be more persuaded by strong than weak arguments. But when value relevance is high, individuals following the central route to persuasion will engage in biased message processing and attend to and elaborate on information that is consistent rather than inconsistent with their views.

PART II: MENTAL SHORTCUTS THAT
INCREASE COMPLIANCE

People are often unable or unwilling to invest the time and/or effort to carefully evaluate a communication. As a result they are forced to follow the peripheral route to persuasion and rely on heuristics to evaluate a communication. Our reliance on the peripheral route is not surprising given the amount of information that comes our way each day. As noted by Cialdini (2009, p. 7),

> [We] "exist in an extraordinarily complicated environment, easily the most rapidly moving and complex that has ever existed on this planet. To deal with it, we *need* shortcuts . . . we must very often use our stereotypes, our rules of thumb,

to classify things according to a few key features and then to respond without thinking when one or another of these trigger features is present."

While relying on these shortcuts may, at first glance, seem unacceptable or even deplorable, it is important to realize that we rely on these heuristics because they typically lead us to good decisions and do so in a manner that is both quick and easy. However, as just noted, these shortcuts, though they often prove to be reliable, are not perfect. Some of the time, relying on a shortcut will lead us to make an error in judgment. This is especially likely when social influence practitioners, including extremists, are purposefully using tactics that force us into relying on our shortcuts or heuristics. For example, if a salesperson informs you that a deal is only available today, it limits your time and therefore your ability to carefully consider the merits of the deal. Depending on the item or idea being "sold" a social influence prac- titioner may use any number of tactics, alone or in combination, to make it more likely that you will agree with them. Typical sales tactics include efforts to establish or enhance attractiveness, credibility, and/or similarity. Or to manipulate the situation in such a way that there is an urgency to the decision and thus no time to carefully consider the merits of the argument. And while these efforts may seem relatively benign when someone is trying to sell you a cellphone or living room set, they are much less so when someone is trying to sell you extremism. And some extremists have become quite savvy at using these tactics by making threats to one's home or family seem imminent or by making false claims about their "product" or about the people who endorse it.

For example, in 2016 Borgeson and I (Valeri & Borgeson, 2016) wrote about the efforts of white supremacists to improve their image so that their messages would be more likely to make it into the mainstream and reach more people. They did this by revamping their image, changing their dress, discourse, and, in some instances, even their organizations' names. For exam- ple, the Keystone State Skinheads rebranded themselves Keystone United so they would have a broader appeal. In fact, some white supremacists were so successful in their rebranding efforts that broadcasters interviewed them as legitimate and credible sources.

So what shortcuts do we rely on to let us know we are making a good decision when we do not have the time and/or ability to carefully examine a message? There are three main shortcuts that often signal we are mak- ing a good decision. These are consensus, this is what most people do, similarity, this is what people like me do, and credibility, this is what the experts say I should do. Consensus can be established through numbers, such as "four out of five people choose," "the number one brand of," or "the most popular . . . sold." Similarity can be manipulated by establishing commonalities between the potential follower and members of the group or using a spokesperson who looks like members of the target group. Finally, credibility can be established by associating one's group or one's views with people who are, or appear to be, experts, trustworthy, or authorities (Cialdini, 2009).

One group that was quite successful at using these mental shortcuts in cyberspace to influence the behaviors and beliefs of others was the terrorist group, the Islamic State of Iraq and Syria (ISIS). While ISIS never hid what it wanted from Muslims or potential converts, which was for them to make hijrah, meaning move to the caliphate, the land occupied by ISIS, and engage in jihad, fighting infidels either from the caliphate or in the countries where their adherents lived; they were quite successful at using authority, consensus, and similarity to convince people to do their bidding. It is estimated that 41,490 people from 81 different countries made hijrah, that is they moved to the Islamic State (Cook & Vale, 2018). It is also estimated that, not including the people killed by ISIS within the lands they occupied, ISIS inspired 143 attacks, which killed 2,043 people in 29 countries (Lister et al., 2018). ISIS was able to garner this success by effectively using the tools of cyberspace, publishing online magazines in a variety of languages, using social media, and creating their own online videos, to recruit and radicalize followers (Berger, 2014; Yan, 2015). Because the terrorist group ISIS was so successful in its propaganda efforts, in 2016 my colleagues and I (Valeri, Furgal, & Russell, 2016) decided to examine the social influence tactics used by them to recruit followers to make hijrah or to engage in jihad, used by ISIS almost exclusively to mean fighting for Islam. For our analysis we conducted a content analysis of *Dabiq*, ISIS's English-language online magazine. Fifteen issues of *Dabiq* were published between July 5, 2014, and July 31, 2016.

In those issues, ISIS repeatedly called for people to make hijrah and to engage in jihad. As shown in the selected quotes, ISIS used authority to establish the injunctive norm that making hijrah and engaging in jihad are moral obligations for Muslims. They used both consensus and similarity to establish the descriptive norm, that making hijrah and engaging in jihad are what most people do. Note that when the behavior advocated by an injunctive norm is consistent with the behavior advocated by a descriptive norm, it is clear and easy for an individual to know how to act. In this case they should make hijrah and engage in jihad.

Hijrah is mentioned in each issue of *Dabiq* approximately 20 times ($M = 19.87$, $SD = 15.65$) except for Issue 5 *Remaining and Expanding*, in which it is not mentioned at all. The two publications with the most frequent mentions of hijrah are Issue 15 *Break the Cross*, in which hijrah is mentioned 47 times, and Issue 3 *Call to Hijrah*, where it is mentioned 45 times. Consistent with its title, the theme of Issue 3 was hijrah and called upon Muslims everywhere, especially doctors, engineers, and religious scholars to come to the Khilafah, the caliphate. Issue 15's theme is that all non-Muslims, with a focus on Christians, should accept Islam and move to the caliphate.

Jihad is mentioned even more frequently. In each of the 15 issues of *Dabiq*, jihad is mentioned almost 50 times ($M = 49.40$, $SD = 23.56$). The minimum number of times jihad is mentioned is 14, which occurs in Issue 2, *Islamic State: It's Either the Islamic State or the Flood*, the theme of which is that the day of judgment is coming and that disbelievers will die on earth in the flood and be condemned to hellfire while the true believers, followers of the Islamic State, will be saved and enjoy life in paradise. The maximum number of times jihad is mentioned is 91, and this occurs in both Issue 12 *Just Terror* and in Issue 14 *The Murtadd Brotherhood. Just Terror* celebrates the attacks on the *Charlie Hebdo* office in Paris, France, on January 7–9, 2015, and encourages Muslims to conduct jihad in the country where they live rather than traveling to the caliphate and engaging in jihad there. *The Murtadd Brotherhood* praises the March 22, 2016, attacks in Brussels, Belgium, names targets, including an Imam in Northern California, and encourages the use of easily accessed weapons, knives, guns, and explosives for carrying out jihad in the country where you live.

The sheer number of calls for hijrah and jihad alone ensure that these two ideas are firmly established in the mind of the reader. The repetition of the calls to make hijrah and engage in jihad also creates the feeling that doing so is imperative.

In Issue 1, ISIS used a religious authority figure to establish the injunctive norm that making hijrah is a moral obligation. Amirul-Mu'minin is quoted as saying,

> Therefore, rush O Muslims to your state. Yes, it is your state. . . . The State is a state for all Muslims. The land is for the Muslims, all the Muslims. O Muslims everywhere, whoever is capable of performing hijrah (emigration) to the Islamic State, then let him do so, because hijrah to the land of Islam is obligatory. (Issue 1, p. 10)

The previous quote is repeated in later issues to remind readers of their obligation to make hijrah (e.g., Issue 15, p. 27). *Dabiq* frames hijrah as being about physically and mentally moving from a state of disbelief to one of belief. In the foreword of Issue 2 it is suggested that many readers probably want to know what their obligations are to the caliphate. *Dabiq* explains, "The first priority is to perform hijrah from wherever you are to the Islamic State, from dārul-kufr [land of disbelief] to dārul-Islām" (Issue 2, p. 3). *Dabiq* also uses parables and historical accounts to establish the injunctive norm for hijrah. For example, in Issue 3, which is devoted to hijrah, an article entitled *Hijarh to Sham* [Syria] *Is from the Millah of Ibrahim* [Prophet Abraham, God's messenger] is included.

The hijrah of the strangers to Shām was in adherence to the path of Ibrāhīm . . . who established for them the tradition of declaring enmity and hatred towards the mushrikīn [polytheist] and their tawāghīt [idolatry]. . . . Allah's Messenger . . . said, "There will be hijrah after hijrah. The best people on earth will be those who keep to the land of Ibrāhīm's hijrah." (Issue 3, p. 10)

Thus someone embarking on hijrah to the caliphate would be following in the footsteps of God's messenger, Abraham. Given that Abraham is God's messenger he is clearly a credible person and, as such, his actions should be emulated. Furthermore, the statement that "There will be hijrah after hijrah," which is frequently repeated throughout the issues of *Dabiq*, suggests that there is a constant flood of people moving to the caliphate, creating the illusion of consensus, that everyone agrees that moving to caliphate is the right thing to do and that they are doing it. Thus the previous quote established both the injunctive norm, what ought to be done, and the descriptive norm, what most people do, to persuade people to move to the Islamic State.

As with hijrah, *Dabiq* presents the decision to engage in jihad as a moral issue by providing examples of historical religious figures and quoting religious leaders—for example, in a parable about Ādam, the devil or Shaytān attempts to tempt Ādam away from jihad and is unsuccessful at doing so.

Then he [Shaytān] sat in wait for him upon the path of jihād and said, "It's exhaustion of oneself and one's wealth; you'll fight and be killed. Your wife will be married [after you], and your wealth will be divided." So he [Ādam] disobeyed him and performed jihād. (Issue 2, p. 19)

To further demonstrate the injunctive norm of jihad, the reader is informed that waging jihad will be rewarded by Allah in this life or the next.

Allah's Messenger (sallallāhu 'alayhi wa sallam) said, "Allah has guaranteed the one who performs jihād in His path, having left his home for no reason other than to perform jihād in His path out of belief in His words, that He would enter him into Jannah [paradise] or return him back home with what he has attained of reward or ghanīmah [booty or prizes taken in battle]." (Issue 6, p. 6; Issue 7, p. 10)

Beginning in Issue 4 Muslims around the world are encouraged to kill nonbelievers where they live. The source of this encouragement is from a speech by an authority, Shaykh Abū Muhammad al-'Adnānī's, parts of which were included in Issues 4 (p. 9), 5 (p. 37), and 6 (p. 4). The Shaykh said,

So O muwahhid, do not let this battle pass you by wherever you may be. You must strike the soldiers, patrons, and troops of the tawāghīt. Strike their police, security, and intelligence members, as well as their treacherous agents. Destroy their beds. Embitter their lives for them and busy them with themselves. If you can kill a disbelieving American or European—especially the spiteful and filthy French—or an Australian, or a Canadian, or any other disbeliever from the disbelievers waging war, including the citizens of the countries that entered into a coalition against the Islamic State, then rely upon Allah, and kill him in any manner or way however it may be. Do not ask for anyone's advice and do not seek anyone's verdict. Kill the disbeliever whether he is civilian or military, for they have the same ruling. (Issue 4, p. 9)

To help establish the descriptive norms for hijrah and jihad, the issues of *Dabiq* included a regular column *Among the Believers Are Men*, in which the stories of average people who made hijrah and/or engaged in jihad are presented. These stories accomplish two things. First, they make it seem like a lot of people are making hijrah or engaging in jihad, and, therefore, these are the right things to do. And second, that people who are similar to you are making hijrah or engaging in jihad, again suggesting that these are things you should be doing and also that these are things you can do.

Now, with the presence of the Islamic State, the opportunity to perform hijrah from dārul-kufr to dārul-islām and wage jihād against the Crusaders . . . is available to every Muslim as well as the chance to live under the shade of the Sharī'ah alone. (Issue 7, p. 61)

Both men and women are making hijrah.

And today, after the Muslims established a state that rules by the Qur'ān and the Sunnah of the Prophet . . . and whose blessed soldiers restored the promised khilāfah by the edge of the sword not through pacifism, the rate of hijrah magnified and now every day there are not only muhājirīn to the land of Islam but also muhājirāt [female migrants] who were sick of living amongst kufr and its people. (Issue 8, p. 33)

Through examples of hijrah success stories by everyday people, *Dabiq* suggests that hijrah is both a common practice and an achievable goal. In Issue 8 there are several stories of women making hijrah, including the stories of two pregnant women who made hijrah:

I met a sister who was six months pregnant accompanied by her husband coming from Britain. I was surprised by this adventurist, so I said, "Why didn't you wait a bit until you gave birth to the baby you are carrying and then perform hijrah!" She answered, "We could not handle waiting any longer. We melted yearning for the Islamic State!" (Issue 8, p. 35)

These hijrah success stories deliver a clear message: if people just like you are deciding to make hijrah and succeeding at it, then this decision is right for you and you can achieve the goal.

Similarly, *Dabiq* establishes the descriptive norm for jihad by suggesting that people yearn to go on jihad as in the case of Abū Qudāmah, who so longed to answer the call of jihad that he left London for Syria two months before the birth of his daughter (Issue 7, p. 46). It suggests that engaging in jihad is a common practice through statements such as "And the numbers of Muslims taking up arms in the name of jihād under the banner of the Islamic State are growing, and they're growing fast" (Issue 5, p. 38). *Dabiq* also presents stories of everyday Muslims engaging in jihad. For example, In Issue 12 it praises the *Charlie Hebdo* attackers and points out that neither their youth nor lack of weapons training deterred them, thus suggesting that nothing should stand in the way of jihad.

[W]e will not forget to commend the martyred "lone" knights of the Khilāfah who struck out against the kāfir and apostate enemies near them [in Australia, Canada, Israel]. These brave men were not content with merely hearing news about jihād battles. . . . They did not use the obstacles laid down by the kuffār on the path to hijrah as an excuse to abandon jihād against the enemies. They did not use a younger age or lack of training as an excuse to be mere bystanders. They sacrificed their souls in the noblest of deeds in pursuit of Allah's pleasure. (Issue 12, p. 3)

Through the use of quotes from authority figures and parables, ISIS makes it clear that making hijrah and engaging in jihad are moral obligations, and it is what every good Muslim should do. Through their stories of individuals engaging in hijrah and jihad, ISIS makes it seem that there is consensus, that everyone agrees that making hijrah and engaging in jihad are the right things to do. Finally, the stories of individuals making hijrah and engaging in jihad make clear that people who are similar to you are doing these things, therefore it is also the right thing for you to do as well as something that you can do.

While the earlier analyses focused on an online magazine, my colleagues and I have also investigated the tactics used by hate websites that hinder people's ability to recognize their hate and extremism.

PART III: RECOGNIZING HATE WEBSITES

Almost 20 years ago Borgeson and I began studying hate in cyberspace. In our first publication on the topic, we noted (Borgeson & Valeri, 2004) that hate had been on the web since the 1980s. Since that time the presence of hate groups in cyberspace has grown to include a presence not only on the web but also on social media platforms, video streaming, and gaming. Hate groups, both then and now, use cyberspace to spread their ideas, communicate with like-minded individuals, recruit new members, incite illegal activity and violence, and make money. Given that 86% of Americans say they get their news from their smartphone, computer, or tablet "often" or "sometimes" (Shearer, 2021) and that the platforms they use for news include not only news websites but also search engines, social media, and podcasts (Shearer, 2021), it has become increasingly important to understand people's ability to recognize hate and extremism.

In our first study, Borgeson and I began investigating people's ability to recognize hate websites. To do this we examined the impact of a webpage's header on perceptions of a webpage by simply manipulating the title of an actual webpage "Jew Watch" (the URL which is no longer available, had been www.JewWatch.com), but not its content, to make it either more explicitly anti-Semitic "Jews Are Taking Over the World" or purposefully deceiving "News Watch" and then asked participants to evaluate the webpage. The results revealed that people judged "Jews Are Taking Over the World" to be significantly more intolerant than either "Jew Watch" or "News Watch." However, participants' evaluations of "Jew Watch" and "News Watch" did not differ significantly from each other. These results suggest that people are relying on a webpage's header, a peripheral cue, rather than the actual content of the webpage to make decisions about its content. Our results reveal that people judge a webpage with a blatantly biased header, which we termed the "In Your Face" approach, to be intolerant but that their judgments are thrown off when the header is ambiguous ("Jew Watch") or misleading ("News Watch"), which we termed the "soft-sell" and "false-information" approaches respectively. In a follow-up study (Valeri & Borgeson, 2005) in which we sought to replicate and extend these findings we examined whether warnings alerted people to the intolerant content of a webpage. In this follow-up study, as with the previous study, participants viewed content from the website *Jew Watch* and, as in the previous study, the title was either kept as "Jew Watch" or changed to "Jews Are Taking Over the World" or "News Watch." Additionally we manipulated a second variable, the presence versus absence of a warning "Whites only." Consistent with our hypothesis there was a main effect for warning—specifically webpages with a warning were rated as significantly more intolerant than those without a warning. When no warning was present, the results replicated our previous findings, and participants rated "Jews Are Taking Over the World" as significantly more intolerant than either of the other two webpages. But when the warning was present, participants rated the three webpages as equally intolerant. While the warning did not impact intolerance ratings for the webpage "Jews Are Taking Over the World," participants rated both "Jew Watch" and "News Watch" as significantly more intolerant when the warning was present versus absent. As with our first study, these results also suggested that participants were relying on peripheral cues, either the blatantly biased webpage header, in the case of "Jews Are Taking Over the World," or the warning "Whites only" to alert them to the biased nature of the webpage.

In the intervening years there has been an increase in the use of cyberspace, both on the web and on social media, by hate groups. The Anti-Defamation League (ADL) in its 2020 survey reported that 44% of Americans who responded to their survey had experienced online harassment and that 77% of those people reported that some of that harassment had occurred on Facebook. Greenblatt (2022) notes

> that social media drives radicalization. It's a font of conspiracy theories, a slow-burning acid weakening our foundations post after post, tweet after tweet, like after like. And the hate festering on social media inevitably targets the most vulnerable—particularly marginalized groups like religious, ethnic, and racial minorities, and members of the LGBTQ community.

Because of the prevalence of hate in cyberspace and its repercussions in the physical world, we decided to revisit this research. As with the previous studies, we (Valeri et al., 2019) focused on people's ability to recognize anti-Semitism. This issue seemed especially important given that both the ADL (ADL, 2018a; 2018b; 2019) and the FBI (2017) had reported increases in anti-Semitism. These acts of anti-Semitism included both the October 27, 2018, attack at the Tree of Life Synagogue in Pittsburgh, Pennsylvania, and the April 27, 2019, attack at the Chabad Synagogue in Poway, California. As you may recall, prior to the attack, the gunman at the Tree of Life Synagogue shooting had posted anti-Semitic comments on the social media platform Gab (Ohlheiser & Shapira, 2018), including his last post on the morning of the attack in which he stated "HIAS [Hebrew Immigrant Aid Society] likes to bring invaders in that kill our people. I can't sit by and watch my people get slaughtered. Screw your optics. I'm going in" (Ohlheiser & Shapira, 2018). The gunman at the Chabad Synagogue also made use of cyberspace, posting his manifesto on 8kun.

While this study, like the previous two, focused on anti-Semitism, unlike our previous research we chose four real websites, two that presented accurate information about the Holocaust, the Jewish Virtual Library (www .jewishvirtuallibrary.org), and the Nizkor Project (www.nizkor.org), and two that presented inaccurate information about the Holocaust, the Institute for Historical Review (www.ihr.org), and Jew Watch (www.jewwatch.com). The two inaccurate websites were selected first. Jew Watch was selected because we had used it in our two previous studies and it still existed online. As you may remember from our first study, Jew Watch represented the "soft-sell" approach because the source and bias are somewhat ambiguous. The Institute for Historical Review was selected as an example of the "false information" approach because the website strives to make it look like they are an educational resource while presenting biased information as factual. The Southern Poverty Law Center (SPLC) has described it as "a pseudo-academic organization that claims to seek 'truth and accuracy in history,' but whose real purpose is to promote Holocaust denial and defend Nazism" (Southern Poverty Law Center, n.d.b). In contrast, the Institute for Historical Review describes itself as

an independent educational center and publisher that works to promote peace, understanding and justice through greater public awareness of the past. . . . We work to provide factual information and sound perspective on US foreign policy, World War Two, the Israel-Palestine conflict, war propaganda, Middle East history, the Jewish-Zionist role in cultural and political life, and much more. (IHR, n.d.)

After selecting the two sites with inaccurate information we then sought to find two websites with accurate information that were similar in appearance to these two webpages. In searching for a webpage similar to that of the Institute for Historical Review, because it falsely presents itself as an educational or news source, we were searching for a website that was clearly educational in nature. The Jewish Virtual Library, which describes itself as an archive with "Anything you need to know from Anti-Semitism to Zionism" (Jewish Virtual Library, n.d.), has a library as the background image on both its "Home" and "About Us" sections was selected. The Jewish Virtual Library is described as "the most comprehensive online Jewish encyclopedia in the world, covering everything from anti-Semitism to Zionism" (WorldCat, n.d.a) and was judged by the researchers to be similar in appearance to that of the Institute for Historical Review. The Nizkor Project was selected because it presents accurate information, having been described as "a memorial to the Jewish Holocaust victims of Nazi atrocities during World War II. Site features a variety of historical facts and research . . . on the victims and their persecutors" (WorldCat, n.d.b) and because of its similarity in appearance to Jew Watch. Participants viewed all four webpages.

To assess participants' perceptions regarding the factual nature of the information presented by an organization, participants rated the information presented on a 7-point semantic differential scale (completely fake–completely factual).

To assess participants' perceptions regarding the credibility of the information presented by an organization, participants rated the information presented on three, 5-point semantic differential scales (very untrustworthy–very trustworthy, very untrue–very true, very unreliable–very reliable). Participants' responses to these three scales, which had good or acceptable correlations (αs = 0.88 Jew Watch, 0.87 Institute for Historical Review, 0.79 Nizkor Project, and 0.80 Jewish Virtual Library), were transformed to agree in direction and averaged to indicate a participant's belief that the information presented was credible. Higher scores indicate that participants viewed the information to be greater in credibility.

To assess participants' ability to recognize an organization's tolerance for others, participants rated the information presented on four, 5-point semantic differential scales (very unbiased–very biased, very unbalanced arguments–very balanced arguments, very close minded–very open minded, and very intolerant of others–very tolerant of others). Participants' responses to these scales, which had good or acceptable correlations (αs = 0.75 Jew Watch, 0.89 Institute for Historical Review, 0.78 Nizkor Project, and 0.84 Jewish Virtual Library), were transformed to agree in direction and averaged to indicate a participant's assessment of the tolerance of an organization.

To assess participants' beliefs about the anti-Semitic nature of the website, participants responded to the 7-point semantic differential scale (completely anti-Jewish to completely pro-Jewish) that asked, "To what extent do you think the information in the links provided on the webpages would be Pro Jewish?" This measure was previously used by Valeri and Borgeson (2005).

In order to examine the data, for each dependent variable, means and standard deviations were calculated for each website and are presented in table 2.1. A one-way within-subjects ANOVA was conducted for each of the dependent variables.

The within-subjects ANOVA examining the factual nature of the content was significant $F(3, 120) = 11.95$, $p < .01$, $\eta^2 = .23$. Post hoc comparisons using the Bonferroni procedure revealed that participants viewed the information presented by the Jewish Virtual Library, true-information, as significantly more factual than that presented by the Institute for Historical Review, inaccurate information, which was rated as somewhat more factual than that presented by Jew Watch, also inaccurate information ($p = .07$). The Nizkor Project, accurate information, was rated as significantly more factual than Jew Watch but did not differ significantly from either the Jewish Virtual Library or the Institute for Historical Review.

Table 2.1   Evaluations of Webpages That Differ in Accuracy and Appearance

	Inaccurate		Accurate	
Webpage Ratings	Jew Watch M (SD)	Institute for Historical Review M (SD)	Nizkor Project M (SD)	Jewish Virtual Library M (SD)
Factual	3.56[a] (1.42)	4.34[ab] (1.18)	4.56[bc] (1.29)	5.15[c] (1.33)
Credible	2.70[a] (1.02)	3.58[b] (0.96)	3.48[b] (0.84)	4.19[c] (0.73)
Tolerant	2.06[a] (0.79)	2.91[bc] (0.93)	2.90[b] (0.83)	3.40[c] (0.85)
Pro-Jewish	4.22[a] (2.25)	4.54[a] (1.38)	5.85[b] (1.65)	6.39[b] (1.07)

Notes: Ratings for factual and pro-Jewish were made on 7-point scales and ratings for credible and tolerant were made on 5-point scales. Higher scores indicate more positive ratings. In a row, means that do not share a superscript are significantly different at $p < .01$ unless otherwise indicated. For factual, Jew Watch versus Institute for Historical Review is significant at $p = .073$. For credible, Jewish Virtual Library versus Institute for Historical Review is significant at $p = .013$. For tolerant, Jewish Virtual Library versus Nizkor is significant at $p = .021$ and Jewish Virtual Library versus Institute for Historical Review is significant at $p = .065$. For Pro-Jewish, Jew Watch versus Nizkor is significant at $p = .014$.
Source: Table created by author based on data from Valeri, Borgeson, Cogley, Hamed, Kindred, & Tripodi, 2019.

The analyses for credibility were significant $F(3, 120) = 19.66$, $p < .01$, $\eta^2 = 0.33$. Post hoc comparisons using the Bonferroni procedure revealed that participants viewed the information presented by Jewish Virtual Library as significantly more credible than that of any of the other organizations ($ps < .01$) and the information presented by both the Nizkor Project and the Institute for Historical Review as significantly more credible than Jew Watch ($ps < .01$). However, participants' credibility ratings for the Nizkor Project did not differ significantly from their credibility ratings for the Institute for Historical Review ($p > .10$).

The within-subjects ANOVA for tolerance was significant $F(3, 120) = 17.99$, $p < .01$, $\eta^2 = .31$. Using the Bonferroni procedure, post hoc comparisons revealed that participants rated the Jewish Virtual Library, the Nizkor Project, and the Institute for Historical Review as significantly more tolerant than Jew Watch ($ps < .01$). Somewhat surprisingly, the Nizkor Project was rated as significantly less tolerant than the Jewish Virtual Library ($p < .05$). While differences between participants' tolerance rating for the Institute for Historical Review and the Jewish Virtual Library only approached significance ($p = .065$). Furthermore, participants' rating of the tolerance for the Institute for Historical Review did not differ from their rating for the Nizkor project ($p > .10$).

Finally, the within-subjects ANOVA for participants' pro-Jewish ratings was significant $F(3, 120) = 15.40$, $p < .01$, $\eta^2 = 0.28$. Post hoc comparisons using the Bonferroni procedure revealed that participants viewed both the Jewish Virtual Library and the Nizkor Project, which did not differ significantly from each other, as significantly more pro-Jewish than either Jew Watch or the Institute for Historical Review, which did not differ significantly from each other.

As mentioned previously, the four websites that participants viewed differed on the accuracy of the information provided. Both the Jewish Virtual Library and the Nizkor Project presented accurate information about Jews and Jewish history while the information provided on the two anti-Semitic websites, Jew Watch and the Institute for Historical Review, was inaccurate.

According to the ELM, participants following the central route to persuasion should examine message content. Therefore, participants attending to message content should rate the Jewish Virtual Library and the Nizkor Project as more factual, more credible, more tolerant, and more pro-Jewish than either Jew Watch or the Institute for Historical Review.

However, if participants are following the peripheral route to persuasion they should be impacted by peripheral cues, in this case the website's header and the professional appearance of the website. Individuals basing their judgments on the website header and professional appearance of the webpage would judge a professional-looking page to be more credible. Therefore, participants who are basing their judgment on appearance should rate the Jewish Virtual Library and Institute for Historical Review as more factual, more credible, more tolerant, and more pro-Jewish than either Jew Watch or the Nizkor Project.

The current results suggest that when both message content and appearance lead to the same conclusion, because the content is accurate and the appearance is professional or, conversely, because the content is inaccurate and the appearance is unprofessional, participants reach the correct conclusion. Thus the Jewish Virtual Library, which had accurate information about Jews and Jewish history and both a professional name and appearance, was rated as significantly more factual, more credible, more tolerant, and more pro-Jewish than either of the two websites with inaccurate information, Jew Watch and the Institute for Historical Review. While Jew Watch, which had inaccurate information coupled with an ambiguous name and an unprofessional appearance, was rated as significantly less factual, less credible, less tolerant, and more anti-Jewish that either of the two websites with accurate information, the Jewish Virtual Library and the Nizkor Project.

However, participants' responses suggested that they had difficulty evaluating a website when there was a mismatch between the accuracy of the information presented and the professional appearance of the webpage. As a result participants had difficulty distinguishing between the Nizkor Project, which provided accurate information about Jews and Jewish history but had an ambiguous name and an unprofessional appearance, and the Institute for Historical Review, which provided inaccurate information but had a professional name and appearance. Essentially participants evaluated these two webpages to be equally credible, factual, and tolerant.

Even though the Nizkor Project has accurate information, evaluations of it suffered, in comparison to that of the Jewish Virtual Library, because of its unprofessional appearance. This is reflected in the fact that the Nizkor Project was rated as significantly less factual, credible, and tolerant than the Jewish Virtual Library.

On the other hand, the Institute for Historical Review, which presents inaccurate information and was identified by the SPLC as a Holocaust denial website, benefited from its professional name and appearance. This is reflected in the fact that it was viewed as significantly more credible, more factual, and more tolerant than Jew Watch, which also had inaccurate information but an unprofessional appearance.

It was only on ratings of how pro-Jewish a webpage was that participants were not overwhelmed by appearance cues. Individuals rated both the Jewish Virtual Library and the Nizkor Project as significantly more pro-Jewish than either Jew Watch or the Institute for Historical Review. However, it should be noted that the Nizkor Project's pro-Jewish ratings were not as strong as those for the Jewish Virtual Library. Although this difference only approached but did not reach statistical significance, it lends credence to the fact that appearance impacts perceptions of credibility.

People are using a website's appearance, specifically how professional it looks, to determine its credibility. A website with a professional appearance is judged to be more credible than one with an unprofessional appearance. This finding is especially important in an age when more people have access to the Internet and are turning to the web as a source for news and information. Given that it is likely that both Internet access and reliance on the Internet as a news source will continue to increase, an important takeaway message of these results is that people need to become savvier at determining the credibility or veracity of the information they encounter on the Internet. People need to understand that because something looks credible, it does not mean that it is credible.

Lastly, given that at the start of this chapter we mentioned the webpage American Renaissance when discussing the American Historical Society's poor selection of a biased reviewer my colleagues and I (Valeri et al., 2018) decided to examine participants' evaluation of this seemingly unbiased but actually biased webpage, the false-information approach, and the perceptions of it compared with those of a mainstream conservative organization and those of an extremist group.

American Renaissance, in the "About Us" section of its webpage (https://www.amren.com/), describes itself as "the Internet's premier race-realist site . . . [that] publish[es] articles, podcasts, videos, and news items from a worldwide race-realist perspective." American Renaissance's "What We Believe" section suggests that they are willing to take on tough questions about race to create a better society. They describe their beliefs as follows:

Race is an important aspect of individual and group identity. Of all the fault lines that divide society—language, religion, class, ideology—it is the most prominent and divisive. Race and racial conflict are at the heart of some of the most serious challenges the Western World faces in the 21st century. The problems of race cannot be solved without adequate understanding. Attempts to gloss over the significance of race or even to deny its reality only make problems worse. Progress requires the study of all aspects of race, whether historical, cultural, or biological. This approach is known as race realism. (https://www.amren.com/about/)

In contrast the SPLC (n.d.a) describes American Renaissance as

a self-styled think tank that promotes pseudo-scientific studies and research that purport to show the inferiority of blacks to whites—although in hifalutin language that avoids open racial slurs and attempts to portray itself as serious scholarship.

Given these descriptions of American Renaissance and our desire to examine how participants viewed the information presented on its website with a mainstream conservative website we selected the Heritage Foundation, a conservative think tank (Ball, 2013; Groppe, 2021: Heritage Foundation, n.d.; Mahler, 2018), as one of the comparison websites. The third website we selected, one that embodies the "soft-sell" approach because of its ambiguous name, was that of Keystone United, which describes itself "as small group of skinheads residing in the state capital of Harrisburg, PA. With the initial goal of uniting all racially aware skinheads in the state of PA." The SPLC (n.d.c) describes the group as "Keystone United, known until 2009 as the Keystone State Skinheads, is one of the largest and most active single-state racist skinhead crews in the country."

The selection of these three websites allowed us to compare participants' perceptions of a mainstream conservative think tank's website to those of a biased website posing as an unbiased think tank, what we have termed false-information, and a clearly biased group, which we have termed "in your face." We asked participants to examine the "Home" and "About Us" sections of American Renaissance, the Heritage Foundation, and Keystone United and to evaluate them on several different scales. Therefore, the study was a one-way within-subjects ANOVA with three conditions for webpage (American Renaissance, Heritage Foundation, and Keystone United). To minimize any carryover effects, webpage order was completely counterbalanced resulting in each possible webpage ordering to be viewed by at least seven but no more than eight participants.

36   *Robin Maria Valeri*

The respective "Home" and "About Us" webpages for the organizations the Heritage Foundation, American Renaissance, and Keystone United served as the experimental materials. Because the length of each of these webpages varied between organizations, three screenshots of the top portion of each organization's home page and two screenshots of the top portion of each organization's "About Us" section were used as stimulus material.

To assess participants' perceptions regarding the accuracy of the information presented by an organization, participants rated the information presented on three, 5-point semantic differential scales (very untrustworthy–very trustworthy, very accurate–very inaccurate, very true–very untrue). Participants' responses to these three scales, which had acceptable to good correlations (αs = 0.75, 0.76, and 0.81 for American Renaissance, Heritage Foundation, and Keystone United, respectively), were transformed to agree in direction and averaged to indicate a participant's belief that the information presented was accurate. Higher scores indicate that participants viewed the information to be greater in accuracy.

To assess participants' ability to recognize an organization's tolerance for others, participants rated the information presented on four, 5-point semantic differential scales (very unbiased–very biased, very balanced arguments–very unbalanced arguments, very open minded–very close minded, and very tolerant of others–very intolerant of others). Participants' responses to these scales, all with good or acceptable correlations (αs = 0.84, 0.80, and 0.79 for American Renaissance, Heritage Foundation, and Keystone United, respectively), were transformed to agree in direction and averaged to indicate a participant's assessment of the tolerance of an organization.

To assess participants' beliefs about the specific types of intolerance espoused by an organization, participants responded to six, 7-point semantic differential scales (completely anti–completely pro) that asked, "To what extent do you think the information in the links provided on the webpages would be Pro _____?" The six groups specified were African American, Hispanic or Latina/o, Immigrant, Jewish, Muslim, and White.

In order to examine the data, a one-way within-subjects ANOVA was conducted for each of the independent variables.

The analyses for accuracy were significant $F(2, 88) = 45.524$, $p < .01$, $\eta^2 = 0.51$. Post hoc comparisons using the Bonferroni procedure revealed that participants viewed the information presented by the Heritage Foundation ($M = 3.73$, $SD = 0.65$) to be significantly more accurate than that presented by American Renaissance ($M = 3.04$, $SD = 0.90$), $p < .01$, which was viewed as significantly more accurate than that presented by Keystone United ($M = 2.24$, $SD = 0.86$), $p < .01$.

The analyses for tolerance were significant $F(2, 88) = 32.59$, $p < .01$, $\eta^2 = 0.43$. Using the Bonferroni procedure, post hoc comparisons revealed that participants viewed both the Heritage Foundation ($M = 2.86$, $SD = 0.92$) and American Renaissance ($M = 2.53$, $SD = 1.12$) as being significantly more tolerant than Keystone United ($M = 1.55$, $SD = 0.68$), $ps < .01$. However, participants' ratings regarding the tolerance of the Heritage Foundation and American Renaissance did not differ significantly from one another ($p > .01$).

In order to examine participants' ability to recognize the specific biases of the webpages, analyses for African American, Hispanic, Immigrant, Jewish, Muslim, and White bias were conducted separately (means and standard deviations are presented in table 2.2).

The analyses for African American bias were significant $F(2, 88) = 30.48$, $p < .01$, $\eta^2 = 0.41$. Using the Bonferroni procedure, post hoc comparisons revealed that participants rated the Heritage Foundation as significantly more pro-African American than American Renaissance ($p < .05$), which was rated as significantly more pro-African American than Keystone United ($p < .01$).

The analyses for bias ratings toward Hispanics, Immigrants, Jews, and Muslims were also significant. In each of these instances the within-subjects ANOVAs were significant at $p < .01$ (Fs (2, 88) = 35.81 Hispanic, 25.00 Immigrant, 32.23 Jewish, and 24.01 Muslim and η^2s = 0.45 Hispanic, 0.36 Immigrant, 0.42 Jewish, and 0.35 Muslim respectively). For each of these bias ratings, the post hoc comparisons, using the Bonferroni procedure, revealed the same pattern of effects. Specifically, participants rated Keystone United as significantly more anti-Hispanic, anti-Immigrant, anti-Jewish, and anti-Muslim than either the Heritage Foundation or American Renaissance ($ps < .01$). However, there was no significant difference between participants' ratings of Hispanic, Immigrant, Jewish, or Muslim bias for the Heritage Foundation and American Renaissance ($ps > .10$).

Finally, analyses for White bias was significant $F(2, 88) = 10.95$, $p < .01$, $\eta^2 = 0.20$. Participants rated Keystone United as being significantly more

Table 2.2 Participants' Perception of Webpage Biases

Ratings	African American M (SD)	Hispanic M (SD)	Immigrant M (SD)	Jewish M (SD)	Muslim M (SD)	White M (SD)
Heritage Foundation	4.28 (1.37)	4.11 (1.42)	3.87 (1.52)	3.64 (1.75)	3.71 (1.52)	5.62 (1.03)
American Renaissance	3.38 (1.96)	3.47 (1.82)	3.33 (1.92)	4.27 (1.36)	3.09 (1.98)	5.80 (1.47)
Keystone United	1.82 (1.44)	1.80 (1.29)	1.82 (1.17)	2.11 (1.39)	1.67 (1.13)	6.58 (1.06)

Note: Ratings were made on 7-point semantic differential scales (completely anti-completely pro) that asked "To what extent do you think the information in the links provided on the webpages would be Pro _____?"

Source: Table created by author based on data from Valeri, Burgio, Full, & Borgeson 2018.

pro-White than either the Heritage Foundation or American Renaissance ($ps < .01$). However, there was no significant difference in participants' ratings of White bias for the Heritage Foundation and American Renaissance ($p = 1.0$).

These results, although somewhat mixed, provide some hope that people can recognize bias. The participants were able to distinguish between the accuracy of the information provided by a legitimate conservative website, the Heritage Foundation, and the ones that provided biased and inaccurate information. However, when it came assessing the tolerance and biases of a website, while participants could clearly recognize the biases of Keystone Skinheads, recognizing its intolerance, pro-White sentiments, and anti-non-White biases, they had a more difficult time recognizing the biases of American Renaissance. As with the previous study, when there is a mismatch between appearance and content, it can bias the judgment of people who lack the motivation and/or ability to carefully scrutinize the information in such a way so that they assume the information is unbiased.

Because of the rise in hate and extremism in cyberspace, companies, governments, and educational institutions are seeking means to protect the public and/or to make the public more knowledgeable about and better at recognizing hate and bias in cyberspace. Some Internet service providers and social media platforms have chosen to ban hate and extremism. Both Facebook and Twitter have rules regulating content (Facebook, n.d.; Twitter Safety, 2020). For example, Facebook has banned hate speech in its advertisements (Rodriquez, 2020), blackface, anti-Semitism (Kastrenakes, 2020), and Holocaust denial (Effron, 2020), while organizations such as the FBI often try to alert the public, especially parents about cyberhate (F.B.I., n.d.). Several libraries (University of California; University of Maryland) and institutions provide resources to educate students as well as the general public about hate and bias on cyberspace. Stanford University's History Education Group offers a robust online program for people to learn how to better evaluate online resources. Unfortunately finding, reviewing, and learning from the educational information provided takes both motivation and ability. While we might have the motivation to process these educational materials, just as we might have the motivation to carefully scrutinize the credibility of the information we find in cyberspace, many of us do not have that time to do so. As was pointed out earlier in the chapter, it is because we are bombarded with information throughout the day as well as myriad demands for our time and attention, many of us lack one or more of the resources, motivation, time, and/or ability, to carefully scrutinize information and carefully evaluate the source. Therefore, we are forced to rely on our shortcuts, the consequences of which can be dangerous.

REFERENCES

American Renaissance (n.d.). *About us: What we believe.* Retrieved from https://www.amren.com/about/

Anti-Defamation League (2018a). *Audit of anti-Semitic incidents: Year in review 2017.* Anti-Defamation League. Retrieved from https://www.adl.org/media/11174/download

Anti-Defamation League (2018b, October). *Computational propaganda, Jewish-Americans and the 2018 midterms: The amplification of anti-Semitic harassment online.* Anti-Defamation League. Retrieved from https://www.adl.org/media/12028/download

Anti-Defamation League (2019). *Audit of anti-Semitic incidents: Year in review 2018.* Anti-Defamation League. Retrieved from https://www.adl.org/media/12857/download

Ball, M. (2013, September 25). The fall of the Heritage Foundation and the death of Republican ideas. *The Atlantic.* Retrieved from https://www.theatlantic.com/politics/archive/2013/09/the-fall-of-the-heritage-foundation-and-the-death-of-republican-ideas/279955/

Berger, J. M. (2014, June 16). How ISIS games Twitter. *The Atlantic.*

Borgeson, K., & Valeri, R. (2004). Faces of hate. *Journal of Applied Sociology, 21*(2), 99–111.

Brigham Young University (n.d.). *Step-by-step guide & research rescue: Evaluating credibility.* Brigham Young University Library. Retrieved from https://guides.lib.byu.edu/c.php?g=216340&p=1428399

Chaiken, S., Liberman, A., & Eagly, A. H. (1989). Heuristic and systematic processing within and beyond the persuasion context. In J. S. Uleman and J. A. Baugh (Eds.), *Unintended thought: Limits of awareness, intention, and control* (pp. 212–232). New York: Guilford.

Cialdini, R. B. (2009). *Influence: Science and practice.* New York: Pearson Education, Inc.

Connolly, N. D. B. (2017, April). Communications: To the editors. *American Historical Review*, 637–638.

Cook, J., & Vale, G. (2018). *From Daesh to "diaspora": Tracing the women and minors of Islamic State.* International Center for the Study of Radicalization. Kings College, London. Retrieved from https://icsr.info/wp-content/uploads/2018/07/ICSR-Report-From-Daesh-to-%E2%80%98Diaspora%E2%80%99-Tracing-the-Women-and-Minors-of-Islamic-State.pdf

Eagly, A. H., & Chaiken, S. (1993). *The psychology of attitudes.* New York: Harcourt, Brace Jovanovich.

Effron, O. (2020, October 12). Facebook will ban holocaust denial posts under hate speech policy. *CNN Business.* Retrieved from https://www.cnn.com/2020/10/12/tech/facebook-holocaust-denial-hate-speech/index.html

Facebook (n.d.). *Community standards: Objectionable content: 12 hate speech.* Retrieved from https://www.facebook.com/communitystandards/hate_speech

FBI (2017). *Hate crime statistics, 2017.* United States Department of Justice, Federal Bureau of Investigation. Retrieved from https://ucr.fbi.gov/hate-crime/2017/topic-pages/tables/table-1.xls

FBI (n.d.). *Protected voices: Social media literacy.* Federal Bureau of Investigation. Retrieved from https://youtu.be/30lPQI1LElk

Greenblatt, J. A. (2020, December 22). Stepping up to stop hate online. *Stanford Social Innovation Review.* Retrieved from https://ssir.org/articles/entry/stepping_up_to_stop_hate_online

Greenwald, A. G. (1968). Cognitive learning, cognitive responses to persuasion, and attitude change. In A. Greenwald, T. Brock, & T. Ostrom (Eds.), *Psychological foundations of attitudes* (pp. 147–170). New York: Academic Press.

Groppe, M. (February 4, 2021). *Mike Pence to join the Heritage Foundation to "lead the Conservative Movement into the future".* Retrieved from https://www.usatoday.com/story/news/politics/2021/02/04/think-tank-pence-wants-lead-conservatives-into-future/4389431001/

The Heritage Foundation (n.d.). Retrieved from www.Heritage.org.

Institute for Historical Review (n.d.). Retrieved from www.IHR.org

Jew Watch (n.d.). Retrieved from www.jewwatch.com

Johnson, B. T., & Eagly, A. H. (1989). Effects of involvement on persuasion: A meta-analysis. *Psychological Bulletin, 104,* 290–314.

Kastrenakes, J. (2020, August 11). *Facebook bans black face and anti-Semitic stereotypes in hate speech update.* The Verge.

Keystone United (n.d.). Retrieved from keystone2001united, worldpress.com

Liberman, A. & Chaiken, S. (1992). Defensive processing of personally relevant health messages. *Personality and Social Psychology Bulletin, 18,* 669–679.

Lichtenstein, A. (2017, October). The AHR editor responds. *American Historical Review,* 1386.

Lister, T., Sanchez, R., Bixler, M., O'Key, S., Hogenmiller, M. & Tawfeeq, M. (2015, December 17, updated 2018, February 12). ISIS goes global: 143 attacks in 29 countries have killed 2,043. *CNN World.* Retrieved from https://www.cnn.com/2015/12/17/world/mapping-isis-attacks-around-the-world/index.html

Mahler, J. (2018, June 20). How one conservative think tank is stocking Trump's government. *The New York Times Magazine.* Retrieved from https://www.nytimes.com/2018/06/20/magazine/trump-government-heritage-foundation-think-tank.html

Ohlheiser, A. & Shapira, I. (2018, October 29). Gab, The white-supremacist sanctuary linked to the Pittsburg suspect goes offline (for now). *The Washington Post.* Retrieved from https://www.washingtonpost.com/technology/2018/10/28/how-gab-became-white-supremacist-sanctuary-before-it-was-linked-pittsburgh-suspect/

Ostrom, T. & Brock, T. C. (1968). A cognitive model of attitudinal involvement. In R. P. Abelson, E. Aronson, W. J. McGuire, T. M. Newcomb, M. J. Rosenberg, & P. H. Tannebaum (Eds.), *Theories of cognitive consistency: A sourcebook* (pp. 373–383). Chicago: Rand-McNally.

Petrzela, N. M. (2017, April) Communications: To the editors. *American Historical Review, 122,* 638–639.

Petty, R. E., & Cacioppo. J. T. (1981). Issue involvement as a moderator of the effects on attitude of advertisement content and context. *Advances in Consumer Research, 8,* 20–24.

Petty, R. E., & Cacioppo, J. T. (1986). *Communication and persuasion: Central and peripheral routes to attitude change.* New York: Springer-Verlag.

Petty, R. E., Cacioppo, J. T., & Goldman, R. (1981). Personal involvement as a determination of argument-based persuasion. *Journal of Personality and Social Psychology, 41,* 847–855.

Petty, R. E., Cacioppo, J., & Schumann, D. (1983). Central and peripheral routes to advertising effectiveness: The moderating role of involvement. *Journal of Consumer Research, 10,* 135–146.

Rodriquez, S. (2020, June 26). Zuckerberg: Facebook will prohibit hate speech in its ads. *CNBC.* Retrieved from https://www.cnbc.com/2020/06/26/zuckerberg-facebook-will-prohibit-hate-speech-in-its-ads.html

Schneider, R. A. (2017, April). Communications: The AHR editor responds. *American Historical Review,* 639.

Scribner, C. F. (2017, April). Communications: To the editors. *American Historical Review,* 637.

Shearer, E. (2021, January 12). More than eight-in-ten Americans get their news from digital devices. *Pew Research Center.* Retrieved from https://www.pewresearch.org/fact-tank/2021/01/12/more-than-eight-in-ten-americans-get-news-from-digital-devices/

Southern Poverty Law Center (n.d.a). *American renaissance.* Retrieved from https://www.splcenter.org/fighting-hate/extremist-files/group/american-renaissance

Southern Poverty Law Center (n.d.b), *Institute for historical review.* Retrieved from https://www.splcenter.org/fighting-hate/extremist-files/group/institute-historical-review

Southern Poverty Law Center (n.d.c). *Keystone united.* Retrieved from https://www.splcenter.org/fighting-hate/extremist-files/group/keystone-united

Twitter Safety (2020, December 2). *Updating our rules against hateful conduct.* Retrieved from https://blog.twitter.com/en_us/topics/company/2019/hatefulconductupdate.html

University of California at Berkeley (n.d.). *Evaluating resources.* Berkeley Library, University of California. Retrieved from https://guides.lib.berkeley.edu/evaluating-resources

University of Maryland, Global Campus (n.d.). *Is my source credible?* Library, University of Maryland: Global Campus. Retrieved from https://sites.umgc.edu/library/libhow/credibility.cfm

University of Wisconsin at Green Bay (n.d.). *How can I tell if a website is credible?* Information Technologies, University of Wisconsin, Green Bay. Retrieved from https://uknowit.uwgb.edu/page.php?id=30276

Valeri, R. M. & Borgeson, K. (2005). Identifying the face of hate. *Journal of Applied Sociology, 22*(1), 91–104.

Valeri, R. M. & Borgeson, K. (2016). Sticks and stones: When the words of hatred become weapons, A social psychological perspective. In S. Harding & M.

Palasinski (Eds.), *Global perspectives on youth gang behavior, violence, and weapons* (pp. 101–132). IGI Global.

Valeri, R. M., Borgeson, K., Cogley, E., Hamed, M., Kindred, E., & Tripodi, S. (2019). *The face of hate: A 15 year follow-up study examining the impact of online anti-semitism*. Unpublished manuscript.

Valeri, R. M., Burgio, S., Full, A. & Borgeson, K. (2018). *Cyberhate gets a make-over: Comparing the face of the right, the alt-right, and the extremist right on the web*. Unpublished manuscript.

Valeri, R. M., Furgal, E., & Russell, R. (2016). *Make hijrah to the Islamic State or jihad at Home*. Unpublished manuscript.

Wolters, R. (2017, February). Review of books: Ansley T. Erickson. Making the unequal metropolis: School desegregation and its limits (Historical studies of urban America) Chicago: University of Chicago Press, 2016. Pp. xviii, 390. $40.00. *American Historical Review*, 210–211.

WorldCat (n.d.a). *Jewish virtual library*. Retrieved from http://www.worldcat.org/title/jewish-virtual-library/oclc/439562962&referer=brief_results

WorldCat (n.d.b). *The Nizkor project*. Retrieved from http://www.worldcat.org/title/nizkor-project/oclc/40593673

Yan, H. (2015, March 23). Why is ISIS so successful at luring Westerners. *CNN.com*. Retrieved from https://www.cnn.com/2015/03/23/world/isis-luring-westerners

Chapter 3

Is Hate against the Law?

Legal Responses to Cyberhate

Janine Fodor

There is a maxim or principle dating back to Roman law that states, "for every wrong, the law provides a remedy." Acts of online cyberhate challenge the truth of this maxim. At times it seems as though our system of laws has fallen behind our technological ability to do harm. Or perhaps, we are struggling to reach consensus on what behavior constitutes a "wrong" that requires a legal response. For instance, in July 2019, three white fraternity brothers from the University of Mississippi posed for a photo in front of a bullet-riddled monument, two carrying rifles, one of which was an AR-15 assault rifle. The photo was posted to social media and obtained hundreds of "likes" before it was taken down. The defaced monument was dedicated to Emmett Till (Noori Fazan, 2019). The lynching of Emmett Till in 1955 in Mississippi was one of the events that ignited the civil rights movement. Accused of flirting with a white woman, the 14-year-old African American boy was abducted by four men, tortured and killed, and then his body was thrown into the Tallahatchie River. His killers were acquitted by an all-white jury. The monument to the lynched child was erected at the place on the river where his body had been found.[1]

The young men who took the photo beside the vandalized monument were suspended from their fraternity. Although the University of Mississippi described the post as offensive, it took no disciplinary actions against the students. As of the date of this writing, the U.S. Department of Justice is investigating the incident, but no formal action has been taken (Noori Fazan, 2019). What should be the legal response to this post? Is this a hate crime? Did the fraternity brothers intend for their conduct to be intimidating? Should their intent matter? Could the students be criminally charged with vandalizing

a monument? Could they be civilly liable to pay damages, not only for repair-
ing the monument but for the emotional harm caused to the survivors of
Emmett Till? Should social media sites be liable for allowing this post? Or
is it better to let conduct like this go unsanctioned, out of fear of inflating its
importance and generating copy-cat acts, or in the hope that the students will
one day grow ashamed of their conduct?

This chapter examines how we answer the aforementioned questions.
There are not necessarily single correct answers. From the outside, the law
can appear to be a set of rules that determines what conduct is permissible,
or alternatively, what conduct might expose its participants to sanctions, but
the reality is more complicated. Understanding the law is more like knowing a city or knowing a hiking trail than memorizing a set of rules. It is not a
finite or definite kind of knowledge. The law is dynamic; it originates from
multiple, sometimes conflicting sources, it changes over time, and its parts
are interconnected in ways that are not immediately obvious. No matter how
familiar you are with the governing laws, there is always uncertainty about
how laws may be applied in a given situation. Confronted with behavior such
as the previous example, lawyers try to design a strategy, utilizing the legally
available tools and limited by the constraints of the law, to redress wrongful
conduct.

The law develops analogically by building upon key examples which are
called *precedents*. In other words, judges look at a set of facts in a case before
them and ask, "Are these facts sufficiently similar to the facts of an already
decided case such that the two cases should be resolved in the same way?"
One way to state the principle of the "rule of law" is that like cases should
be treated alike. Because the law develops by this kind of similarity analysis,
important precedents set the standard for other cases to follow. Thus, the
chapter is organized around particular cases that have set, or may be setting,
precedent.

Part I of the chapter is a brief introduction to the sources and types of law.
The remaining sections examine different types of legal actions that have
been taken against perpetrators of cyberhate, as well as the limitations on
such actions. Part II focuses on the criminal law and explores hate crimes
statutes and circumstances in which speech of verbal communications alone
may constitute a crime. Part III looks at personal injury law or cases in which
a private party has sued another person or group for money damages to
compensate for a physical or emotional injury. Part IV deals with efforts by
administrative agencies to regulate the Internet. As the chapter demonstrates,
we are in uncharted territory. The injured and their advocates will have to
engage in creative thinking to both fairly and effectively design legal remedies for the wrong of cyberhate.

PART I: SOURCES AND TYPES OF LAW

Where Do Laws Come From?

Laws come from multiple different sources. In the United States, we have three branches of government: the legislative branch, the executive branch, and the judicial branch, and each is involved in lawmaking. The division of the authority of government into three branches is called the "separation of powers," and it is a key organizing principle of the U.S. Constitution.

The legislative branch, the U.S. Congress at the federal level of government, has the primary responsibility of passing laws. Laws passed by Congress are called "statutes." Statutes are organized topically and numerically and published as "codes." For example, one of several federal hate crimes statutes is codified at Chapter 18 of the U.S. Code, section 249; the reference is usually abbreviated as follows: 18 U.S.C. §249.

The other branches of government are also involved in lawmaking. The executive branch, which consists primarily of the president and cabinet, includes administrative agencies, such as the Federal Trade Commission (FTC) and the Federal Communications Commission (FCC). Administrative agencies have authority to issue "regulations," which are also organized by number in an "administrative code." Regulations are subordinate to statutes, meaning that if Congress is dissatisfied with a regulation, it can pass a statute to overrule the regulation, but it is often politically difficult to do so. In addition to drafting regulations, administrative agencies have enforcement powers. Agencies investigate violations of certain laws or regulations and impose sanctions, such as fines or penalties, or revoke licenses or permits. For example, the FTC has the authority to investigate and sanction violations of Internet privacy rules, such as the Children's Online Privacy Protection Act[2] and the regulations adopted under this act.

Courts are involved in lawmaking in two ways. First, it is the duty of courts to interpret laws. This is a critically important lawmaking function because adversarial parties, which are promoting alternative interpretations of certain laws, must ultimately turn to the courts to resolve their dispute about what a certain law or regulation requires. In particular, courts have the authority to interpret the Constitution of the United States. The authority to determine the meaning of the Constitution gives courts the power of *judicial review*, which allows courts to decide whether a statute or regulation, passed by another branch of government, is consistent with the U.S. Constitution. Because the Constitution is the highest law of the land, if a statute or regulation is unconstitutional, it is invalid and cannot be enforced. For example, if Congress passed a statute that criminalized political speech and violated the First Amendment to the U.S. Constitution, the statute could not be enforced.

In addition to their role in interpreting laws passed by the other branches, most states in the United States are *common law* jurisdictions. This means that certain legal rules are made only by the courts and are not codified into statutes or regulations. Technically, the federal government is not a common law jurisdiction, but some of the laws that federal courts interpret, such as the First Amendment, are so broad that the process of interpreting these laws gives rise to a great many court-made rules. Courts make common law rules by issuing written opinions to decide cases. The legal rule set forth in an opinion is called a *precedent.* In order to be fair and treat like cases alike, courts tend to follow precedent. In other words, once a legal rule is settled by one court, other judges in other courts tend to rely on that rule and decide the matter the same way in their own opinions. Also, courts are hierarchical. Each state has a high court, and the U.S. Supreme Court is the highest court in the land. If a high court issues a precedent, all the courts below the high court in the hierarchy *must* follow its precedent. When the U.S. Supreme Court issues a ruling interpreting the U.S. Constitution, that ruling is binding on the entire country.

Federal and State Laws

In the United States, governmental power or authority is divided between the federal government and the states. The federal government and each of the fifty states create laws. Federal laws apply throughout the country, but state laws are only valid in the state which has passed or adopted the law. Sometimes the federal government will *preempt* state law by stating that the federal law is the only allowable law or standard governing a particular topic, and the states are not permitted to have their own, potentially inconsistent laws, on the issue. In many situations, however, federal law and state law coexist. For instance, the federal government and most states have hate-crimes statutes, and an offender, who is alleged to have committed a hate crime, might be tried by the federal government, the state government, or both.

The federal government is intended to be a limited government; it only has the powers that are specifically enumerated or spelled out in the Constitution. As a practical matter, the federal government has very broad powers, arising primarily from its constitutional duty to regulate interstate commerce. Congress is explicitly given the power to pass laws governing interstate commerce in Article I, Section 8, Clause 3 of the U.S. Constitution.

Most businesses and most forms of communication, including Internet communications, cross state lines and involve interstate commerce. Thus, the federal government has adopted both criminal and civil laws governing behavior that occurs over the Internet, and many of the laws we will examine in this chapter are federal laws. Conversely, states have limited power to enforce laws regarding Internet behavior because the perpetrator or violator of the state law may be located in another state and beyond the jurisdiction or reach of the state law.

Criminal Law and Civil Law

Laws made at both levels of government, federal and state, can be divided into two broad categories: (i) criminal law and (ii) civil or private law. Criminal prosecutions can be brought *only* by the executive branch of the government. Private individuals, even if they are victims of crimes, cannot initiate criminal prosecutions. A person who violates a criminal law or commits a crime can be subject to criminal penalties, such as imprisonment or probation. Criminal prosecutions are subject to strict procedural requirements. For example, a person charged with a serious crime has the right to be represented by a lawyer, and the government must prove its case to a jury beyond a reasonable doubt. Civil actions, by contrast, are cases initiated by private individuals or groups of individuals alleging that another person or company has harmed them. The remedy available for civil actions is almost always money damages. Civil actions are subject to different procedural rules than criminal cases. A person who brings a civil action, called a *plaintiff*, has a less demanding burden of proof. A plaintiff need only prove that it is *more likely than not* that a defendant harmed him or her and does not have to prove their case beyond a reasonable doubt. A person sued in a civil case has a right to be represented by an attorney but not at public or state expense. Thus, a person sued in a civil case who cannot afford counsel must represent himself or herself. The same conduct can result in both a civil suit and a criminal prosecution. Someone who commits a hate crime may be criminally prosecuted by the government for that conduct and simultaneously sued by the victims for money damages.

Regulatory enforcement actions brought by administrative agencies are a hybrid between criminal and civil actions. Enforcement actions are civil actions initiated by the government. Such actions seek the imposition of fines or penalties, not imprisonment. Fines or penalties are paid to the government, not to the victims. Regulatory agencies also have the authority to issue orders or injunctions that prohibit individuals or corporations from taking certain actions. If a corporation violates an administrative order, it may be subject to various penalties, including a loss of a license to engage in its business.

PART II: CRIMINAL LAWS AGAINST CYBERHATE

General Principles of Criminal Law

A *crime* can be defined as conduct which pairs an *actus reus* or bad act, with a *mens rea* or malicious intent. Unintentional car accidents are not crimes even though the individuals involved can suffer serious injury or even death, because the driver who caused the accident did not have malicious intent. Conversely, a person who has malicious intent but never acts on that intent in any way—their malicious intent is nothing but a private thought—also has not committed a crime.

The *actus reus* or wrongful act requirement makes it difficult to criminally convict a potential perpetrator in the planning stages of a crime, before a violent act has occurred. There are a set of offenses called *inchoate crimes* that permit the prosecution of unfinished crimes. The three most common inchoate crimes are attempt, conspiracy, and solicitation. An *attempt* to commit a crime occurs when a person intends a crime, that is, has the *mens rea* to commit a crime and takes some step toward committing the *actus reus* but fails to complete it. Similarly, a *conspiracy* occurs when two or more people plan a crime, evidencing their joint criminal intent and start but fail to complete the intended act. *Solicitation* is when one person pays a person to commit a crime; an individual may be guilty of solicitation even if the recipient of the payment never follows through.

All inchoate crimes require some overt action toward committing the crime, beyond simply expressing an intent. For example, in the case of *United States v. Graham*,[3] the defendant, Randy Graham, was a member of an antigovernment group called the North American Militia, located in western Michigan, which had planned attacks on various federal government targets. Mr. Graham admitted being a member of the militia but defended himself on the grounds that "words alone," that is expressing support for the militia, did not constitute a crime (*United States v. Graham*, 2001, pp. 500–501). The government obtained a conviction of conspiracy by showing that Mr. Graham had engaged in more than mere words; he was involved in growing marijuana to fund the militia, and he engaged in paramilitary training exercises, scoped out particular targets, and purchased weapons for the organization (*United States v. Graham*, 2001, pp. 501–502).

While the *actus reus* requirement limits the ability of law enforcement to stop criminal activity at the planning stages, the *mens rea* requirement makes it hard to hold groups or organizations criminally liable for the actions of one person. *Mens rea*, or malicious intent, is an individual attribute. Several people may participate in the same act, but each person's state of mind is his or her own. Generally speaking, to be criminally responsible for someone else's act, it must be proved that the responsible person shared the *mens rea* or criminal intent of the actor or actors. For instance, individuals who merely sat in on meetings of a militia group like the North American Militia described earlier or read online chats about impending violent actions, but never said or wrote anything themselves nor took any action to show that they shared the goal to commit violence would likely not be guilty of conspiracy.

These principles of criminal law constrain the kinds of cyberhate that can be criminalized. In the sections that follow, we look at several kinds of criminal laws directed at trying to redress cyberhate.

Hate Crimes Statutes

On October 27, 2018, Robert Bowers, armed with an AR-15-style assault rifle and three handguns, rushed into the Tree of Life Synagogue in Pittsburgh during Saturday morning services and fired at the congregants, killing eleven people. Mr. Bowers had a history of posting anti-Semitic diatribes on a social media site called Gab. Hours before the shooting he accused a Jewish non-profit organization of "bring[ing] invaders in that kill our people. I can't sit by and watch my people get slaughtered. Screw your optics, I'm going in" (Turkewitz & Roose, 2018). After his arrest, Mr. Bowers told a police officer, "they're committing genocide to my people. I just want to kill Jews."[4] Mr. Bowers was charged with 29 federal crimes including 11 hate crimes under the federal statute codified at Chapter 18 U.S.C. §247 (Complaint, *United States v. Bowers*, 2018). The case against Mr. Bowers is still pending; he has been arrested and charged but not convicted.

The statute, Chapter 18 of the U.S. Code, section 247, under which Mr. Bowers is charged, reads as follows:

(a) Whoever, in any of the circumstances referred to in subsection (b) of this section—

. . .

intentionally obstructs, by force or threat of force, including by threat of force against religious real property, any person in the enjoyment of that person's free exercise of religious beliefs, or attempts to do so;

shall be punished as provided in subsection (d).

(b) The circumstances referred to in subsection (a) are that the offense is in or affects interstate or foreign commerce.

. . .

(d) The punishment for a violation of subsection (a) . . .

(1) if death results from acts committed in violation of this section or if such acts include kidnapping or an attempt to kidnap, aggravated sexual abuse or an attempt to commit aggravated sexual abuse, or an attempt to kill, a fine in

accordance with this title and imprisonment for any term of years or for life, or both, or may be sentenced to death. (18 U.S.C. § 247)

The aforementioned law is a federal statute, creating a federal crime. Mr. Bowers is charged with committing this crime eleven times, one for each of the persons killed.[5] This statute, like virtually all hate crime statutes, has several important characteristics. First, it focuses on the motivation of the perpetrator. Subsection (a) of the statute requires the government to prove that the offender committed the crime for a discriminatory purpose, in this case interfering with the victims' freedom of religion. Second, the law is a sentencing enhancement law. The statute does not create a separate crime called hate but instead it increases the possible punishment to be imposed for other underlying crimes, such as murder or attempted murder, or kidnapping. In other words, Mr. Bowers could not be charged with a hate crime offense until after he had committed another serious violent offense, such as murder or assault. Third, and finally, the sentences that can be imposed for a racially or religiously motivated crime are severe; Mr. Bowers may face a sentence of life imprisonment or even death.

Hate crimes statutes are important and effective at exposing the motivations behind those who commit violent acts for reasons of racial or religious bigotry. One purpose of high-profile prosecutions of persons like Mr. Bowers is to deter others from engaging in similar conduct. However, hate crimes statutes have their limitations. These statutes are invoked *after* an atrocity has occurred. The next section examines the ability of the legal system to prevent acts of violence by initiating criminal prosecutions *before* a killing or assault occurs.

RICO and the Ancillary Crimes Approach

In addition to hate crimes statutes, federal prosecutors may prosecute organized groups expressing an ideology of hate under the Racketeer Influenced and Corrupt Organizations (RICO) Act.[6] The statute is usually referred to by its acronym "RICO." RICO is designed to prevent proceeds from criminal activity from being used to support businesses, even if the businesses themselves are not illegal. White supremacist and other ideologically based organizations count as "businesses" for RICO purposes. A person convicted of a RICO offense can be sentenced to a long term of imprisonment. Just as importantly, all property acquired through the criminal enterprise is forfeited to the government. In other words, RICO allows the government to go after the money.

All organized groups need money to operate and often fringe groups, including white supremacist organizations, turn to criminal enterprises such as drug trafficking, human trafficking, or illegal arms sales to make money. Recently, in Arkansas, the federal government initiated a RICO prosecution against 54 members of the New Aryan Empire, alleging that it is a racketeering enterprise, which committed crimes such as drug trafficking, kidnapping, and murder in support of its organization. If successful, not only the prosecution may result in multiple criminal convictions but the New Aryan Empire may have to forfeit its assets (Dept. of Justice, 2019).

While not explicitly relying on RICO, a similar kind of prosecution recently took place in Texas. In 2017, a consortium of state and federal law enforcement agencies successfully prosecuted 89 members of several white supremacist groups that were active in Texas, including the Aryan Brotherhood of Texas, the Aryan Circle, the Irish Mob, Dirty White Boys, and the White Knights. The defendants were not convicted of belonging to white supremacist organizations but for their ancillary criminal conduct, which was used to raise money for the groups. The 89 defendants were convicted in total of over 700 offenses, including drug possession, sale and distribution, gun possession violations, burglaries and other crimes of violence, and sex crimes against children. All defendants combined were sentenced to over 1,000 years' imprisonment (Dept. of Homeland Security, 2017). Due to the number of people convicted, and the interruption of their sources of funding, the U.S. attorney involved in the prosecution stated, "The Aryan Brotherhood of Texas and the Aryan Circle have essentially been decimated in North Texas" (Dept. of Homeland Security, 2017).

In sum, one tool that the government utilizes to prevent extremist groups from carrying out acts of violence is to rigorously pursue crimes of vice such as drug and sex trafficking, illegal weapons dealing, and financial crimes. When extremist groups rely on crimes of vice to fund their operations, the prosecutions not only result in the imprisonment of group leaders, but the money supply is cut off.

When Does Speech Alone Constitute a Crime?

The First Amendment to the U.S. Constitution states in part that "Congress shall make no law . . . abridging the freedom of speech" (U.S. Const. Amend. I). The Supreme Court has held that most speech, even hate speech, is protected by the First Amendment.[7] The right to free speech, however, is not absolute. The Supreme Court has identified categories of speech that are not protected by the First Amendment and may be criminalized. One such category is the act of communicating threats.[8]

Both the federal government and the states have criminal statutes that prohibit communicating threats.[9] In order to be criminal, and outside the protection of the First Amendment, a threat must be both specific and credible. For

example, in the case of *United States v. White*,[10] William White, who identified himself as the commander of a neo-Nazi organization, the American
National Socialist Workers Party, left an intimidating telephone message for
a University of Delaware administrator, who was responsible for starting a
diversity training program at the university. When the administrator's secretary answered the phone call from Mr. White and asked if she could take a
message, Mr. White answered, "Yes. Just tell her that people that think the
way she thinks, we hunt down and shoot" (*United States v. White*, 2012, p.
504). Mr. White was criminally convicted by a jury, and his conviction was
upheld by the appellate court, because his threat targeted a certain individual
and he, along with unidentified others, threatened to shoot the victim (*United
States v. White*, 2012, pp. 508–513).

By contrast, in *United States v. Bagdasarian*,[11] the Ninth Circuit Court of
Appeals out of California vacated Mr. Bagdasarian's convictions for communicating a threat against President Obama. Upset at Mr. Obama's election,
Mr. Bagdasarian posted the following two statements to an online message
board: (1) "Re: Obama fk the niggar, he will have a 50 cal in the head soon"
and (2) "shoot the nig" (*United States v. Bagdasarian*, 2011, p. 1115). He
was initially convicted of the crime of communicating threats, but the reviewing court on appeal held that neither communication was a direct threat
against Mr. Obama; Mr. Bagdasarian was asking some unidentified person
to assault the president; he was not actually threatening to take action himself. The Court also found that there was no showing that Mr. Bagdasarian
had the power or ability to command anyone to shoot the president. Because
the threat was not credible, it did not qualify as a crime (*United States v.
Bagdasarian*, 2011, pp. 1120–1124).

Communicating a threat can involve nonverbal, expressive acts. For example, the Supreme Court held that the state of Virginia could pass a criminal
law prohibiting cross-burning with the intent to intimidate. The Supreme
Court explained that given the historical meaning of cross-burning and its
association with the Ku Klux Klan, the act of burning a cross with the intent
to intimidate was effectively a threat. Thus, this activity was outside the protections of the First Amendment.[12]

Both the federal and state governments also criminalize Internet harassment or cyber stalking, when such harassment includes threats of physical
violence or is likely to cause substantial emotional distress.[13] Cyber stalking
statutes were enacted in part to protect women from domestic violence and
are used primarily in the context of domestic abuse. In those situations, the
victim knows his or her stalker, and the stalker often knows enough about the
victim that the stalking is continuous and the threat of escalation into physical harm is real. In instances of racially or religiously based cyberhate, the

opposite is often true. Frequently, the victims of the harassment don't know the identity of the perpetrators, except perhaps by a pseudonym, and have no way of assessing how real a threat may be. Thus, prosecution of Internet harassment cases in instances of racially or religiously based cyberhate is difficult.[14]

Another kind of speech, which is not protected by the First Amendment, is speech that specifically and directly incites violence. This is a very difficult exception to meet. The leading U.S. Supreme Court case explaining this exception is *Brandenburg v. Ohio*.[15] In that case, Mr. Brandenburg, who was a leader in the Ku Klux Klan, gave a public speech in Ohio in which he advocated seeking revenge against the government if it did not stop suppressing the white race. Specifically, Mr. Brandenburg said, "we're not a revengent organization, but if our President . . . continues to suppress the white, Caucasian race, it's possible that there might have to be some revengeance taken" (*Brandenburg v. Ohio*, 1969, p. 446). Mr. Brandenburg initially was convicted of violating an Ohio criminal law that prohibited "teaching or advocating violence or terrorism as a means of achieving political reform." However, the U.S. Supreme Court, exercising its power of *judicial review*, held that the Ohio statute was unconstitutional under the First Amendment and the Court vacated Mr. Brandenburg's conviction. Brandenburg holds that the only kind of "advocacy" or public speech that may be criminalized is speech that directly calls for "immediate imminent lawless action and where the speaker has power and the speech is likely to produce such action" (*Brandenburg v. Ohio*, 1969, pp. 448–449).

One example of a criminal prosecution for speech that incited violence is the case of *Pennsylvania v. Knox*.[16] In this case, rap artists were criminally prosecuted under a Pennsylvania state law for publicizing lyrics that named and threatened violence against police officers. The court held that the lyrics, while not threats directly communicated to the police officers, put the officers at risk of being targeted by other persons influenced by the lyrics.[17]

In summary, the First Amendment limits the kinds of hate speech that can be prosecuted as a crime. In order for speech alone to be a crime, the speech must be a direct and credible threat by the speaker, or the speech must credibly incite others to act violently.

PART III: CIVIL ACTIONS

The previous section outlined criminal laws that have been used to sanction and deter cyberhate. This section looks at civil causes of action used to accomplish the same ends.

General Principles of Civil Actions

Civil cases are cases initiated by private individuals or groups of individuals, called *plaintiffs*. Civil actions seek money damages as a remedy for harms committed by the person or organization that is sued. The person or organization sued in a civil case is called a *defendant*. The claims made in a civil action are called *causes of action*. Sometimes causes of action are created by statutes, passed by federal or state legislatures. For example, the federal government has passed civil rights statutes, one of which is examined in detail further, that grant private individuals the ability to sue for money damages if the plaintiff(s)' constitutional rights are violated. Other civil causes of action are created by *common law*. Common law consists of court-made rules. Defamation, discussed later in more detail, is a common law cause of action. Recall that the federal government is not a common law jurisdiction, so that common law rules are a matter of state law. It is common for plaintiffs to include multiple causes of action in a single lawsuit. An individual who is alleging causes of action under both federal and state laws can combine these allegations into a single lawsuit and can choose whether to bring the action in state court or federal court. The First Amendment does not apply to private civil actions; it only limits the actions of the government. In other words, even if certain verbal conduct may not be criminalized because of the First Amendment, it may still be the subject of a civil action and the speaker may be required to pay money damages if the speech is negligent and harmful.

There are practical limitations on civil actions. Plaintiffs and the defendants who are sued must pay the costs of litigation. Because of the costs, many cases are settled without a clear or publicly announced result. Sometimes attorneys will provide legal services to a plaintiff in exchange for a share of the damages won in the lawsuit. Occasionally, plaintiffs may obtain the support of an advocacy group that can either provide legal representation or pay for a lawyer. For example, the Southern Poverty Law Center (SPLC) has helped victims of hate crimes initiate lawsuits. Even if a plaintiff wins an award of money, it might not be easy to collect the money. Sometimes defendants simply do not have the money to pay, and in other cases, they take steps to move their money out of reach of the plaintiff.

This part examines three different kinds of civil actions that have been used against white supremacist organizations or individuals involved with such organizations. The first are personal injury or *tort* cases, in which the plaintiff alleges that the defendant(s) caused the plaintiff either physical or severe emotional injury.

Personal Injury Cases

A "tort," which derives from the French word for "wrong," is a common law cause of action that allows private individuals to sue persons or organizations that have harmed them. Under the common law, in order to establish liability or responsibility in a tort case, the plaintiff must prove that the defendant engaged in wrongful conduct, either intentionally or negligently, that the defendant's conduct *caused* the plaintiff's injury, and the plaintiff must show that he or she was actually harmed. Traditionally, the only kind of harm that the law recognized as compensable in a tort case was actual physical harm. However, more recent cases have allowed recovery for severe cases of emotional or psychological harm. The remedy available in a tort case is that the defendants must pay money to the plaintiff to compensate for the harm that has been caused. When the harm is not easily susceptible to measurement, our legal system leaves it up to the jury to determine how much the harm is worth.

While the federal government is not a common law jurisdiction, the U.S. Congress passed a statute, based on the common law of tort, which permits private citizens to sue for monetary compensation on two conditions: if the citizen's constitutional rights are violated, and if the deprivation of rights results in injury to a person or damage to property.[18]

The constitutional tort statute was the basis of a case brought by a group of church leaders in Arizona against the Patriot Movement AZ and several individual members of the Patriot Movement group.[19] The plaintiffs in the case were churches and church leaders who were involved in assisting recent immigrants and asylum seekers from Central America. Pastors, church members, and volunteers provided shelter, food, clothing, basic medical treatment, and transportation to court dates or other appointments. The churches were operating within the law; in fact, immigration officials often dropped off migrants at the churches (Complaint, *Alliance of Christian Leaders v. Patriot Movement AZ*, 2019, pp. 7–8).

The defendants in the case, who were members of the "Patriot Movement AZ," strongly objected to any assistance given to migrants. The movement has been designated as a hate group by the SPLC, which provided legal counsel to the plaintiffs. The Patriot Movement has a substantial online presence, including a Facebook page, a YouTube channel, and a Twitter account. According to the allegations in the Complaint, members of the Patriot Group went to the church sites, where immigrants were being assisted and housed and intimidated the migrants and their supporters. The group members, sometimes carrying guns, yelled insults at the migrants, calling them dogs, illegals, and criminals, and telling them they were not welcome in the United States. The group members often filmed their interactions with the migrants, church leaders, and volunteers and posted photos and videos to their Internet sites. Some of the videos and images received tens of thousands of views. The postings would include recognizable faces, as well as video images of name tags and license plates, or would list the names and addresses of church leaders and volunteers (Complaint, *Alliance of Christian Leaders v. Patriot Movement AZ*, 2019, pp. 8–10).

As a result of the posts, the plaintiff church leaders were harassed and threatened online. One pastor received a voice mail message stating that his children should be raped (Simon & Sidner, September 24, 2019). In another incident a member of the Patriot Group filmed children playing outside a church and published the video online, accusing the pastor by name as a human trafficker. As a result of the Patriot Group's behavior, the church leaders and volunteers constantly feared for their personal safety and the safety of family members. Many volunteers quit and some churches had to hire guards (Complaint, *Alliance of Christian Leaders v. Patriot Movement AZ*, 2019, pp. 10, 14–15). Although, at least of the time of this writing, no pastor or volunteer had actually been physically hurt as a result of the defendants' activities, the risk of harm is real, and the psychological damage caused by intimidation and threats is serious.

The complaint against the Patriot Group states that members of the group are motivated by racial hatred and animus and are violating the constitutional rights of the pastors and church leaders to freely practice their religious beliefs and to be free of racial discrimination. The lawsuit seeks both money damages and an injunction, or court order, that prevent the defendants from continuing to trespass on church property and film there (Complaint, *Alliance of Christian Leaders v. Patriot Movement AZ*, 2019, pp. 20–22). Realizing that they might otherwise have to pay money to the churches and pastors, some of the defendants in the case recently settled and agreed to cease their harassing activity. Other defendants have refused to settle and claim that they have a First Amendment right to post the images, names, and innuendos (Simon & Sidner, September 24, 2019). If the case moves forward, a jury will eventually decide whether the plaintiffs have been injured by the defendants' conduct, and if so, the jury will also decide how much to award in damages.

Defamation

Defamation is a special kind of tort case, created by the common law. Defamation occurs when the tort or wrongful act is lying about a person or falsely accusing them of criminal or unethical conduct. To prove defamation as a cause of action, the plaintiff must show that (i) the defendant made a false claim about the plaintiff, (ii) the defendant publicized that false claim to others, and (iii) as a result of the publication of the falsity, the plaintiff suffered either emotional or reputational harm.

When acts of cyberhate are based on falsehoods, lawsuits for defamation can result in awards of money damages against the defendants, as well as court orders requiring that the false information be removed from online sources. For example, in December 2012, twenty children and six teachers were killed in a mass shooting at the Sandy Hook Elementary School in Newtown, Connecticut. In the aftermath of this tragedy, an online conspiracy theory began to evolve claiming that the massacre was not real, but rather was a fake event staged by advocates for gun control. Parents of the children killed in the massacre then became targets of online harassment and threats. Several parents of children killed in the massacre at Sandy Hook Elementary School have brought defamation lawsuits against proponents of the conspiracy theory. The father of one of the victims, Leonard Pozner, sued James Fetzer and Michael Palacek, who coedited a book called *Nobody Died at Sandyhook*.[20] Mr. Fetzer and Mr. Palacek wrote that Mr. Pozner had faked his son's death certificate and questioned whether the deceased child had ever existed. Mr. Pozner argued that the claim that he had faked his son's death was both false and extremely harmful to him, causing emotional distress that compounded the trauma of the massacre itself and the loss of his child (Complaint, *Pozner v. Fetzer*, 2018). Mr. Pozner settled with one of the defendants, Michael Palecek, who agreed to publicly renounce his earlier views and apologized for the distress he caused. Mr. Pozner won his case against the other defendant, James Fetzer, and recently was awarded damages in the amount of $450,000 (Svriuga, 2019).

Civil Harassment

As discussed in Part II, the federal government and many states have anti-harassment criminal laws, but those laws can be hard to enforce. It is also possible for a private citizen to sue a defendant for harassment in a civil action.

On May 1, 2017, Taylor Dumpson was elected president of the student government at American University in Washington D.C. She was the first African American female to be elected to head the student government. Almost immediately, she was subject to acts of racially motivated harassment and name-calling. When neo-Nazi Andrew Anglin learned of Dumpson's election, he posted an article about her in his online publication, *Daily Stormer*, encouraging his followers to "troll storm" Ms. Dumpson by subjecting her to cyberbullying on all of her social media sites. A troll storm indeed took place, and Ms. Dumpson was overwhelmed with racist taunts and threats (Sidner & Simon, 2019). Ms. Dumpson sued Andrew Anglin as well as two other individuals whose identities she was able to discern. Ms. Dumpson claimed that Mr. Anglin and the perpetrators of the troll storm had interfered with her right to pursue her education free from racial discrimination and that they had intentionally inflicted extreme emotional distress.[21] Mr. Anglin failed to respond to the lawsuit, and a $725,000 judgment has been entered against him. Due to numerous large judgments against him, Mr. Anglin is not currently living in the United States. Because Mr. Anglin is out of reach of the U.S. courts, Ms. Dumpson will probably never collect her money. Her lawsuit, however, was not futile. Due in part to her lawsuit (and others against Mr. Anglin) mainstream website hosts have refused to publish the *Daily Stormer*, and Mr. Anglin is reduced to living in exile. Moreover, one of the other defendants, Evan James McCarty, did respond to the lawsuit. Mr. McCarty entered into a settlement with Ms. Dumpson under which he agreed to publicly apologize and renounce white supremacism. He also agreed to complete 200 hours of community service advocating against racial hatred (Zraick, 2018). Ms. Dumpson's lawsuit shows the impact that ordinary individuals can have in combating Internet hate.

PART IV: LIMITS OF THE LAW—CAN WE REGULATE THE INTERNET?

The previous sections discussed cybercrimes and ways in which individual citizens may initiate private lawsuits to win money damages against defendants who have harmed them. This section explores a third approach, using administrative agencies to regulate the Internet.

What Are Administrative Agencies?

Administrative agencies are a part of the executive branch of government, and they exist at both the state and federal levels of government. Administrative agencies are the workhorses of government. They carry out the detailed work of implementing and enforcing laws passed by Congress or state legislatures. Administrative agencies carry out laws in two ways. First, the agencies issue regulations giving detailed guidance on what a specific law means. Second, the agencies often have the authority to take enforcement actions against individuals or corporations that violate laws or regulations within the jurisdiction or scope of the agency. Enforcement may involve both investigations, much like a law enforcement agency might investigate a crime, and quasi-judicial hearings, like mini trials before a hearing officer, where fact findings are made and penalties can be imposed.

The federal administrative agency that has been most heavily involved in regulating activity on the Internet is the FTC. Section 5 of the Federal Trade Commission Act prohibits businesses from engaging in *unfair and deceptive trade practices.*[22] The FTC Act dates back to 1914. Over the years, the FTC has issued regulations setting forth in more detail what constitutes an unfair and deceptive trade practice. It has also taken enforcement actions, resulting in findings that companies have violated the law, and it has issued sanctions against those companies. For instance, recently the FTC imposed a $5 billion penalty against Facebook. The penalty was part of a settlement arising from Facebook's failure to comply with an earlier order issued by the FTC, in 2012, that limited Facebook's ability to use or sell data it collected from its customers (Miller & Favors, 2019). Unlike private cases against companies, penalties collected by administrative agencies are paid to the government, not to the individuals who were hurt by the company's conduct.

What Can the FTC Do with Respect to Internet Content?

The FTC has not yet given clear guidelines about hate speech on the Internet. Various stakeholders, including social media corporations and advocacy groups on all sides of the issue, are lobbying both Congress and the FTC to try to shape the law.

The FTC is a part of the government and must abide by the First Amendment. The First Amendment restricts the ability of the FTC to control the publication of hate speech on the Internet. However, utilizing its authority to ban unfair and deceptive trade practices, there are two methods by which the FTC may be able to indirectly exercise some control over Internet content. First, social media sites and Internet providers, which are private actors and are not bound by the First Amendment, often have community use or community standards policies. Twitter, for example, has a community standards policy that precludes using Twitter to threaten violence against individuals or groups, or to glorify violence.[23] Twitter users arguably choose its platform over others because the customers do not want to be confronted with hate speech or other objectionable content. The FTC could take the position that if a social media site or web publisher creates a community standards policy but does not proactively enforce that policy, it is deceiving its customers and the FTC could sanction the site. This approach is problematic, however, because if the FTC sought to penalize social media sites for not complying with their own voluntary community standards policies, it would reduce the incentive for social media sites to adopt such policies. This approach also leaves platforms that are less socially responsible beyond the reach of the FTC.

A second approach would focus on banning fraudulent content. The FTC could adopt regulations stating that social media sites or Internet platforms which knowingly permit false information to be published on their platforms are engaged in "unfair and deceptive trade practices" and could be subject to administrative penalties. The U.S. Congress has indicated an interest in the anti-fraud approach to Internet regulation.

Mark Zuckerberg, the founder of Facebook, recently appeared before the House Financial Services Committee of the U.S. Congress.[24] He was questioned about whether Congress should seek to regulate false political advertisements that are published online. Congresswoman Alexandria Ocasio-Cortez, a liberal Democrat who is the lead proponent of a legislative plan called the Green New Deal, asked Mr. Zuckerberg whether Facebook would allow a political advertisement stating, falsely, that certain Republicans, running for reelection, had voted for her Green New Deal. Mr. Zuckerberg struggled to answer but ultimately responded that Facebook would allow such an advertisement. He reasoned that by not removing the advertisement, viewers would recognize its falsity and would, in the end, penalize Ms. Cortez or other Democrats at the ballot box for engaging in fraud and deception (Zuckerberg, Congressional Testimony, October 23, 2019). Mr. Zuckerberg was arguing for the self-corrective power of truth, that a discerning and informed public will not only recognize truth but will ultimately reward the truth speaker. He did not appear to convince many committee members. The committee could ask the FTC to draft regulations to preclude the publication of intentionally false political advertisements on the Internet. Even if given this directive, the agency will likely struggle to define and identify exactly what constitutes an intentionally false claim.

The exchange between Ms. Cortez and Mr. Zuckerberg captures the legal dilemma in which we now find ourselves with respect to the Internet. The Internet's great strength—it can give a voice to people oppressed by governments and be a platform for speaking truth to power—is also a great threat, when Internet speakers advocate for dangerous and morally indefensible ideologies. Over the next few years, Congress and the FTC will struggle to find the right balance. They will seek to protect victims of cyberhate and prevent further victims, without giving up the idealism that Mr. Zuckerberg expressed in the power of speech and the hope that truth eventually prevails in a marketplace of ideas.

CONCLUSION

This chapter has presented a broad overview of some of the legal strategies that have been employed against acts of cyberhate. When cyberhate escalates into acts of violence, the perpetrators can be criminally prosecuted, and their sentences may be enhanced if the crime was motivated by racial or religious animosity. Words alone, even words of hate, rarely constitute a crime, unless those words communicate a direct and credible threat. Private individuals can sue the perpetrators of cyberhate for money damages, and there are examples where this strategy has been successful. However, there are practical limitations to private lawsuits, such as finding lawyers and ways to fund the litigation, and it is often hard to collect money even if a case is won. Finally, the FTC is exploring ways it may more closely regulate the Internet, but there are countervailing interests that may limit its involvement. In short, the legal landscape around cyberhate is uncertain and evolving. For those who are injured by cyberhate, and their attorneys, the task of crafting and refining legal remedies to redress this wrong is an ongoing journey.

NOTES

1. An account of the incident can be found at Latson, J. (2015, August 28). How Emmett Till's murder changed the world. *Time Magazine*, retrieved from https://time.com/4008545/emmett-till-history/
2. The Children's Online Privacy Protection Act (COPPA) is codified at 15 U.S.C. §§ 6501–6506.
3. *United States v. Graham*, 275 F.3d 490 (6th Cir. 2001).
4. The statements and charges are set forth in the Affidavit of FBI Special Agent Brian Collins, in support of the Criminal Complaint in *United States v. Robert Bowers*, ___ F. Supp. _____ case no. 18-1396 (W.D. Pa filed 10/27/2018).
5. The federal government has the authority to prosecute Mr. Bowers because his conduct, namely purchasing weapons, involved interstate activity. Mr. Bowers was also charged with multiple state crimes. In theory, both the state of Pennsylvania and the federal government could separately prosecute Mr. Bowers, but if Mr. Bowers receives a sentence of life imprisonment or death as a result of the federal prosecution, there is little to be gained by a second state prosecution.
6. RICO is codified at Chapter 18 U.S.C. §§ 1961–1968.
7. The United States recently restated its position on hate speech in the case of *Matal v. Tam*, 582 U.S. ____, 198 L.Ed.2d 336 (2017). The Court held that the Trademark Office could not refuse to grant trademark protection to a potentially racially offensive mark, in this case an Asian American band that wanted to call itself "the Slants." The First Amendment, on its face, places limits on the federal government. The Supreme Court has interpreted the Fourteenth Amendment to require that state governments too must protect most of the rights set forth in the Bill of Rights, set forth in the first ten amendments to the Constitution.
8. The U.S. Supreme Court held that threats were not protected by the First Amendment in the case of *Chaplinsky v. New Hampshire*, 315 U.S. 568 (1942).

9. The federal statute making it a crime to communicate a threat is codified at 18 U.S.C. § 875.

10. *United States v. White*, 670 F.3d 498 (4th Cir. 2012).

11. *United States v. Bagdasarian*, 652 F.3d 1113 (9th Cir. 2011).

12. See *Virginia v. Black*, 538 U.S. 243 (2003).

13. The federal cyber stalking statute is codified at 18 U.S.C. § 2261A(2). Like the statute that criminalizes communicating threats, the penalties for violating the statute depend on the type of injury that results.

14. Danielle Citron, the author of *Hate Crime in Cyberspace* (Harvard University Press, 2016), discussed the difficulty of pursuing perpetrators of cyber stalking in an interview with Brianna Wu, who is a female developer of online games, in an interview on WNYC's radio talk show "The Takeaway," on February 18, 2016, available at https://www.wnyc.org/story/gamergate-will-not-go-trial/.

15. *Brandenburg v. Ohio*, 395 U.S. 444 (1969).

16. *Pennsylvania v. Knox*, 190 A.3d 1146 (Pa. Sup. Ct. 2018).

17. In a similar case, *Elonis v. United States*, 575 U.S. ___, 192 L.Ed2d. 1 (2015), the U.S. Supreme Court held that a rap artist could not be held criminally liable for violent lyrics unless he intended his lyrics as a threat.

18. The statute enabling private individuals to sue for violations of their constitutional rights is codified at 42 U.S.C. § 1985(3).

19. See Complaint, *Alliance of Christian Leaders v. Patriot Movement AZ*, ____ F. Supp. (D. AZ filed 6/4/2019).

20. The book was initially published by Moon Rock Books Publishing in 2015. It has been removed by Amazon, but Mr. Fetzer has posted a free version online.

21. The case is entitled *Taylor v. Ade, et. al*, case no. cv 1:18-01011 (D.C. Dist. Ct., filed 4/30/2018), retrieved from https://www.courthousenews.com/wp-content/uploads/2018/05/DUMPSON-v-Ade.pdf).

22. The FTC Act is codified at 15 U.S.C §§ 41–58.

23. The Twitter community use policy is set forth at https://help.twitter.com/en/rules-and-policies/twitter-rules.

24. See Zuckerberg's testimony, House Financial Services Committee (10/23/2019). A video of his testimony may be viewed at https://www.bing.com/videos/search?q=zuckerberg+testimony+aoc&view=detail&mid=150EB8F0916845352510150EB

REFERENCES

Alliance of Christian Leaders v. Patriot Movement AZ, ____ F. Supp. ____, case no. 2: 2019 cv 04347 (D. AZ filed 6/4/2019).

Brandenburg v. Ohio, 395 U.S. 444 (1969).

Chaplinsky v. New Hampshire, 315 U.S. 568 (1942).

Children's Online Privacy Protection Act (COPPA), 15 U.S.C. §§ 6501–6506.

Conspiracy to Interfere with Civil Rights, 42 U.S.C. § 1985.

Damage to Religious Property; Obstruction of Persons in Free Exercise of Religious Beliefs, 18 U.S.C. § 247.

Elonis v. United States, 575 U.S. ___, 192 L.Ed.2d. 1 (2015).

Federal Trade Commission Act, 15 U.S.C §§ 41–58.

Interstate Communications, 18 U.S.C. § 875.

Latson, J. (2015, August 28). How Emmett Till's murder changed the world. *Time Magazine*. Retrieved from https://time.com/4008545/emmett-till-history/

Matal v. Tam, 582 U.S. ____, 198 L.Ed.2d 366 (2017).

Miller, M. & Favors, J. (2019, July 29). *The Facebook settlement*. Harvard Law School Forum on Corporate Governance and Financial Regulation [pdf]. Retrieved from https://corpgov.law.harvard.edu/2019/07/29/the-facebook-settlement

Noori Farzan, A. (2019, July 26). Ole Miss frat brothers brought guns to an Emmett Till memorial. They're not the first. *Washington Post*. Retrieved from https://www.washingtonpost.com/nation/2019/07/26/ole-miss-emmitt-till-guns-kappa-alpha-fraternity/

Pennsylvania v. Knox, 190 A.3d 1146 (Pa. Sup. Ct. 2018).

Pozner v. Fetzer, case no. 2018 cv 003122 (Cir. Court Dane Cty, Wisc., filed 11/27/2018).

Racketeer Influenced and Corrupt Organizations Act, 18 U.S. C. §§ 1961–1968.

Simon, M. & Sidner, S. (2019, September 22). He tweeted hate at her. She sued. Then she met him. *CNN Report*. Retrieved from https://www.wthitv.com/content/national/560947002.html

Simon, M. & Sidner, S. (2019, September 24). Arizona group agrees to stop harassing churches that are helping immigrants. *CNN Report*. Retrieved from https://www.cnn.com/2019/09/23/us/arizona-patriot-groups-churches-lawsuit-soh/index.html

Stalking, 18 U.S.C. § 2261A(2).

Svriuga, S. (2019, October 16). Jury awards $450,000 to father of Sandy Hook victim in defamation case. *Washington Post*. Retrieved from https://www.washingtonpost.com/education/2019/10/16/jury-awards-father-sandy-hook-victim-defamation-case/

Taylor v. Ade, et. al, case no. cv 1:18-01011 (D.C. Dist. Ct., filed 4/30/2018).

Turkewitz, J. & Roose, K. (2018, October 27). Who is Robert Bowers, the suspect in the Pittsburgh synagogue shooting. *New York Times*. Retrieved from https://www.nytimes.com/2018/10/27/us/robert-bowers-pittsburgh-synagogue-shooter.html

United States v. Bagdasarian, 652 F.3d 1113 (9th Cir. 2011).

United States v. Bowers, ___ F. Supp. _____ case no. 18-1396 (W.D. Pa filed 10/27/2018).

United States Dept. of Homeland Security (2017, August 8). Last of 89 members/associates of Aryan brotherhood of Texas and Aryan circle sentenced to 20 years in federal prison. *U.S. Immigration and Customs Enforcement News Release*. Retrieved from https://www.ice.gov/news/releases/last-89-membersassociates-aryan-brotherhood-texas-and-aryan-circle-sentenced-20-years

United States Dept. of Justice (2019, February 12). Multiple white supremacist gang members among 54 defendants charged in RICO Indictment. *Press Release.* [pdf] Retrieved from https://www.justice.gov/usao-edar/pr/multiple-white-supremacist-gang-members-among-54-defendants-charged-rico-indictment

United States v. Graham, 275 F.3d 490 (6th Cir. 2001).

United States v. White, 670 F.3d 498 (4th Cir. 2012).

Virginia v. Black, 538 U.S. 243 (2003).

Zraik, K. (2018, December 21). Student targeted by troll storm hopes settlement will send message to white supremacists. *New York Times.* Retrieved from https://www.amren.com/news/2018/12/student-targeted-by-troll-storm-hopes-settlement-will-send-message-to-white-supremacists/

Zuckerberg, M. (2019, October 23). Testimony before House Financial Services Committee. Retrieved from https://www.bing.com/videos/search?q=zuckerberg+testimony+aoc&view=detail&mid=150EB8F0916845352510150EB

Chapter 4

Bitcoin

The Currency of White Supremacists

John Bambenek

Hate groups and terrorist organizations have often raised funds to support their operations. In some cases, those funds were used to support the lifestyles of their leaders, in other cases it was to fund tangible efforts the groups were undertaking or literature they were producing. With the creation of the Internet, much of that has been made easier. Technology generally has enabled people to produce information and disseminate it at greater scale, with lower cost, and cover greater distance than ever before.

The recent cyberhate groups have utilized technology to reach larger audiences and operate online communities that cater to like-minded individuals. In many cases, they run their own infrastructure with relatively strong cybersecurity and extend their reach internationally. It also means they are able to raise funds from a relatively global audience. As the groups have evolved and gained influence, they've shifted tactics from traditional methods like mailing checks and PayPal to using cryptocurrency.

Their move to cryptocurrency creates some difficulties but also provides a rare opportunity to get insight into how these organizations raise and spend money. First, it requires an overview of bitcoin and cryptocurrency.

OVERVIEW OF BITCOIN

Part of that shift has occurred due to the activities of those who are seeking to limit the ability of cyberhate groups to operate. The phenomena of "deplatforming" has been relatively successful at getting banks, credit card processing firms, and PayPal to stop doing business with these groups, especially after the Unite the Right rally in Charlottesville. The result was to accelerate their move to using alternative means of fundraising from the traditional financial system into cryptocurrency.

Cryptocurrency is a new digital asset that allows for transferring assets around the traditional banking system without respect to national borders. While many people are familiar with bitcoin specifically and cryptocurrency generally, some explanation of the underlying technology is warranted as it can help explain how and why cyberhate groups (and other criminals) have shifted to cryptocurrency and how aspects of the technology make it possible to track their financial activities.

Blockchain is the underlying technology that makes bitcoin possible. In reality, there are many blockchains and many are not tied to cryptocurrencies at all. At its core, blockchain is a decentralized peer-to-peer network that exchanges information in a trustworthy and reliable way that prevents tampering and does not require an "authority." It requires systems (called nodes) to be set up in the peer-to-peer system, which means all nodes are "equal" and exchange and synchronize information with each other.

This technology empowers bitcoin (and other cryptocurrencies) to create a decentralized financial system. Each node receives transactions from clients and that validity is determined by enough nodes seeing the same unaltered transaction so it can be presumed valid. In essence, because there is no authority in bitcoin, all transactions must be made public so they can be verified enough nodes to prove that it has not been a tampered transaction. Each transaction on the blockchain contains the following elements: a source wallet address, a destination wallet address, a timestamp, and the amount of bitcoin sent.

This public ledger must be unaltered in its entirety as each block of the blockchain builds upon the previous one. The blockchain is a file downloadable by anyone that contains the entirety of the public ledger from bitcoin's inception in 2010. A blockchain node will continue to update this file as new transactions are received and validated.

A wallet is created by an individual that is identified by a wallet address, an alphanumeric string of characters such as 1FnVXX84Ap VtyuuNfNJFN4bmyx1jkjp5dA that correspond to one private encryption key stored by the owner of that wallet. Any transactions signed by that private key will be presumed to be valid. Thus, if a victim has 100 bitcoin in their wallet and someone steals their wallet's private key, they can then sign a transaction sending that 100 bitcoin to wherever they want, and there is no undoing of the transaction as there is no "authority" to say a transaction is invalid.

Wallets may also be stored by third parties (called "web wallets") for organizations to maintain the security of the private key. Often these entities will also operate as exchanges where one can turn bitcoin into hard currency and hard currency into bitcoin. Some also enable moving money between bitcoin and other cryptocurrencies. There are, in fact, over 800 cryptocurrencies, though an overwhelming majority of the money is in bitcoin.

All anyone can do with bitcoin is to send it somewhere else. If you control your own wallet private key, there is no way for a third party such as law enforcement to blacklist, intercept, or escrow funds. The various financial sanction regimes many governments have are generally difficult to enforce in cryptocurrency. In fact, every seizure of bitcoin that has been covered in the media has involved seizing control of the wallet's private encryption key that has enabled law enforcement to control the underlying bitcoin that wallet contains.

As mentioned earlier, exchanges allow individuals to turn their real money into cryptocurrency and vice versa. These exchanges are often highly regulated with "know your customer" and anti-money laundering regulations that require them to identify who their customers are. The value of bitcoin has generally risen since 2010, but there is no entity setting its exchange rates. As of this writing, the value of 1 bitcoin is about 9,300 USD. It is mostly controlled by the price people are willing to buy and sell them at exchanges. As such, bitcoin and other cryptocurrencies have had very wild fluctuations in value. In theory, the value could go drop to $0 (Cheah & Fry, 2015). It is not necessary to trade in full bitcoins; one can also trade in fractional values of bitcoin.

One can also send their bitcoin to others in exchange for goods and services. There has not been widespread adoption of bitcoin as a currency of commerce, however. That said, there is nothing preventing one party for doing something for another party based on receipt of an agreed upon amount of bitcoin.

It is also possible to "mine" bitcoin using computer hardware. When bitcoin was first created in 2010, it was possible to use commodity hardware to mine bitcoin with good returns. Mining involved running processes on a computer to essentially solve cryptographic algorithms but those have increased in difficulty over time. Now, mining bitcoin requires specialized hardware, which has led to interesting effects of the pricing of graphics cards (which can be used for mining). There are those, however, who mined a great deal of bitcoin in the early years and now that the value of bitcoin is orders of magnitude higher, those individuals are essentially multi-millionaires.

Bitcoin provides a strong measure of anonymity of the users, but the transactions are all public. The confusion between anonymity and privacy has led some to think they can simply transact in bitcoin without any accountability. The reality is all the transactions are public and if you can turn wallet addresses into an identity, you have complete visibility into what the individual is doing without needing a warrant, court order, or some other legal process.

Transactions within the bitcoin ecosystem are unregulated and mostly unregulatable. Anyone with a wallet can send bitcoin to any other wallet. Regulation does come into play at exchanges (Gikay, 2018) where individuals can turn traditional currency to bitcoin (or other cryptocurrency) and vice versa. This means exchanges not only store a great deal of information, but that the flow of hard capital into cryptocurrency and, more importantly, the flow of cryptocurrency into hard cash is limited.

There are other cryptocurrencies, notably monero, that encrypt the public ledger so individuals can still verify the integrity of the transactions but only the participants can decrypt the details of those transactions. This cryptocurrency makes looking into the financial activity of cyberhate groups more difficult, but there are also no established and credible direct cash-to-monero exchanges at present, so cyberhate and other groups still need to use an intermediate cryptocurrency (like bitcoin) to conduct their operations.

CYBERHATE GROUPS' USE OF BITCOIN

Cyberhate groups generally operate various forms of Internet media presences. Radio Aryan, for instance, runs several podcasts. Andrew Anglin runs *Daily Stormer* as a neo-Nazi "news site." Redice.tv runs both podcasts and videos. They also run various Discord channels or bulletin boards to encourage engagement with their followers. Many of them, until recently, overtly operated YouTube channels where they produced video content for their followers.

Like many other "new media" figures, they use this content generation as a way to make money. All of their blog posts, social media accounts, video and podcast stations include means to donate for their followers as a way to monetize their content. Until recent changes by Google, they were also able to monetize their content on YouTube via advertising revenue. With some exceptions discussed later, almost all of their known financing comes from donations from their viewership/listenership.

Many cyberhate groups started out using PayPal and Patreon. Some used traditional credit card processors which they placed on their various web presences so people could donate with credit cards. With a few notable exceptions, they generally raised money via electronic means as opposed to getting checks in the mail. They generally did not have events for their followers, so in-person fundraising or "passing the hat" was not an option for them. After the Unite the Right rally, they began to shift their fundraising due to the large increase in scrutiny these groups received.

As they were deplatformed (Jardine, 2019), some moved to Hatreon (a Patreon-like site catering to cyberhate groups) and cryptocurrency

(Blekkenhorst, 2019). Ultimately, Hatreon closed, so the alternatives to these groups raising money have become quite limited. Not every group or individual has been deplatformed, but a great deal has been. In part, due to the work of groups like the Southern Poverty Law Center that actively work to financially disrupt these groups, pressure has been effectively put on organizations to not do business with cyberhate groups.

As most followers of cyberhate groups generally also operate under pseudonyms, in part, due to fear their views would be exposed to others that would create difficulties in their "real life," many members and followers have no real connection to each other in these communities except online and via pseudonyms. While older hate groups could raise money with PO Boxes and passing that hat at gatherings, these groups required a new method that doesn't require the donor to have meaningful knowledge of the recipient.

There are techniques to obfuscate transactions in bitcoin, most notably the use of bitcoin "mixers" or "tumblers." What these services do is aggregate several incoming transactions and split them up into many smaller transactions sent through networks of dozens or hundreds of other wallets several times and then output those transactions to a destination wallet (minus the fee for the service). If many users are using such a service at the same time, it becomes disproportionately difficult to attribute specific output transactions to the correct input transaction. This break between a known wallet and an unknown (destination) wallet also makes it difficult to follow the chain of transactions of a specific person due to the inherent ambiguity created. While these services exist, at least for their donation wallets, cyberhate groups did not make use of them.

One important dynamic of bitcoin which is unrelated to cyberhate groups has helped grow their financial holdings. In 2013, bitcoin went from around $20 per bitcoin to $1,000 per bitcoin. In 2017, there was also another spike, from around $1,000 bitcoin to peaking just below $20,000 bitcoin. For reference, the Unite the Right rally was August 11 and 12, 2017. Bitcoin then fell again, falling to $3,300 in 2019 before going back to its current value of $9,300. This is relevant because many cyberhate groups received bitcoin (some as early as 2013) that they sat on. They became "wealthy," almost overnight, with the surge in value of bitcoin. Most turned to bitcoin for reasons unrelated to cryptocurrency speculation, but they happened to be at the right place at the right time and were able to take advantage in the surge in the value of bitcoin.

Of note, no "left" cyberhate groups were identified because none of them appear to raise money in bitcoin. The list of cyberhate groups cited here all are various flavors of neo-Nazi or white supremacist groups (figure 4.1).

These groups turned to bitcoin for its anonymity and perceived privacy. However, cyberhate groups wanted to receive funds from fans who were

John Bambenek

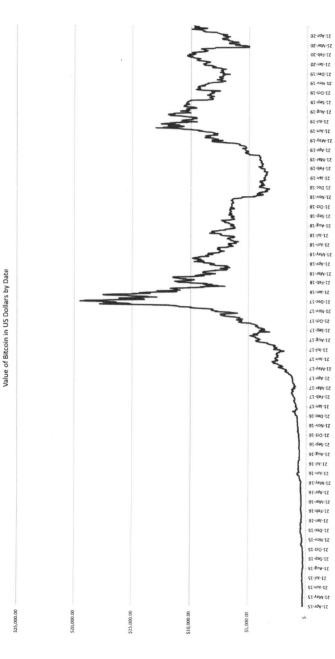

Figure 4.1 Value of Bitcoin in U.S. Dollars by Date. Figure created by author based on data from Chainalysis

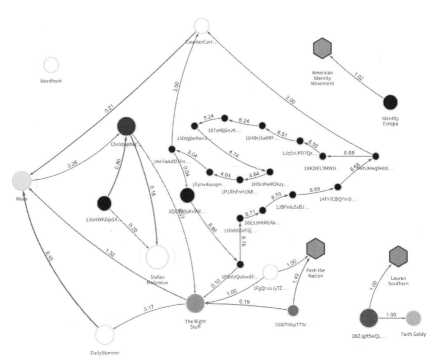

Figure 4.2 Bitcoin Transaction Map Showing Relationships between Cyberhate Groups. Figure created by author based on data from Chainalysis

consuming their media who they didn't know and often didn't have trusted private channels to communicate with. So they published their bitcoin address on their websites, YouTube videos, social media accounts, and the like. This made it immediately possible to track the financial activities of those groups because one could query the blockchain public ledger for all transactions in or out. In short, as a necessary step to raise funds from those they had no close connection with, leaders of cyberhate groups broke the anonymity of their wallets by openly publishing them so donors knew where to send the money. This wouldn't inherently identify the owners, but it does give a large amount of visibility into their financial operations.

Tracking Cyberhate Groups' Finances

With the rise of cryptocurrency also came the rise of scrutiny of cryptocurrency transactions. Commercial tools like Chainalysis and Elliptic are available to help researchers and investigators follow the money. The technique essentials boil down to entering a starting wallet or transaction ID and then follow the chain of transactions before and/or after that.

With these commercial services, some wallets are labeled, either because they belong to established cryptocurrency services (like Coinbase or Binance) or because the owner of the wallet somehow identifies themselves. In the present case, almost all cyberhate groups publish a wallet to receive donations which makes attribution trivial. In other cases, they rely on open-source research to link wallets to posts on various online forums, YouTube comments, Twitter accounts, and so on to give researchers some context on where a specific wallet has been mentioned. As wallets are random-looking strings of text, a wallet identifier will not organically occur in any other way except as a reference to that specific wallet.

There are other services, such as Bitcoinabuse.com, which operate as a crowd-sourced public repository of "abusive" bitcoin wallets, such as those used in ransomware and sextortion attacks. Occasionally such sites also list wallets of interest, such as those by cyberhate groups. This leads to two important scientific limitations of this analysis: the lack of "perfect knowledge" due to no centralized authority and the potential for false or misleading information.

Unlike in traditional financial accounts, there are no organizations with transaction records with the notable exception of cryptocurrency exchanges if they comply with know-your-customer laws. For instance, if one had subpoena power, one could not send a subpoena to "bitcoin" or an exchange for all accounts related to a specific individual. Inherently, wallets have no identifying information so something "external" to the blockchain is needed to identify the owner of an account.

Exchanges, at least reputable ones operating in rule of law countries, do require strong identification documents to open an account (Jackson, 2019), but it would be on the investigator to prove that a given account belongs to an exchange before legal process would be appropriate. While many cyberhate groups have accepted donations from users of exchanges, the groups themselves tend not to be exchange users (especially after the Unite the Right rally). These groups may also have other wallets that aren't publicly identified that they accept funds from. There are a wide variety of reasons they would wish to do that, most importantly because if an investigator doesn't know a wallet exists, they would have no way to identify transactions to it.

Additionally, the identities of donors, by and large, are unknown absent some legal process to identify those who donated through the exchanges and, in many cases, it is not possible to know with any certainty what the cryptocurrency was spent on. Some inferences can, of course, be made. That said, typically the cyberhate groups have more technical savvy to protect their anonymity than their donors, so this will limit the precision of the analysis that can happen here.

The presence of potentially false information is a potentially bigger problem. The confidence on "external" linkages between wallets and open-source information can vary widely. For instance, it is effectively certain when a cyberhate group is advertising their own wallet, one can be sure it is, in fact, their wallet for donations. If the group puts up a false wallet, then their own donations would be going elsewhere and not to them.

The same cannot be said for wallets mentioned in YouTube comments, Bitcoinabuse, or other content that may or may not be under the control of the cyberhate group. To illustrate this risk, one anecdote involving Faith Goldy, a Canadian white nationalist, will be discussed in depth later. Her bitcoin wallet is 1Ej6qC5zuNAz4xhBjowxDWD9XRjzSpadVm. During the rise of sextortion scams (emails that threatened to expose a victim's nude photographs or scandalous online behavior), a security blogger Brian Krebs had posted some research on this threat (see Krebs, 2018). In the comments section of the blog, commenters described their own experiences with seeing these scams in their own emails. One commenter references Faith Goldy's wallet saying "Same, but BTC address was 1Ej6qC5zuNAz4xhBjowxDWD9XRjzSpadVm. Demanded $4000 Canadian. Old password. I ignored the email, deadline passed, nothing happened."

If Faith Goldy was using sextortion to raise funds days before she announced she was running for Mayor of Ontario, this would be explosive information. Examining the wallet, however, showed no transactions equivalent to 4,000 Canadian dollars. On a deeper examination of the commenter who left the post, however, it was shown that the individual was, in fact, a supporter of Faith Goldy. It's unclear if Ms. Goldy was aware of this post but if someone took the data point of the wallet being used in sextortion without further examination and went public suggesting she was financing her mayor campaign with sextortion funds, it would have led to strong groups of a defamation suit.

This shows that a great deal of care has to be used in the analysis of these transactions and not to jump to conclusions as to what they mean. It doesn't seem that cyberhate groups have an organized effort to deceive researchers in this way, but the possibility of overt deception has to be accounted for.

Stefan Molyneux

Stefan Molyneux is a far-right Canadian podcaster known for promoting so-called scientific racism. He operates a call-in show, organizes podcasts, sells books, and provides subscription-based content. He has both the longest running use of bitcoin and a long history of producing content that, in effect, provides "intellectual" support for various cyberhate movements. He runs a media community at Freedomain.com, which has podcasts and videos, and links to "documentaries" and his blog. He has produced a wide variety of articles, some of which can be seen at Google Scholar.

He began to raise money in bitcoin starting in January 2013. His first transaction was for 5 bitcoins with a value of $83 at the time. As of this writing, 5 bitcoins are worth about $46,500. This was also before there was a popular knowledge of bitcoin and implies some (but by no stretch all) early adopters of cryptocurrency had white supremacist leanings. It is impossible to know for sure, but if one believes the various forms of the "Jewish banking conspiracy" there really is no other place to go besides cryptocurrency.

From January 25, 2013, to May 19, 2020, there have been 4,877 contributions to Mr. Molyneux for an average of $49 in bitcoin (conversion to dollars based on value of bitcoin at the time of transaction) for total contributions of about $238,000. 2,983 of the donor wallets were unique and 296 wallets were repeat donors. Mr. Molyneux is unique among other recipients of cyberhate donations as he has seemed to curate recurring small-dollar donors. One wallet, 14XuM7u3LhkCPBWXfj78dyi8EKx2BgXs7p, donated 26 times in 2014 and 2015 but in the aggregate for only about $30 at time of transaction.

There have only been 16 transactions over $1,000 with the largest donation being $21,000 (200 BTC) received on April 2, 2013. The next month, a 52 BTC transaction (5,500 USD equivalent) was sent to Stefan Molyneux. The wallet that sent that still has 20 BTC left over balance. In 2013, there was worth about $2,000. As of this writing, those 20 BTC are worth $186,000. Some of the major donors behind these groups are sitting on large sums of bitcoin, though the reason that amount hasn't been spent in seven years is unclear.

Almost 850 of those transactions were from Coinbase, the largest bitcoin exchange that makes small transactions in bitcoin possible for those who have little knowledge of bitcoin and cryptocurrency.

As an example of how the rise in value of bitcoin has coincidentally made certain people very rich, the amount of money given to Mr. Molyneux has been relatively modest at the time of the transaction. However, he has been receiving bitcoin since 2013. In total, he has received 598 bitcoin. There are three wallets he has transferred what hasn't been spent which contain, as of this writing, 132, 152, and 239 bitcoins for a total of 521 bitcoin. At its current exchange value, that means Mr. Molyneux is likely sitting on $4.6 million worth of bitcoin that can be used at his leisure making him, in effect, independently wealthy.

Daily Stormer/Andrew Anglin

The Daily Stormer is a neo-Nazi website created by Andrew Anglin. Inspired by Der Stürmer, a World War II–era German propaganda publication promoting Nazism, the site caters to the more virulent of hard-right and anti-Semitic cyberhate followers. The site overtly calls for genocide against the Jews. While some cyberhate groups try to conceal or whitewash their activities, Mr. Anglin is extremely overt in his opinions and activities.

The most defining characteristic of the site is the troll army it commands to harass various individuals online. Even before Unite the Right, this site was active in a variety of harassment campaigns including against radio host Dean Obeidallah (of Palestinian and Italian decent), who they accused of orchestrating the Manchester Arena bombing in 2017, and against Tanya Gersh, a Jewish realtor in Montana, who they accused of trying to force the mother of another white supremacist, Richard Spencer, out of a Montana community.

Most of Mr. Anglin's fundraising stems from the fact that the previous two activities, as well as others, have made him the target of lawsuits. His fundraising efforts have been tied to raising money for his legal defense. It is unclear how much of the funds raised have actually been spent on lawyers as he has never shown up to a court room claiming he is not in the United States, and he believes it would be too dangerous to travel here for legal proceedings. This led to his lawyer, Marc Randazza, to withdraw from his case over Tanya Gersh (Associated Press, 2019).

Mr. Anglin's first donation was June 23, 2016. Up until May 25, 2020, he has received $411,591 worth of bitcoin donations (at time of transaction) across 2,884 donations for an average of $143 each. Of those, 45 donations were over $1,000 totaling almost $219,000. He received approximately $61,000 on August 20, 2017 (days after Unite the Right), $33,000 on July 5, 2019, $12,000 in January 2017, and $10,000 in March 2017. Notably, the donation for over $60,000 was in precisely 14.88 BTC, 14 for a popular 14-word neo-Nazi slogan ("We must secure the existence of our people and a future for white children") and 88 for Heil Hitler (*H* being the 8th letter of the alphabet).

Due to an ongoing federal lawsuit, some visibility into Mr. Anglin's private finances is known. In *Obeidallah v. Anglin*, case 2:17-cv-00720, in the Southern District of Ohio, this author testified in open court that in the period from January 1, 2017, to June 5, 2019, Mr. Anglin received $260,000 worth of bitcoin. From June 1, 2017, to December 31, 2018, bank records showed he received $106,000 in traditional funds. This shows Mr. Anglin was far more successful and consistent in his fundraising via cryptocurrency than so-called traditional means.

Mr. Anglin's best online fundraising month was the same month as Unite the Right (in part due to the large transaction). It is impossible to say for certain but seems like Mr. Anglin gets a boost in fundraising after "successful" acts of cyberhate. Unlike Mr. Molyneux, Mr. Anglin has been spending his cryptocurrency. Payments to Andrew "Weev" Auernheimer (discussed later) make up the largest portion of these payments. He also has expenses tied to his web presence as it is frequently taken down due to its hateful content and he frequently has providers who cut him off.

The more recent donation of about $33,000 came from wallet 14EtQeD1zSGWCBxHY6pUbLSY3er1pxFs2R, which has been active since 2011. That individual acquired 270 bitcoins around May 10, 2011. The market was less established at that point, but the value was like around $2,500 at that time. The wallet currently has a balance of just under 288 bitcoin that is worth over $2.5 million at the time of this writing. This individual got involved with bitcoin extremely early and became wealthy as a result and shared a nominal portion of that wealth with Mr. Anglin.

The $60,000 donation was likely from a different individual but follows a similar pattern. This individual acquired 3,900 bitcoins on November 13, 2012. Of that, 2,995 bitcoin remains for a current value of 26.7 million dollars. This individual also sent a nominal .88 bitcoin donation ($3,677 at the time) to Mr. Anglin before his $60,000 contribution. Not much can definitely be said about either of these donors except that they do not appear to be related (aside of both contributing), they have been involved in bitcoin long before the alt-right came along, the fast rise of bitcoin made them very wealthy, and they shared that wealth with Mr. Anglin, in part, to keep his web presence online so he can continue to command his troll army and engage in harassment campaigns.

Andrew "Weev" Auernheimer

Of the various cyberhate actors' behavior in cryptocurrency, Mr. Auernheimer is unique. While he does accept donations, his activity in bitcoin predates most other cyberhate groups. He was a member of Goatse Security and the Gay Nigger Association of America, both hacking and online trolling groups. In 2010, he exposed a flaw in AT&T's website that made it possible to get e-mail addresses of iPad users. He published this information and was ultimately arrested and convicted on hacking charges (O'Neill, 2014).

Eventually those charges were dropped on appear due to technical issues, and he was released in 2014 at which point he has not returned to the United States. After this point, he overtly identified himself as a white nationalist and neo-Nazi (Wall, 2018). He infamously abused printers that were connected to the open Internet to print out flyers at universities throughout the United States that advertised *The Daily Stormer* website.

It is these technical and security skills that have led Mr. Auernheimer to both have a following in cyberhate group and contract out his services to other groups. He has been paid by *The Daily Stormer, The Right Stuff*, and Counter Currents. Interestingly, Mr. Auernheimer contributed to Christopher Cantwell in September 2017. As Mr. Auernheimer has a variety of cryptocurrency activity (online gambling and underground marketplaces), it is not easy to separate out what are donations and what are payments or other transactions to him.

That being said, his bitcoin wallet has received over $220,000 worth of bitcoin across 514 transactions for an average of about $429. Mr. Auernheimer also has both a heightened sense of security and technical ability compared to the others. He routinely moves money into monero and back to make full visibility into his cryptocurrency holdings unclear. Due to a flaw in an exchange, it is possible to see several organizations such as the *Daily Stormer* pay him directly to his monero wallet. Mr. Auernheimer did receive what looks like a $11,000 donation on November 9, 2016, from an individual who received 400 bitcoins ($290,000 at time) from an online gambling site Fairlay.com just days prior.

Nordfront/Nordic Resistance Movement

Nordfront, or the Nordic Resistance Movement, is a far-right neo-Nazi group based in Sweden with affiliates in other Nordic countries. It is a relatively new organization started in 2016 and is also a recognized political party in Sweden. From January 26, 2018, to May 26, 2020, it has received almost $76,000 in bitcoin donations, $68,000 from large donors of over $1,000. The largest donation was received on July 16, 2019, for $33,500 worth of bitcoin. That same donor also donated about $2,300 worth of bitcoin on May 17, 2019.

Only 197 donations in total have been received for an average of $387 each. Currently, the organization still holds about $29,000 of those donations in their wallets they have yet to move or spend. Unlike some of the other groups mentioned here, they have no obvious common donors or movement of bitcoin between other groups. This can likely be attributed to their specific geographic focus and ideology emphasizing Nordic ethnicity.

Counter Currents

Counter Currents is run by Greg Johnson as a book publisher of various white nationalist authors including himself. It has accepted traditional credit card payments in the past but that is currently down. The only means of payment he accepts currently is bitcoin and mailing payments. While he accepts donations the bulk of the transactions seems to be selling his publications. He has received almost $60,000 in bitcoin from March 19, 2013, to May 23, 2020, in 120 transactions for an average of approximately $500. He has notably received about $40,000 in bitcoin from exchanges across three transactions that are presumably donations.

He has also paid Mr. Auernheimer about .21 bitcoin across four transactions. Millennial Woes (discussed later) paid him .2 bitcoin in June 2019 (about $1,800). Unlike other groups, Counter Currents more or less hasn't used any of the bitcoin that it has been sent. Of the 13.2 bitcoin it has received, 12.8 bitcoin remain in the same wallet that is worth about $113,000 as of this writing.

Fash the Nation

Fash the Nation is a white supremacist podcast and website. It is affiliated with *The Right Stuff* and run by "Alex McNabb" and "Jazzhands McFeels." Interestingly, they no longer advertise their bitcoin wallet for donations, but from the ones they used to advertise it can be seen that from August 11, 2016, to July 14, 2018, they raised over $153,000 in bitcoin. Of that, almost all of that was from large donors ($149,000), $50,000 of that was from a Coinbase user (or users) alone. As those donations ultimately derived from exchanges, it is not easy to determine whether they were multiple individuals or not. In total, there were 96 donations for an average of $1,615 worth of bitcoin.

The Right Stuff/Mike Enoch

Mike Enoch founded *The Right Stuff* as a media network for cyberhate content and hosts his own podcast, the Daily Shoah, on the site. Like *Fash the Nation*, it no longer advertises their donation bitcoin wallet but as of this writing they are using a merchant service to allow for subscriptions to paid content. Some of the other shows on the website do advertise their bitcoin wallets so the content creator can take donations or payments directly.

Unlike other groups, Mr. Enoch doesn't have any large benefactors and has received no large donations. He has received a little less than $20,000 in bitcoin from December 8, 2005, to August 13, 2018. He has received 448 donations for an average of $44 per donation. Of note, Mr. Enoch has paid Mr. Anglin .165 bitcoin in 2017 and made two payments to Mr. Auernheimer (presumably for technology support) in 2016 for .66 bitcoin each.

Christopher "the Crying Nazi" Cantwell

Christopher Cantwell is a prominent public neo-Nazi and participant in the Unite the Right rally. He was convicted on two misdemeanor counts based on his actions at the rally (Moyer, 2019) and is currently awaiting trial on federal charges over an unrelated extortion plot (Mathias, 2020). Despite his large public presence, his cryptocurrency donations have been much more modest. He has only raised about $21,000 over 665 donations for an average of about $32 from June 25, 2013, to the last recorded transaction of May 12, 2019.

His first cryptocurrency activities are tied to a black-market exchange known as Silk Road (now defunct). He has largely spent the cryptocurrency donations he has received and was using Coinbase until he was deplatformed. Unlike other cyberhate groups, Mr. Cantwell only received one $1,000 donation as most of his transactions were much smaller. His donations started drying up in 2018 to completely disappear in 2019. Notably, Mr. Cantwell sent five donations to Mr. Molyneux totaling .18 bitcoin from 2014 to 2017 indicating the influence Molyneux has had on Mr. Cantwell's thinking.

Identity Evropa/American Identity Movement

As far as cryptocurrency activity, the previous groups have the most volume, but a few of the other groups of individuals are worth mentioning. American Identity Movement, a successor organization of Identity Evropa, is active in various flyering movements. It targets college-aged men, in particular, to recruit members. After the Unite the Right rally, Identity Evropa essentially disbanded and American Identity Movement was formed as ostensibly a separate and distinct group with a less "hostile" message. Examining the bitcoin wallets for both shows that virtually the entire balance of donations sent to the Identity Evropa bitcoin wallet was sent to American Identity Movement, another indication that the difference between the groups is more a rebranding effort.

Identity Evropa only received $5,800 in bitcoin contributions from December 4, 2017, to August 13, 2019. American Identity Movement, however, has received over $41,000 in bitcoin donations (excluding the balance that was sent from the Identity Evropa wallet) from June 10, 2019, to May 3, 2020, $39,000 of that was from large donors of over $1,000. The largest donation of $14,500 was received on January 2, 2020.

Lauren Southern

Lauren Southern is a former candidate for Canadian political office as a Libertarian candidate and new media personality. She was active from 2015 to 2019 having recently reporting she would step away from political activism to resume her education. During her time of being active she has received about $54,000 in bitcoin donations across 270 transactions for about $200 each. She was active on Twitter and YouTube and attempted a tour in New Zealand with Stefan Molyneux that was not overly successful due to venue cancellations and protests.

Faith Goldy

Faith Goldy, in addition to her mayor campaign previously mentioned, is also an active social media user supporting white nationalism. She has received about $20,000 in bitcoin transactions from December 18, 2017, to May 12, 2020, across 131 transactions for an average of $155. She is currently active on social media and accepts donations via traditional credit card or bitcoin and has a subscription content service at Subscribe Star.

Common Donors

What is interesting is that among the relatively wealthy donors that have backed some of these groups, there is not significant overlap between donors of one group with another. There are some exceptions. The same wallet (1BZJgft5wQLZx2fLirv42fEr31XSyiwVEp) that donated 1 bitcoin to Faith Goldy also donated to Lauren Southern. That wallet has used bitcoin mixers to receive its funding and has received over 1,800 bitcoin over its existence. Likely, this is one individual who has followed both female activists.

Another wallet (13bHWFZqxSX7Cp36hPgA38cCpPJQZ1Am9N) donated to Christopher Cantwell and either donated or purchased books from Counter Currents. *The Right Stuff* and *Fash the Nation* have a common donor (1FgQrvuJyTZgMj7Luo524kheFFpfRWrRWS) who gave 1 bitcoin to both wallets. That wallet has a balance of 42 bitcoin or over $400,000. *The Right Stuff* and Counter Currents also have a common donor. The largest donors tended not to be related to another group that could easily be discerned. This seems to suggest that the followers and donors to one group are more or less captive to that group, even though these groups have cooperated in the past (such as the Unite the Right rally) and may appear on each other's podcasts and/or referenced on each other's blogs.

Figure 4.2 shows the various cyberhate groups referenced here and, where appropriate, chains of transactions that show common donors or financial relationships between groups.

PATTERNS OF ACTIVITY

Table 4.1 shows bitcoin revenue by month in dollars at the time of the donation being received. The following legend identifies who the recipients are. Figure 4.3 is a graph of this table that shows the relative ebb and flow of financial transactions throughout the cyberhate ecosystem described here.

Table 4.1 Bitcoin Donations to Cyberhate Groups and Individuals by Month in U.S. Dollar Equivalent

Month	AA	CC	SM	FTN	ME	GJ	IE	NF	LS	FG	Total
Jan			$706								$706
Feb			$1916								$1916
Mar			$1061								$1061
Apr			$22591								$22591
May			$9249								$9249
Jun		$17	$1171								$1188
Jul			$824								$824
Aug		$65	$418								$483
Sep		$6	$1494								$1500
Oct		$11	$884								$895
Nov		$2	$2802								$2804
Dec			$5029								$5029
Total 2013		**$101**	**$48144**								**$48245**
Jan			$3060								$3060
Feb		$1	$2742								$2743
Mar			$2187								$2187
Apr		$13	$4697								$4709
May		$43	$3587								$3630
Jun		$172	$3659								$3831
Jul		$399	$3234								$3633
Aug		$243	$4325								$4569
Sep		$41	$2182								$2222
Oct		$47	$1847								$1894
Nov		$609	$4537								$5146
Dec		$196	$2406								$2602
Total 2014		**$1764**	**$38463**								**$40227**
Jan		$118	$1612								$1730
Feb		$377	$977								$1354
Mar		$261	$975								$1236
Apr		$266	$1332								$1598
May		$814	$1090								$1904
Jun		$152	$1160								$1313
Jul		$199	$1455								$1654
Aug		$165	$1521								$1686
Sep		$458	$1492								$1950
Oct		$151	$1662								$1813
Nov		$288	$2864								$3153
Dec		$220	$2412		$166						$2797
Total 2015		**$3469**	**$18552**		**$166**						**$22187**
Jan		$87	$2002		$584						$2674
Feb		$341	$2338		$903						$3582
Mar		$241	$2141		$1280	$14					$3676
Apr		$351	$2809		$586	$26					$3772
May		$706	$2381		$452	$888					$4427
Jun	$16	$342	$1270		$670	$1750					$4048
Jul		$268	$1315		$911						$2494
Aug	$73	$228	$1041	$136	$526	$50					$2053
Sep	$166	$160	$3705	$452	$1273						$5756
Oct	$119	$329	$1349	$871	$443	$1					$3113
Nov	$292	$419	$2219	$1608	$1425	$251					$6214
Dec	$374	$70	$2573	$411	$916						$4344
Total 2016	**$1039**	**$3544**	**$25142**	**$3478**	**$9971**	**$2978**					**$46153**
Jan	$12744	$66	$1367	$236	$3863						$18275
Feb	$3590	$100	$738		$701	$8					$5137
Mar	$15198	$209	$1735		$651	$108			$519		$18418
Apr	$9913	$248	$2562		$983				$25		$13731

(Continued)

John Bambenek

Table 4.1 Bitcoin Donations to Cyberhate Groups and Individuals by Month in U.S. Dollar Equivalent (*Continued*)

Month	AA	CC	SM	FTN	ME	GJ	IE	NF	LS	FG	Total
May	$6658	$763	$3389	$15	$2085				$397		$13308
Jun	$5174	$166	$898	$19	$272				$1048		$7577
Jul	$3889	$322	$1492	$285	$532				$3479		$10000
Aug	$80129	$2255	$3934	$82		$9473			$1643		$97515
Sep	$3084	$3512	$430	$38208		$27			$4770		$50031
Oct	$2918	$411	$7373	$29743		$161			$320		$40927
Nov	$7294	$308	$3218	$29369		$133			$485		$40806
Dec	$3418	$1523	$4262	$370		$146	$400		$492	$19	$10631
Total 2017	**$154009**	**$9884**	**$31399**	**$98327**	**$9087**	**$10056**	**$400**		**$13177**	**$19**	**$326357**
Jan	$2384	$237	$3924			$1571	$272	$42	$14056	$13691	$36177
Feb	$4702	$299	$1290			$1	$106	$162	$934		$7495
Mar	$7507	$93	$14298			$12	$657	$51	$13041		$35659
Apr	$1938	$57	$2146	$17772		$75	$52	$2966	$494		$25500
May	$5283	$189	$1945	$8548		$155	$506	$205	$374	$233	$17438
Jun	$23410	$20	$163	$6127		$111	$110	$271	$436		$30649
Jul	$13261	$72	$634	$19241		$813	$282	$214	$1073	$1503	$37093
Aug	$3592	$303	$32304		$418	$146	$285	$382	$3496	$973	$41899
Sep	$1896	$209	$538				$15	$58	$76	$110	$2903
Oct	$9787	$19	$233			$35	$518	$117	$108	$1049	$11866
Nov	$3593	$242	$168				$923	$205	$1911	$22	$7065
Dec	$7821	$291	$593			$162	$180	$287	$1726	$490	$11549
Total 2018	**$85178**	**$2031**	**$58236**	**$51689**	**$418**	**$3081**	**$3907**	**$4959**	**$37724**	**$18070**	**$265292**
Jan	$12606	$90	$594				$1085	$115	$544	$46	$15081
Feb	$3294		$185			$307	$378	$8	$25	$84	$4283
Mar	$2387		$1249			$229	$120	$29	$1120	$71	$5205
Apr	$8965		$219					$1494	$59	$1237	$11974
May	$4108	$65	$4240			$377		$3373	$1246	$53	$13461
Jun	$5975		$80			$15957	$17445	$298	$19	$34	$39806
Jul	$37367		$2408			$269	$115	$51847		$137	$92143
Aug	$4539		$369			$1396	$178	$380		$111	$6974
Sep	$18878		$1416			$99	$301	$179		$88	$20960
Oct	$3121		$2792			$571	$8269	$99		$8	$14861
Nov	$3566		$194			$2772	$235	$880	$128		$7775
Dec	$14411		$1653			$1153	$245	$4881			$22343
Total 2019	**$119219**	**$156**	**$15399**			**$23130**	**$28371**	**$63583**	**$3141**	**$1868**	**$254866**
Jan	$14832		$1783			$16656	$14578	$93			$47942
Feb	$20782		$680			$3149	$50	$95		$290	$25046
Mar	$5399		$389			$200	$65	$103			$6156
Apr	$7436		$231			$7	$12	$13			$7698
May	$3697		$333			$379	$42	$6907		$88	$11446
Total 2020	**$52146**		**$3416**			**$20390**	**$14747**	**$7211**		**$378**	**$98288**
Total	**$411591**	**$20949**	**$238751**	**$153493**	**$19642**	**$59635**	**$47425**	**$75753**	**$54042**	**$20335**	**$1101616**

Source: Table created by author based on data by Chainalysis.

AA—Andrew Anglin
CC—Christopher Cantwell
SM—Stefan Molyneux
FTN—Fash the Nation
ME—Mike Enoch/*The Right Stuff*
GJ—Greg Johnson/Counter Currents
IE—Identity Evropa/American Identity Movement
NF—Nordfront
LS—Lauren Southern
FG—Faith Goldy

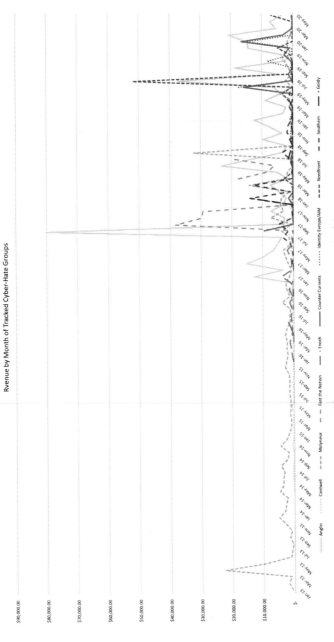

Figure 4.3 Revenue by Month of Tracked Cyberhate Groups. Figure created by author based on data from Chainalysis

Most groups have large donors, and in some cases, the groups are almost entirely dependent on those large donors for their bitcoin revenue. The interesting question is what these groups do with these funds. It is clear many of them use some amount of bitcoin on technology and services (notably with some being paid to Mr. Auernheimer). Counter Currents and *The Right Stuff* provide media services and American Identity Movement does flyer various communities.

What is notable is that there is no evidence that they are using the revenue in a systematic way to further their cause. Mr. Anglin, for instance, has received over $400,000 in cryptocurrency, ostensibly for his legal defense. He likely has used a small amount for hosting charges for his website. However, he has never shown up to a courtroom, and he hasn't incurred much in legal fees which begs the question if the funds are being used for anything other than his personal enjoyment.

Mr. Molyneux is notable in how much he has not spent and saved instead. Among all the other groups here, he has singularly become independently wealthy for his efforts in spreading his cyberhate message.

Also of interest is the effect of the COVID-19 epidemic on cyberhate fundraising. There are spikes in the overall ecosystem of right-wing cyberhate fundraising in August 2017 (the Unite the Right rally), July 2018, and July 2019. Those spikes are universally related to solitary donors spending large sums on a group during these times. There appears to be a baseline of general fundraising of about $10,000 a month in bitcoin. As COVID-19 ramped up, spending has generally fallen but it does not appear the amount of revenue going into these groups has gone down.

It appears that despite the economic downturn, there is still support for these groups and their activities which could lead to unrest in the following months. That said, after Unite the Right and the wave of lawsuits that have resulted, these groups have gotten more careful about advertising their activities openly. Some cyberhate groups are not advertising their bitcoin wallets, which makes this analysis more difficult. Some groups have rebranded to attempt to whitewash their involvement in the violence that occurred at Unite the Right. There is likely more assets behind these groups than is known at this point.

CONCLUSION

Cyberhate groups have flourished online which has led them also using their larger reach to increase their pool of potential donors. No left-leaning cyberhate groups were identified that raise significant funds in bitcoin. Most of the groups analyzed here have at least one, sometimes more than one, large benefactor that make up the bulk of their cryptocurrency revenue. Mr. Molyneux and Mr. Anglin have done well in cultivating a following who also donate small sums of money that have helped them build their cryptocurrency wealth.

The groups that have done the best are those who started accumulating cryptocurrency before it reached its peak at the end of 2017. However, the increased scrutiny and deplatforming from traditional bitcoin exchanges have caused them to be more careful in advertising their wallets and to start using alternative cryptocurrencies that are harder to track.

While the amount of money these cyberhate groups have raised could be effectively used to organize their efforts in more profound and concerning ways, it seems based on the available evidence that they have only used it for technology needs and for their own personal enjoyment. Especially as these groups start facing legal judgments against their activities, it is likely they will take even more steps to conceal their cryptocurrency finances and protect them against seizure.

REFERENCES

Blekkenhorst, M. (2019). Moderating online extremism on fringe and mainstream platforms: An analysis of governance by Gab & Twitter (Master's thesis, Utrecht University, Utrecht, Netherlands). Retrieved from https://dspace.library.uu.nl/handle/1874/383832

Cheah, E-T., & Fry, F. (2015). Speculative bubbles in bitcoin markets? An empirical investigation into the fundamental value of bitcoin. *Economics Letters* 130, 32–36.

Gikay, A. A. (2018). Regulating decentralized cryptocurrencies under payment services law: Lessons from European Union Law. *JL Tech. & Internet*, 9, 1–39.

Jackson, O. (2019, February 28). Primer: Regulating cryptocurrency exchanges. *International Financial Law Review*. Retrieved from https://search.proquest.com/docview/2200496443?pq-origsite=gscholar&fromopenview=true

Jardine, E. (2019). Online content moderation and the dark web: Policy responses to radicalizing hate speech and malicious content on the darknet. *First Monday, 24*(12).

Johnson, A. (2016, March 28). Infamous hacker "Weev" says he blasted college printers with antisemitic message. *NBC News*. Retrieved from https://www.nbcnews.com/news/us-news/infamous-hacker-weev-says-he-blasted-college-printers-antisemitic-message-n547001

Krebs, B. (2018, July 12). Sextortion scams uses recipient's hacked passwords. *Krebs on Security*. Retrieved from https://krebsonsecurity.com/2018/07/sextortion-scam-uses-recipients-hacked-passwords/comment-page-18/

Kunzelman, M. (2019, April 26). Neo-Nazi website founder's lawyers are backing out of case. *Associated Press*. Retrieved from https://abcnews.go.com/US/wireStory/neo-nazi-website-founders-lawyers-backing-case-62653042

Mathias, C. (2020, January 23). "Crying Nazi" Christopher Cantwell arrested in attempt to extort information about rival Nazi. *Huffington Post*. Retrieved from https://www.huffpost.com/entry/christopher-cantwell-arrested-crying-nazi_n_5e29e32ec5b6779e9c2f5f17

Moyer, J. Wm. (2018, July 20). "Crying Nazi" pleads guilty to assault committed during Charlottesville rally. *The Washington Post*. Retrieved from https://www.washingtonpost.com/local/public-safety/crying-nazi-barred-from-virginia-after-pleading-guilty-to-assault-during-charlottesville-rally/2018/07/20/164480a4-8c5f-11e8-81bf-28c7cd96bbc2_story.html

O'Neill, P. H. (2014, October 2). The fall of hacker-troll Andrew "weev" Auernheimer. *The Daily Dot*. Retrieved from https://www.dailydot.com/debug/weev-hates-jewish-people/

Wall, J. T. (2019). Where to prosecute cybercrimes. *Duke Law & Technology Review, 17*, 146–161.

Chapter 5

Accelerating Hate

Atomwaffen Division, Contemporary Digital Fascism, and Insurrectionary Accelerationism

Michael Loadenthal, Samantha Hausserman,
and Matthew Thierry

MASS SHOOTINGS, FASCISM, AND
WHITE POWER ACCELERATIONISM

Awareness of the threat of far-right, fascist, white nationalist, and neo-Nazi terror networks has risen throughout the past few years, capturing the attention of many following mass killings at two mosques in Christchurch, New Zealand, synagogues in Pittsburgh, Pennsylvania, and Poway, California, a Wal-Mart in El Paso, Texas, and another attempt at a mosque in Baerum, Norway. Media focus in the United States seemingly peaked in January 2020 when eight members of a neo-Nazi survivalist organization known as the Base were arrested on a variety of charges related to weapons possession, "swatting,"[1] harboring fugitives, aiding and abetting, violating civil rights, and conspiring to commit murder. In a series of four arrests, Base members were captured in Georgia,[2] Maryland,[3] Wisconsin,[4] and Virginia.[5] Days prior to the completion of this chapter, and only weeks after the Base arrests, five members of the clandestine neo-Nazi network the Atomwaffen Division (AWD) were arrested for threatening journalists and antifascist activists (including the use of swatting),[6] while a sixth member of AWD was sentenced to prison[7] (Weiner & Zapotosky, 2020). The arrests exposed numerous plots including plans to murder antifascists and subsequently open fire on a Richmond, Virginia, Second Amendment rally to "accelerate the downfall of the U.S. government, incite a race war, and establish a white ethnostate"

(Gurman, 2020). More recently, police arrested twelve men in six German states suspected of planning attacks on politicians, Muslims, and asylum-seekers, to spark "a civil-war-like situation," "to shake the state and social order in Germany and in the end to overturn it" (AFP, 2020).

This strategic frame has come to be known as *accelerationism*, defined in a poster (figure 5.1) allegedly authored by the Base as

> The belief that a social system's internal contradictions should be pushed to their limits in order to encourage rather than overcome the system's self-destructive tendencies. This is done to hasten the system's collapse or demise as well as create space for radical social change to take root. (The Base Official, n.d.)

In this paradigm of accelerationist violence, Western governments thought to be "irreparably corrupt" are attacked by agents "sowing chaos and creating political tension" through mass shootings, terror attacks, and real-world violence to disrupt political discourse (Beauchamp, 2019). One fascist platform detailed the strategy:

> Propaganda addressing the system and its agents needs to instill fear, uncertainty, and a sense of insecurity—it should lead to headlines that remind the public of the danger and seriousness of our message . . . propaganda addressed to the masses should be strictly employed to increase societal tensions, division,

Figure 5.1 Recruitment Poster for Neo-Nazi Survivalists, the Base. *Source*: Telegram user Misanthropik Mayhem (2020).

and hostility between various opposing blocs, with special attention given to anything that agitates the masses against the system. (Ross & Bevensee, 2019)

These so-called accelerationists seek to catalyze and spread systemic breakdown, inflame racial, ethnic, and religious tensions already present in society, and prepare to fill a prophesied future power vacuum with revolutionary, white supremacist violence. Beginning in 2017, and spurred on by a national convergence in Charlottesville, Virginia, dubbed "Unite the Right," these groups have expanded, diversified, and "gone dark"[8] in an effort to develop and grow clandestine networks to communicate, recruit, and plan attacks.

AWD is one such accelerationist organization, named after the German translation of nuclear warfare and described as following an ideology of "esoteric Hitlerism"—a mystical take on Nazism (Lamoureux & Makuch, 2019). AWD was founded in 2015 by a young national guardsman, Brandon Russel, in Tampa, Florida. This group was discovered when law enforcement arrested one of Russel's roommates, Devon Arthurs, for killing their other two roommates after which police found an array of Nazi paraphernalia, radioactive material, guns, and homemade explosives upon searching their apartment. After being detained, questioned, and released, Russel drove south and was eventually intercepted by officers who found two semi-automatic rifles and more than 1,000 rounds of ammunition, believing a mass shooting may have been imminent due to the absence of personal items such as clothes and toiletries in the car.

AWD members or affiliates have since been responsible for a series of murders, assassination attempts, bomb plots, and providing hit lists targeting journalists (Ross & Bevensee, 2019). The group has also been accused of planning to blow up nuclear power plants, crippling public water systems, and attacking the U.S. power grid to cause nuclear meltdown and prompt a race war thought to inaugurate a fascist regime.

The rise of white terror, accelerationist fascism, and its broader support base (i.e., the "alt-right," neo-confederates, identitarian, and others) should be placed in the context of a global transnational fascism extending beyond the United States. Fascism as a political, social, and revolutionary movement is as amorphous and difficult to define as the movements, cells, individuals, and networks seeking to advance this dystopian model. Although a single definition does not exist, fascist ideology was broadly defined by historian Robert Paxton as

a form of political behavior marked by obsessive preoccupation with community decline, humiliation, or victimhood and by compensatory cults of unity, energy, and purity, in which a mass-based party of committed nationalist militants, working in uneasy but effective collaboration with traditional elites, abandons democratic liberties and pursues with redemptive violence . . . goals of internal cleansing and external expansion. (Paxton, 2005, p. 218)

The strategy excavated by Paxton reveals a number of additional elements hidden within a fascist worldview including "a sense of overwhelming crisis," "the primacy of the group," "the belief that one's group is the victim" and thus justified in their authoritarian pursuits, a fear of decline via liberalism, "the need for closer integration of a purer community," "the need for [male] authority," "the superiority of the leader's instincts," a belief in the utility and efficacy of violence, and, finally, "the right of the chosen people to dominate others without restraint from any kind of human or divine law" (Paxton, 2005, pp. 219–220). This broader global framework is key to understanding and contextualizing the rise of U.S.-based accelerationist networks, the focus of the current chapter.

A New Wave of Rebel Terror?

This chapter puts forth an explanatory framework for both AWD and the wider accelerationist movement through an analysis of the network's video communiqués and key written texts. Through a mixed methodological, quantitative, and qualitative approach, we explore the process of white insurrectionary radicalization and path toward accelerationism known colloquially as "Siege-pilling."[9] This process is understood by examining the wider movement's digital communication strategies within the social media ecosystem. Breaking with the typical alt-right political engagement, AWD's strategy to rupture civic life through terrorist actions—propaganda of the deed—to drive media narratives problematizes the nature of system transformation and with it, classical notions of civic participation.

After introducing the reader to the dense concentration of fascist imagery and language that makes up the worldview of AWD, we consider the semiotic chains operationalized in the group's propaganda that serves as a locus of accelerationist discourse, the "Siege-pill." We next link the Siege-pilled worldview to the wider accelerationist movement, demonstrating how it both breaks with and continues as an iteration of the white power movement, introducing new elements to shape discourse in novel ways. By highlighting the process and media ecosystems by which these narratives flow toward secondary and tertiary audiences, we are better positioned to consider its potential for political disruption, as well as possibilities to disrupt its efficacy.

The adoption of accelerationist terrorism as a more effective strategy toward the objective of fascist empowerment indicates a distorted interpretation of environmental signals, thereby opening itself up to more complex approaches to systemic and structural transformation. At the same time, we attempt to offer a more nuanced interpretation of insurrectionary accelerationism itself, demystifying its philosophy of violent reaction to deny the strategy a sense of legitimacy, viability, and desirability.

On Method

To understand AWD's inner experience, complex relations, and narrative frame, our initial study focused on 19 video communiqués produced and distributed by the group, located on an online archive and redundantly circulated through the group's Telegram channel (Atomwaffen Division Videos, 2019) and various websites. Situating our approach in grounded theory, we watched each video in totality before creating an extensive coding scheme constructed around 12 variables, each with 7–24 categorical values. These materials were used to compile a visual coding dictionary to improve intercoder reliability and a written account of variable values. The variables included discrete, quantifiable objects (the environment, time of day, types of flags, presence of weapons, use of clothing and concealment, deployment of symbols, use of music, etc.) as well as structural qualitative codes we felt could be quantified (type of bias displayed, discursive themes, etc.).[10] After familiarizing ourselves with the videos and the coding scheme, we individually reviewed the videos, coding the frequency of each value-type, later comparing individual results with one another.

Following the completion of the visual, video-based analysis, we engaged in additional text-based analyses centered around corpora developed from AWD's writings and that of its ideological figurehead, American neo-Nazi James Mason. The textual analysis evaluated observations from the visual analysis with insights concerning the core text promoted by AWD, Mason's *Siege*, a collection of articles emphasizing power acquisition through armed struggle rather than political means. These texts offer a tentative definition for what is informally meant by "Siege-pilled," the inspiration of radicals to commit lone-wolf terror attacks.

By integrating quantitative visual analysis with a quantitative corpus linguistic analysis, along with an historical and philosophical approach to the sociopolitical context, we are thus able to develop a more comprehensive framework to better understand and deconstruct the lifeworld of AWD that underlies accelerationist violence.

Visual Content Analysis of AWD Video Propaganda

Nineteen videos produced and distributed by AWD were selected to establish the visual corpus. The activities showcased in AWD's videos focus primarily around displaying flags (17% of activities documented).[11] This is presumably done to distinguish a clear group identity and produce a boundary between group affinities such as the wider Iron March network of fascist, underground accelerationists and European-based groups such as the National Socialist German Workers' Party and England-based National Action.

Along with these activities, the AWD videos include flyering (16%), displaying weapons (16%), and giving Nazi salutes (12%), often while concealing their identity with black masks bearing white skulls and often dressed in camouflaged gear. This repertoire of action suggests a willingness to reach out to like-minded potential recruits, position themselves as threats to the communities they target, proliferate provocative hate speech, and advance revolutionary narratives and strategies of violence through increasingly networked affinity groups. An examination of the location and time frames of activities centered on wilderness or semi-wilderness settings (50%), where paramilitary and firearms training could be carried out. Those activities that take place in urban settings usually take place at night (45%), presumably when activities like flyering on campuses and in commercial districts are less visible and prone to disruption. These flyers typically included some sort of bias, typically anti-Semitic, anti-black, or anti-multicultural, yet also implicitly anti-liberal, anti-intellectual, and/or anti-antifascist. These flyers were shown to be placed in order to cover other groups' stickers and were posted primarily on college campuses and used to critique long-standing liberal policies such as pro-immigration policies.

The tactic of using liberal values like free speech (through stickering, flyering, and banner drops) to promote illiberal hate speech, or using the U.S. Second Amendment to insinuate threats against a democratic system, is central to AWD's message. The esthetic dimension AWD cultivates regarding wilderness events at night, organizing regional gatherings dubbed "hate camps," which include symbolic actions like burning the U.S. Constitution and destroying a USSR flag, presumably represent a rejection of representational democracy, communism, or international Bolshevism, and capitalism in favor of some idealized set of pseudo-frontier warrior value system. The anti-systemic nature of this imagery and language is highlighted through consistent imagery of war, government protests, antipolice sentiment, the burning of symbols of liberal democracy, along with an implicit condemnation of the "New World Order" or "Zionist Occupational Government," recurrent anti-Semitic tropes wherein Jews are presented as controlling international banking, media, culture, and governance.

A focus on strategy and tactics is core to AWD's messaging, as is the infatuation with specific white power "celebrities," as opposed to traditional white power groups like skin heads crews, the American Nazi Party, the Ku Klux Klan, or movements like the White Aryan Resistance. Instead, there is consistent deployment of specific leaders from these movements, such as George

Lincoln Rockwell, James Mason, Tom Metzger, and Charles Manson, along with visuals and speeches from Adolf Hitler. For example, Rockwell, an influential leader in the American Nazi Party, explains how support is won by fighting Jews in the street, as opposed to talking (The Atomwaffen Division, 2017a). A speech from Metzger emphasizes "white racists" need to refuse public demonstrations, realize they are in a civil war, and prepare for battle, avoiding above-ground actions but instead attacking enemies in covert strikes where they are (The Atomwaffen Division, 2017b).

Finally, there is significant critique of both the alt-right and conservative movements. While certain affinities are suggested (anonymous members mimicking alt-right Pepe memes, Moon Man images on racist flyers, etc.), AWD promotes images of Nazi supremacy over the alt-right, while framing conservative or alt-right events like the Charlottesville, Virginia, protests as a failure, detailing the weaknesses and vulnerabilities of right-wing movements, and encouraging further polarization toward more extreme measures in a spectrum of violence. *Siege*, the text repeatedly promoted throughout these videos, then offers the necessary "antidote" to what is understood as passivity toward the system: a more extreme approach through a blueprint for decentralized attacks carried out by autonomous cells.

Linguistic Analysis of AWD and Siege

After reviewing the themes and activities displayed in the AWD *video* corpus, our team assembled a textual corpus of AWD and related canonical material for additional review. In order to establish a sizable sample of AWD written material, we assembled a 194,909-word corpus derived from two authors: AWD and James Mason. Five percent of the total corpus (9,886 words) was made up of texts explicitly authored by AWD. This was constructed from a complete transcription of the audio and written text contained in the video corpus, website text from AWD's .org and .onion websites, and the text displayed in flyers and posters designed by the group and hosted online. The remaining 95% of the corpus (185,023 words) was assembled from *Siege*, the collected works of James Mason consistently advocated by AWD. These two corpora—the smaller AWD-specific collection and the larger *Siege*—linguistically confirm many of the politics, worldviews, ethics, and themes of our video content analysis.

Our linguistic analysis of the AWD-only corpus revealed frequent usage of words like "join," "plans," "revolution," and "war." These words were used in much higher frequency than in Standard English, suggesting the network's organizing efforts for future-oriented violence. The network also established strict in-group/out-group boundaries with words like "join," "family," and "group," used in high frequency, emphasizing purposeful recruitment into explicitly defined communities rooted in racial and fascist characteristics, as well as community threats sometimes termed "enemy communities." Beyond function and other *helper* words, we see the word "system" in high frequency indicating a focus on a system-level critique of the social-political-economic order. Other highly occurring words focus on identity, specifically an exclusionary lexicon of words such as "Nazi," "white," "race," and "revolution" (figure 5.2).

Throughout the AWD corpus, words like "siege" and "rope" allude to core movement literature, for instance, James Mason's *Siege*, explicitly and vigorously promoted, or William Luther Pierce's *The Turner Diaries* (written under the pen name Andrew Macdonald), which speaks of the "day of the rope," a postrevolutionary period wherein "race traitors" are killed. According to historian Kathleen Belew (2018), these core movement texts promote a strategy of leaderless resistance, where autonomous cells use literature as decentralized blueprints to hone a vision, seek out targets, and implement strategies of racial insurrection. *The Turner Diaries* (Macdonald, 2019), for instance, suggests insurgent attacks against the federal government and has been found in possession of numerous far-right attackers including Timothy McVeigh, who modeled the 1995 bombing of the Oklahoma City federal building on the text.

An explicit examination of pronoun usage within the AWD-only corpus finds that "you" and "we" are the most commonly used pronouns (8th and 10th most commonly used words, respectively), indicating messaging directed outward at a collective, community identity. When these words

Figure 5.2   List of "Sainted Accelerationists, Noting Accelerating Frequency of Attacks."
Source: Telegram user Death Kvlt (2019).

are viewed in context, one observes the clustered use of "you have," "you can," "you must," "you will," and "you are." However outward their focus, what AWD talks about most is itself, its brand, and its online presence. In the AWD-only corpus, the most commonly occurring words, even more frequently used than those previously discussed, were "Atomwaffen Division" and "Ironmarch." They consistently mention the wider networking hub (e.g., Ironmarch and their later .onion site) seemingly to network individuals and build connections. Interestingly, in comparing AWD's use of so-called being verbs, we see "is" (164 times) used nearly four times more frequently than "will" (44 times) or "was" (35 times), which speaks to a focus on the present state of affairs and less on the future or past.

When examining the much larger *Siege* corpus only, we can observe the ideas, linguistic characteristics, and themes present in AWD's most prominent ideological source. Within Mason's 553-page tome, there is an atypically high rate of "I" (as opposed to we, our, your, yours), highlighting Mason's self-referential writing style and focus, a lesson AWD learned well. Beyond pronouns, in both *Siege* and AWD's writings, the word "system" is the most frequently occurring, notable word. In *Siege*, it occurs as the 47th most frequently used word in the entire book including pronouns, and articles.

Within *Siege*, there are other words which appear in notably higher frequencies, far higher than they would appear in typical, standard British or American English.[12] Words occurring frequently include "movement," "white," "national," "Hitler," "[Charles] Manson," "revolution," "against," "revolutionary," and "[George Lincoln] Rockwell." This survey of high-use words paints an apt picture of the elements of *Siege* that AWD adopted, such as the critical focus on targeting the "system" and identity-based categories. As one would expect, AWD's videos, flyers, and texts frequently quote and borrow from the ideologies of Charles Manson, Hitler, and Rockwell (as well as Mason himself) to offer a revolutionary vision based on strict in-group/out-group divisions.

While it is instructive to understand the AWD texts as distinct from Mason's larger assemblage, when these collections are taken as a whole, they exhibit interesting patterns which speak to the symbiotic nature of the two neo-Nazi nodes. For example, when examining the article "the" through a cluster analysis throughout the combined corpus, its most frequent usage occurs within the phrase "the system," followed by the use of "the movement." Farther down the list, the frequent pairing of "the enemy" and "the Jews" is telling. When examining the article "a" and its clusters, there is a high use of "a few," "a revolution/ary," "a man," "a new," "a movement," and others which give a good sense of the topics covered and frames established in Mason and AWD's writings. Further confirmation of the patterned focus and bias in both can easily be seen through cluster analyses of words such as "Jew" frequently clustered as "Jews are" and "Jews have"—or a word such as "white"—frequently clustered with "white man" and "white race." These textual peeks into the sociolinguistic reality of AWD demonstrate the network's tendency to borrow from its forebears while attempting to remix and re-invigor these ideas with a modern twist. AWD's communications are self-promotional, predictable, and champion an us-versus-them mentality seeking to exacerbate social tension, threaten enemies, and set the stage for the fight to come.

"Siege-Pilling" the Alt-Right

To highlight the core message of our findings ("message" being another keyword in our linguistic analysis), AWD promotes a naturalized racial hierarchy embedded within fascist politics, portraying "the system's" promotion of multiculturalism as an existential threat to the white race, alongside academic institutions, ethnic/religious minorities, liberal policies, and antifascist efforts. AWD adopts the rhetoric of free speech to provoke hatred in legal ways while encouraging militant training for insurrectionary attacks as part of an underground, fascistic white supremacist network.

This wider network communicates through online encrypted services (e.g., Wire, Rocket Chat, Telegram, Discord) and message boards (e.g., Reddit, 4-Chan, 8-Chan, Fascist Forge, and the now defunct Iron March) to encourage real-world activity working toward civil war (i.e., "the boogaloo"), white revolution, and the purging of undesirable racial, ethnic, and political opponents. The effect of this rhetoric aims to polarize discourse in conservative, alt-right, and fascist groups, normalizing political violence, displaying affinities to contemporary fascist organizations around the world, and recruiting others toward these ends through flyers, photos, websites, links, and emails. Many of these themes present in AWD's materials are similarly articulated in Kathleen Belew's *Bring the War Home* (2018), where she traces the post-Vietnam white power movement's attempt to undermine the New World Order/Zionist Occupied Government by bombing infrastructure, assassinating political leaders, undermining currency, and conducting autonomous attacks to engage in apocalyptic confrontation with state forces. Similar general themes are found in AWD's communiques, from the Vietnam-era camo fatigues to their "hate camp" training sites, to the militia-driven cell-style underground leaderless resistance, to the various celebrities connected to the wider tradition of the white power movement.

AWD simultaneously draws philosophically from the alt-right movement. Described in journalist Angela Nagle's book *Kill All Normies* (2017), the so-called alt-right movement feeds off of a love of transgression, motivated by deep cynicism and reactive nihilism shrouded in irony, a leaderless digital counterrevolution against political correctness and virtue signaling. The repudiation of morality becomes an attack on civility itself, rationalizing dehumanization, yet doing so satirically and in a detached manner. The intentional triggering can therefore be understood as an antiestablishment attack, targeting the hegemony of liberal elite sensibilities so as to accelerate the collapse of a multicultural, feminist, cultural Marxism through anti-conformity, antiauthoritarian approaches to promote misogyny, racism, sexism, homophobia, xenophobia, and anti-Semitism. If politics are rooted in culture, the alt-right, as a "cultural factory," produces the psychic, social, and philosophical space to shift culture through a form of mimetic warfare ("meme magic"), using technology for an open-source insurgency that seeks to come off as a type of radical evil (Goldenberg & Finkelstein, 2020).

AWD, in intensifying this insurgency and emphasizing its most violent tendencies, seeks joy in the escape from and destruction of the liberal order it finds meaningless, with its notions of universal ethics and human rights. At the same time, by clowning around through "free speech extremism," AWD invites a disinhibition of fascist tendencies, naturalized as morally justifiable, uniting a eugenic theory with a romantic rejection of the modern world for a "blood and soil" narrative to promote a race-based approach to land and politics.

Here, identity is produced in opposition to such a culture, seeking to destroy unrepresentative structures. The violent rejection of the politics of multicultural solidarity and Marxist critique is similarly extended to the academy, seen as a symbol of the destruction of traditional identities (and location for much of AWD's flyering activities). In this regard, a willingness to collapse the complexity of socioeconomic conditions into a symbol of apocalyptic war between the white race and multicultural globalism is apparent.

In the current political context, then, fascism becomes an omnipresent possibility: the potential to derail into a perspective constituted by the eternal struggle and longing for family, home, resolution, and tradition becomes a primary motivating desire. Yet while the alt-right has on occasion used a baseline ideological framework taken from the Nazi Party, as well as employed democratic strategies that brought the Nazi Party to power in Germany, the rejection of party politics suggests no such political solution exists. Instead, political violence is proposed and enacted to control the system, promoting terror meant to quicken the destruction of the system.

The preceding analysis focused on three components: a linguistic analysis of AWD's spoken and projected language, a linguistic analysis of the core text promoted by the group (i.e., Mason's *Siege*), and a qualitatively coded visual analysis. In this three-pronged approach, we are able to better consider, using the heuristic of "Siege-pilling," essential characteristics around which organizations like AWD organize and recruit, yet which may undergo further iterations after they disintegrate. These aspects center around the following:

1. Leveraging core values and ideas of authoritarianism, racial identity, and hierarchy.
2. Cultivating a hatred of others based on racial, ethnic, sexual, religious, gender, or political identity.
3. Alignment to wider historical and contemporary international white power, neo-Nazi, and neo-fascist movements.
4. Desire to escape modernity, capitalism, and the neoliberal corporate state as embodied in New World Order/Zionist Occupied Government tropes.
5. Finding spiritual resources in apocalyptic, Satanic, esoteric Hitlerist, or occult traditions to invert mainstream values of progress, hope, liberalism, and equality.
6. Recruiting alternative family dynamic based in an imagined past marked by strength, virtue, and traditional conservative values.
7. Generating publicity to delegitimize the system, principally through social media and propaganda of the deed.
8. Mobilizing violent direct action and terrorism to accelerate the collapse of the liberal world order while preparing to survive and thrive in the post-collapse era.

By cultivating leaderless resistance and training underground terror cells, AWD foments insurrection through a spectrum of violence to destabilize governments through race war and inaugurate a transnational fascist order. The editor of Mason's *Siege* explicates the strategy writing: "Much of the solution rests within the pages of the book you now hold. At this juncture social malaise cannot be halted, only accelerated onward to the abyss, capitulating the whole vile episode of this end cycle" (2003, p. 13). In this sense, journalist Nate Thayer (2019b) perhaps most appropriately describes AWD as a "satanic Nazi death cult terror group," one that establishes and maintains rigid ideological boundaries to preserve a sense of identity and purity existentially threatened by the system it in turn sets out to escalate attacks on.

Spreading and Harvesting the Seed of Hate

J. M. Berger defines *extremism* as the construction of an in-group identity existentially threatened by a crisis supposedly generated by a constructed enemy, against whom violence is mobilized to destroy this other (2018, pp. 51–74). AWD and its allies view the modern world's multiculturalism as itself representative of a crisis, understanding their own revolutionary vision as an "extraordinary solution" to the perceived crisis (Berger, 2018, pp.

79–83). In this regard, AWD can clearly be defined as violent extremists, in a permanent state of crisis and anxiety defined by race war apocalypticism, naturalized hierarchy, and a spectrum of violence, indicated by the symbols and language it promotes.

AWD's worldview seeks to accelerate anti-systemic violence through leaderless resistance. In this strategy, networks of autonomous cells borrow from open-source blueprints (*The Turner Diaries*, anonymous Telegram posts, etc.) to adopt common targets and operationalize strategic violence to destabilize the social order and precipitate social collapse to initiate race war, white revolution, and an emergent global fascism. This network structure allows for broad involvement from ideological adherents while avoiding traditional organizational models which are prone to observation, infiltration, and disruption by law enforcement. In modern history, this model has been at the forefront of clandestine, lethally minded, U.S.-based neo-Nazi, white power, militant anti-abortion, and allied networks, including the Phinehas Priesthood, the Order, White Aryan Resistance, Army of God, R.B. DePugh's Minutemen, and the National Socialist Liberation Front (Davis, 2010, pp. 45–57).

This approach is essentially the "Siege-pill" around which networks self-organize, recruit, and propagate through social media, using esthetic images and provocative language, drawing from multiple traditions (e.g., white power, skinhead, alt-right, identitarian) while seeking to intensify extreme violence against enemy communities. In this regard, AWD is perhaps less important to our analysis than the Siege-pill itself, considering the group has virtually collapsed after a series of arrests, including the imprisonment of its leader, former members' cooperation with law enforcement, and periodic doxings[13] from hacked chat logs. Yet even if the group disintegrates, the essential aspects we outlined earlier will likely continue to proliferate. People and movements will continue to be Siege-pilled.

Digital Discourse: Catloaf, Fissionwaffen, Ecogang, and Mimetic Warfare

In the following discussion, we demonstrate how the Telegram ecosystem in particular offers fertile ground for the seed of accelerationist violence to grow. Telegram is an end-to-end encrypted messaging app that has been around since 2013 and reports having around 200 million monthly active users as of 2018 (Durov, 2018). Perhaps because it originated to combat restrictions to speech by offering a means to engage in a safe, anonymous exchange of ideas, Telegram quickly became the platform for the growing white nationalist, alt-right, and accelerationist networks (Glaser, 2019; Owen, 2019).

Despite the difficulties inherent in studying a cloud-based, encrypted, instant messaging application through which users create group channels to share messages, photos, videos, memes, audio, and other files anonymously, we are able to partially observe the Siege-pilling process undertaken by the "Terrorgram" community by following discourse as it flowed from the digital ecosystem into real-world public activity and discourse. In one example, attempts were made to turn a seemingly innocuous image of a cat sitting with paws and tail tucked underneath the body ("a cat in the loaf position") into a hate symbol to troll the ADL's Hate Symbol Database inclusion of other memes like the "Ok hand symbol," appropriated as a common trolling tactic (Anti-Defamation League, 2019).

One user, Catloaf, "started a meme where all the channels and groups change their names and [profile pictures] in reference of Catloaf" (The Watering Hole, n.d.a). Another explained: "We got 20 channels to change into a spawn of catloaf in 12 hours, this is the power of the Nat Soc and *Siege* community, oh and yeah also if it becomes a hate symbol" (The Watering Hole, n.d.d). Users had difficulty finding their own channels because the catloaf meme, and its many violent iterations, had been made into the visual icon for so many. Users in turn shared pictures, changed them, and made new ones, helping to map the flow system of "Terrorgram," renamed "Kittygram" (Catloaf News, 2020).

The iterative process marks a knowledge transmission concept map, whereby a meme is created and read by insurrectionary sympathizers, received and redistributed among insurrectionary hubs, and re-authored by other participants as the information flows through the Telegram and wider cyber ecosystem (Loadenthal, 2017, p. 222, Image 7.3). The process further parallels the communiqué/attack-form/function concept map process that AWD and the Siege-pilled community engage in, where a canon detailing a history of past attacks, communiqués, statements, letters, and other texts inspire an attack, creating new content for communiqués to explain, contextualize, and justify the attack, in turn influencing other attacks and communiqués which explain and influence yet more (Loadenthal, 2017, p. 219, Image 7.2) (figure 5.3).

One can see this in the AWD communiqués themselves, where stickers and pamphlets around college campuses garner news coverage, whose footage is ripped to create new communiqués, eventually commenting on events like the Unite the Right rally by overlaying White Aryan Resistance founder Tom Metzger's voice in their video, "Unite the Right: The Lessons of Charlottesville":

> We view all politicians including the President as our deadly enemy. You won't see us at polling booths. You won't see us at cluster fucks like took place in

Figure 5.3 Graphic Circulated on Telegram Channel during COVID-19 Pandemic.
Source: Telegram user Survive Now! (2020).

Virginia this weekend. We have been through that years ago and found it was not a viable tactic in combating our opposition. . . . I would seek out my opposition's meeting places and rallies and their homes and pay them a visit at our own opportune time. . . . If they had taken all the money . . . and put it into equipment and prepare for a real struggle that's in the future, it would have been some good effect. The struggle is going to take more time to develop for what you could call an insurrection or maybe even a civil war, it's coming. So don't get excited. Keep your powder dry. Be extremely careful who your friends are, and realize every politician from the top down to the bottom, and the media, and the churches, and the corporations are all enemies of the white working class survival. (The Atomwaffen Division, 2017b)

The video highlights the theme of evolving critique. In the same way the Siege-pilled lone wolf is declared more potent than movement politicking, a similar commentary is eventually made about AWD after a new video surfaced in October 2019, purporting to be from the group (The Atomwaffen Division, 2019), yet which the group itself denied (Mason, 2019). While many of the same elements of earlier AWD communiqués were present (clothing, logos, burning flags, tactical training, assault weapons, etc.), a subsequent meme signaled an irreparable "fission," even demise of AWD, that the Siege community used to highlight key differences through critique and commentary. As one Telegram user wrote:

As for The Atomwaffen Division, I need to thank them for recent events. The video we released from them caused a big splash and I think really set the bar for any future AW [Atomwaffen] videos and NS [National Socialist] videos in general I hope that their work and the exposure I helped bring will lead to more cells popping up, who I would be glad to post as well. As for pre-Fission AW: you know who Fission-AW want to speak to. Neither side will back down proper, best you get a line to one another sooner than later. I hope sooner than later. Hail the Division! Hail the Fission! HH [Heil Hitler]. (T E R R O R W A V E R E F I N E D, 2019)

The posting exhibits the inevitable fracturing these groups undergo over time. After the AWD fission and subsequent arrests, members flowed toward a similar organization, the Base, another far-right extremist coalition inspired by Mason's *Siege*, seeking to accelerate "race war" (Makuch & Lamoureux, 2018). The Base describes themselves as "A fraternal survivalism & self-defense network of like-minded comrades," noting their "primary mission is to facilitate & organize training events & meetups worldwide" (The Base Official, 2020). Included in the same promotional image are three additional claims:

We are also a collective repository of survivalism & self-defense expertise [.] Our ultimate goal is to serve as a robust international network of mutual support [.] Participation is open to all nationalists including members of other nationalist organizations [.] (The Base Official, 2020)

While the increasing fragmentation of perspectives would presumably disrupt a unified front, these conflicts only seem to drive the development of new imagery (figures 5.4 and 5.5).

In a Telegram channel called the Watering Hole, one user writes, following a dispute as to whether a failed mass shooter in Halle, Germany, deserved "Sainthood" like the shooter Tarrant who killed 51 in the March 2019 Christchurch massacre in New Zealand if he "throws his life away with no results" (Slovak's Siege Relief Shack, 2019b): "we honestly don't need two equally right sides duking it out over this specific shooting. We need to move forward and work towards the next" (The Watering Hole, n.d.b). Another user responds:

It's pretty night and day on what is the divide. If you haven't swallowed the accelerationism pill then you probably hate the guy. If you did (Like me) you like him but is probably disappointed he didn't get passed that door and clean out the 80 kikes that were behind it but you'll learn from his mistakes. As long as they are those who don't want to swallow that pill the divide will always

Figure 5.4   Telegram Post Showing the Gamification of Right-Wing Mass Shootings as Scoreboard. *Source*: Telegram user Brenton Tarrant's lads (2019).

exist. Just look at "There is no political solution" channel compared against the shit posted at the "Random Anon Channel," 2 big channels who took it differently. (The Watering Hole, n.d.c)

In turn, a meme emerged to represent the debate surrounding the objective of destroying "industrial society and initiating the urbanite holocaust," whether it would be more appropriate to attack the "vulnerable pillars of the industrial system like infrastructure, finance, mechanized food production and power generation" or go after "soft targets for 15 minutes of fame and life in a globohomo prison while having done nothing substantial in the wider picture" (Slovak's Siege Relief Shack, 2019).

The critique then suggests even mass shootings are not extreme enough. Rather, the Oklahoma City Bombing is depicted as an ideal attack on state infrastructure to create as much destruction as possible and accelerate the

Figure 5.5 **Site of Christchurch, NZ, Terrorist Attack Gamified in First-Person Shooter Perspective.** *Source*: Telegram user Misanthropik Mayhem (2020).

downfall of the system. Arrested Canadian Base member Patrick Jordan Matthews recorded a video making such an intent clear. According to U.S. attorney's motion to detain pending trial, Matthews states:

> The time for violent revolution is now, that time is already here, it's here right now as we speak. You have one of two options if you understand the truth and you understand the gravity of the situation. . . . Option number one, prepare for the collapse. Option number two, bring the collapse. That is it. If you are not getting physically fit, if you are not getting armed, if you do not acquiring weapons [sic], ammunition, and training right fucking now, then you should be preparing to do what needs to be done. Derail some fucking trains, kill some people, and poison some water supplies. You better be fucking ready to do those things. (*USA v. Brian Mark Lemley, Jr., Patrik Jordan Mathews, and William Garfield Bilbrough IV*, 2020, p. 19)

More recently, the "eco-fascist wing" of the Base was reported to have committed ecologically motivated sabotage in Sweden (Kamel et al., 2020), driving the narrative of eco-fascist revolt against the modern world forward with memes and videos increasingly "greenpilled" or "Ted-pilled" (after the so-called Unabomber Ted Kaczynski's 1995 manifesto, *Industrial Society and Its Future*, that calls for waging war against technological industrial civilization).

Similar eco-fascist channels link to media like the Mexican eco-extremist network Individualists Tending Toward the Wild (see Eco-Fascist Central, 2020; Eco Gang, 2020; Esoteric Ecology, 2020; the Green Brigade, 2020), with memes promoting primitivism, ludditism, animal liberation, Kaczynski's domestic terrorism, Earth First! symbols, new movement literature like Mike Ma's *Harassment Architecture* (2019), even linking to a channel named after the radical feminist anti-reformist resistance Deep Green Resistance, an aboveground group promoting militant underground networks to carry out asymmetric attacks and sabotage to disrupt industrial systems and dismantle industrial infrastructure via "Decisive Ecological Warfare" (Jensen et al., 2011).

One sees how the Ted-pilled/Siege-pilled worldviews are united, as when one Telegram user modifies a popular Rick and Morty copypasta meme:

> To be honest, you have to have a very high IQ to understand SIEGE. The humor is extremely subtle and without a solid grasp on domestic terrorism, most of the jokes will go over a typical reader's head. The Authors nihilistic outlook is definitely woven into his autism. His personal philosophy draws heavily from Ted Kaczynski's literature. The fans understand this stuff, they have the true intellectual capacity to understand these domestic terror plots. They're not just funny, they say something *deep* about life. As a consequence, people who dislike SIEGE truly are idiots. Of course, they for instance, wouldn't understand the humor in James Mason's existential catchphrase. "Kill your local mailman." Which of course is an ebbik reference to Ted Kaczynski's ebbik Unibomber manifesto. Hah, I'm smirking right now. Just imagining one of those addlepated urbanite simpletons scratching their heads in confusion as James Mason's genius wit unfolds itself on their CNN news feeds. What fools, how I pity them. (There Is No Political Solution, 2019)

This promotion of Kaczynski through eco-fascism is perhaps not surprising—Tarrant, who was inspired by Anders Behring Breivik and livestreamed his attacks on the mosque to inspire others, described himself in his manifesto, "The Great Replacement" (Tarrant, 2019), as an eco-fascist, connecting immigration to environmentalism through overpopulation, in turn inspiring other attacks, including the Norway mosque attack, whose perpetrator described himself as "chosen by Saint Tarrant" and needing to "bump the race war threat in real life" (Burke, 2019).

The goal of committing terrorism on behalf of environmental concerns is explicitly promoted by new groups within the Siege-pilled community like the eco-fascist group the Green Brigade, described as

> [an] organization consisting of openly accelerationist, Eco-Extremist members focused on tearing down the system that exploits our land, animals, and people.

These individuals prioritize and practice an autonomous environmentalist life-style, with a fascist emphasis and with a hatred for modern civilization. (The Green Brigade, 2019)

Like AWD and the Base before them, the group's visible activity is pri-marily flyering and recruitment, promoting quotes, memes, videos, and mes-sages that reflect and develop the worldview. Yet at the same time, these and similar Telegram channels circulate documents for how to use chemicals to make firearms, body armor, explosive devices, poisons, and many other lethal components (Owen, 2019; SITE Intelligence Group, 2019; X, 2019). One meme, for instance, suggests "Siege-planting" in black and brown neighbor-hoods, cultivating poisonous and harmful landscapes that harm vulnerable communities. Another hints at the desired objective, where a dark skull-masked figure points to an electrical substation alongside a quote from Ma's *Harassment Architecture* (2019, p. 28) as seen in figure 5.6

Figure 5.6 Siege-Masked Accelerationist with Bolt Cutters Stands in Front of Infrastructure. Captioned with text from Mike Ma's (2019) *Harassment Architecture*. *Source*: Telegram user Terrorwave Revived (2019).

A final example of how operations inspire new ones. Not long after an African American man with "no history of like violent acts and no convictions for any crime . . . no known history of anti-Semitism" and "not a member of any hate groups" (AP, 2019) yet who had reportedly conducted a number of online anti-Semitic searches on "why Hitler hated Jews" stabbed and slashed five Jewish worshippers during Hanukkah celebrations with a machete amid a series of violent attacks targeting Jews, Telegram channels began to disseminate materials on what was called "Operation Kang versus Kike," propaganda meant to incite black hatred against Jews by emphasizing the Holocaust as more important than slavery, blaming Jews for slavery, while suggesting Jews enriched themselves through Jim Crow laws, using Twitter accounts to spread the message. As one user writes:

> Kang versus kike has potential to wreak havoc on the system. But we should not fall into the mindset that they are necessary allies for our long term success. There can be no long term success for our folk if we are to rely on billions of starving, diseased, low iq nogs. Our cause transcends the end of the jew. Our cause is for eternity. Total Victory must be ours and ours alone. So long as we recognize that fact; by all means, set the apes loose on the rats nest in the meantime. (Scrimshaw Saga, 2020)

The cynical nature of this operation is not unlike the attempt to sow discord through other channels, creating flyers mimicking environmental protest group Extinction Rebellion while introducing racist and anti-immigration narratives into environmental concerns or, with "Operation Mickey Mouse" or "Operation Marketfuck," attempting to link Disney figures like Mickey Mouse to protesters in Hong Kong so that China might force companies to clarify their position on the protests or face intellectual property being banned. As one user writes:

> Forcing them to alienate either Chinese or western markets and lose BILLIONS in market cap in the process. How you feel about the HK protests is irrelevant, what matters is that we have been presented with a situation which allows to strip billions from the pockets of our enemies. This is 4th Generation Warfare. (/BMW/ - The Bureau of Memetic Warfare, 2019)

In each of these cases, whether catloaf, the coevolution of the accelerationist terrorist community from AWD through fission to the Base, eco-fascist groups, commentary on mass shooters, pushing extremist narratives guiding terror attacks, and heightening the potential for social conflict, system disruption, and economic or grid collapse, new mass casualty events are the objective, uniting different channels through forwarded posts to accelerate chaotic violence, waging asymmetric anti-systemic warfare, yet hiding behind a cloak of irony for protection. At the time of this writing, users are cheering on the coronavirus, suggesting ways it might facilitate fear, factionalism, and race war.

Across each of these operations, Siege-pilled memes offer a kind of dark, farcical parody of murderous violence, promoted through memes with the intention of having them operationalized, indirectly getting others killed, becoming promoted in media, creating contagions, and accelerating the conditions for social collapse. This idea of "white jihad," adopted by fascist and accelerationist groups, is "satire," "so ridiculous that it mocks comparison— humour is the most fantastic weapon because with it we can make ourselves understood while alienating those who are driving the narrative" (Jackson, 2020). In Durham, UK, for example, a 16-year-old neo-Nazi, writing about an "inevitable race war" in a journal he titled "A Manual for Practical and Sensible Guerrilla Warfare against the Kike System in the Durham City Area, Sieg Heil," became the youngest person convicted of preparing a terrorist act in the UK, defending himself by stating he only "adopted a fake right-wing persona for 'shock value'" (Davies, 2019).

In this section, we have shown how shared targets and methods are used by groups seeking similar outcomes through self-reinforcing feedback loops via open-source digital networks, driving social contagion to further accelerate momentum toward chaos and social violence. While accelerationists may attempt to destabilize society, destroy democracy, and overthrow capitalism, what our research makes clear is that such a strategy transcends the fascist, white supremacist, neo-Nazi, Satanic apocalyptic esoteric Hitlerism of AWD toward the wider Siege-pilled, Ted-pilled, or green-pilled communities operating in encrypted group channels and messaging systems. One user writes of the potential for Telegram as a means toward this end:

> Telegram as a platform is DEFINITELY more promising than Twitter and other kiked social media, so I expect it to grow exponentially as censorship on other platforms intensifies. Here's to a 2020 full of new memes to life our spirits, new people joining the cause, new wignats earning their Sainthood. HAIL VICTORY! (Slovak's Siege Relief Shack, 2020)

Hidden Dynamics

Our coding scheme will likely remain relevant even after accelerationist groups like AWD or the Base disintegrates, providing a framework and coding system to explain new iterations of accelerationist terror. A quantitative analysis of symbolic imagery does much to explain the insurrectionary accelerationist worldview, around which communiqués, memes, channels, networks, and terroristic violence accrete. The provocative imagery, the hate language, the violent aesthetic all serve a greater purpose: accelerating the collapse of liberal democracy and the political-social-economic order.

This tendency to precipitate social collapse transcends fascist and white power movements to define radical political approaches across the political spectrum, whether ecological, feminist, anarchist, or any other. While linguistic analysis could likely detect accelerationist language beyond the Siege-pilled community, we suggest another pathway for research: AWD and the Siege-pilled worldview represent a distortion in the semiotic chain between environmental signal and intentional response, where an oppressive sociopolitical order is interpreted as an existential threat to "white culture," necessitating attacks against it.

Commonly cited on fascist Telegram channels, Mike Ma's *Harassment Architecture* reads as a last ditch effort to escape the apathy and nihilism of the modern world, funneling hatred against a society held responsible for killing beauty. Its disappearance prompts inquiry into what destroys beauty, rejecting anti-beauty while refusing to compromise with the ugly, and so burning down the modern world. For Ma, modern man is "against the next renaissance" (2019, p. 138), "he glamorizes the ugly . . . he destroys art, destroys music, he destroys good taste" (2019, p. 140). Such perspectives take pleasure in causing offense to such a society. The willingness to cause offense, indeed destroy the infrastructure sustaining modern civilization, is the core message, the concretized hatred for all that maintains society: "I hear people are making homemade explosives and knocking down cell towers. I hear some people are making homemade explosives and disintegrating local power substations" (Ma, 2019, pp. 94–95).

In his book *Humankind* (2017) philosopher Tim Morton suggests fascism is the result of intensifying humanity's severance from nature, or the "symbiotic whole," a division maintained by "agrilogistics," accelerated through the neoliberal industrial economy and further intensified through fascist politics that seek not to heal this separation but to maintain it, embracing the chasm dividing the "human" from "inhuman." Included in the category of nonhuman people then are those of certain racial, gendered, sexual, political, and religious characteristics, to be subjugated to a rigid hierarchy. AWD's neo-Nazi fascism may then not so much *produce* marginalization but rather exists as an *expression* of it, its worldview a formalized distortion of the environment it is situated within, severed from the ontological reality of symbiotic interdependence, a place of both division and struggle for reunion where strained relationships, violent tensions, and hyper-alienation find violent expression. Yet the desire for violent insurgency (and with it an escape from suffering) perhaps further signals the anxiety and rage of those who feel altogether unfree and systematically threatened, where revolutionary suicide is preferable to what is internally felt as enslavement.

Fascism offers, then, an alternative reaction to alienation and systematic oppression, yet which does not in fact address it, but only accelerates it, setting itself up against this "system" while seeking salvation in its collapse. If technology and capitalism are inextricably linked, transforming both society and self through the advancement of modern life, as accelerationist philosopher Nick Land suggests, then capital, as the modern motor escalating this techno-commercial complex, would seem to similarly intensify conditions for alienation, and with it, rates of any resulting reactionary violence (Beauchamp, 2019). Here, accelerationist terror becomes a reaction against the "material experience of life under global capitalism (Hughes, 2019, p. 24)," its movement literature providing a philosophy and program to guide "necessary" responses. To quote James Mason's *Siege*:

> It means—scientifically and irrefutably—that the country isn't going but has gone MAD; that the final END of society is accelerating; that the entire foundation itself is thoroughly corroded; and that there is no longer any place to go to hide (save maybe a tent in the North Woods). Now isn't that the most encouraging thing anyone has reported to you in a long, long time? [. . .] It is up for grabs how many moments or seconds remain before the whole repulsive, putrefying mess comes crashing through. (Mason, 2003, p. 199)

While white supremacy manifests racial and ethnic violence, this violence may itself be driven by a polarization driving people toward extremist positions. We should not therefore discount the underlying structural causes for polarization, but perhaps consider extremism less an individual problem, instead rooted in the infrastructure and economic mode ("the system") whose context structurally marginalizes communities across the political spectrum that in turn revolt and attack it—a tendency that transcends white insurrectionary accelerationism (Loadenthal, 2017, chapter 7, esp. pgs. 203–209, 222–225). Any solution then will necessarily be constrained and determined by those logistics generating and reproducing (accelerating) alienation, unless it seeks to negate those underlying dynamics (figures 5.7 and 5.8).

We propose any counter-extremism strategy may necessarily fail if it merely conditions and habituates extremists to a fragmented neoliberal order without addressing the root crisis being resisted, invisibilizing rather than explicitly confronting those conditions that structure hate. Moreover, as the root of accelerationism is deeper than any ideology, bound up in the infrastructure, economic mode, and logistics of capital, simply repressing the impulse to resist, rebel, or violently attack this system may actually provoke violent catharsis, where groups embrace the system's own structural violence, scapegoating marginalized communities rather than effectively addressing

Figure 5.7 **Meme Circulated on Accelerationist Video Sharing Site.** *Source*: Sadlark's (2019) Bitchute channel.

Figure 5.8 **Meme Circulated on Accelerationist Telegram Channel.** *Source*: Telegram user Feuerkrieg Division (2019).

the root causes of suffering to begin with. Indeed, this may be the state of accelerationist terror today.

CONCLUSION

In one of their banner drops, AWD calls to "Resist Racial Eclipse," invoking the white genocide conspiracy theory that inspired mass shooters like Breivik, Tarrant, Bowers, Earnest, and Crusius. Through their video communiqués, AWD thus offers insight into the white power narrative as influenced by movement texts like *Siege* and newer philosophies like accelerationism.

The coding scheme we provide offers ways to understand aspects of the worldview, contextualize it within the wider white power milieu, and demonstrate its functionality in the wider media ecosystem and real-world spaces. In so doing, we point to the question of how such violent extremist orientations are generated, suggesting the role of sociopolitical and environmental forces driving ideological positions, along with strategies for countering violent extremism that prioritize system transformation, of conceptual spaces (identity construction) certainly, but also infrastructural, technical, and economic modes of production that may generate the conditions that acceleration is thought to solve.

Violence like that envisioned by AWD, the Base, and their many contemporaries must therefore be understood as grounded in the same structural violence that generates demographic shifts, inequality, and forms of social, economic, and community exclusion. In her discussion of how violence (and nonviolence) is discursively labeled, philosopher Judith Butler (2020, p. 2) writes, "Sometimes the physical strike to the head or the body is an expression of systemic violence, at which point one has to be able to understand the relationship of act to structure, or system." These young men whom we come to know first as Internet shitposters, then voices in ominously narrated videos, and finally as criminal defendants, these individuals are radicalized by poverty, structural racism, xenophobia, misogyny, homophobia, and a host of other systems, which if left unaddressed, perpetuate and intensify the root causes of the problem. To fight white supremacy without addressing the context that produces it as a viable option runs the risk of scapegoating its violence while leaving the conditions that generate it intact.

It is not yet clear whether the accelerationist violence we are seeing is a stochastic terrorism whose focal point is cultivated in online spaces through propaganda and disinformation; or indeed if it is being carried out intentionally by specific networks targeting and mobilizing vulnerable individuals toward those same ends. Certainly, intelligence services have warned against authoritarian powers like Russia conducting political warfare operations to polarize Western countries to create political stagnation (Pronk, 2019).

According to U.S. law enforcement and intelligence sources, the leader of the Base, Rinaldo Nazzaro, is "working for Russia and operating a violent neo-Nazi, white supremacist organization directing violent terror attacks on U.S. soil from St. Petersburg, Russia" (Thayer, 2019a), though speculation abounds as to his former connections to the U.S. intelligence community as well. Nazzaro, self-described as a "former CIA field intelligence officer," offered services including "server software for use in a proprietary computer system for providing unified operational intelligence awareness to command centers and intelligence analysts via automated information sharing and data process" (Thayer, 2019a). Alexander Slavros, a likely pseudonym for the founder of the website Iron March where many of the fascist groups began, is similarly thought to be living in a district "close to the Kremlin," promoting neo-Nazi and fascist extremism as well (Ross & Bevensee, 2019). Alexander Reid Ross (2020) points out this increased collaboration between Russia and far-right U.S. groups for funding and sanctuary, covertly disrupting U.S. stability and social political norms, while Russian ideologues Alexander Dugin, Eduard Limonov, and others promote the "third positionism" of National Bolshevism, "a violent form of Russian fascism that synthesizing Soviet-style socialism with ultranationalist geopolitics." The ascendency of a transnational global fascist terrorist network has drawn accelerationists seeking military training with openly neo-Nazi, white supremacist, anti-Semitic organizations like the Azov battalion, who recruited from AWD, the Base, Patriot Front, and the Rise Above Movement as well as in other countries, selling translated copies of the Christchurch shooter's manifesto at the Azov literature club, while "presenting a tangible model for how the far right could topple a government and wage a nationalist war to forge a new society in a predominantly white country" (Green, 2020).

Certainly, the tendency to find salvation in apocalyptic violence transcends any particular organization, bordering on ideological incoherence at times, yet if we are able to look through the violence toward the desire for structural and systemic change, alternative modes for dwelling arise in the possibility to root community into the landscape. We can perhaps consider how the semiotic-material reality shared through accelerationist communiqués and Telegram channels might offer pathways to heal the trauma of severance, inviting pathways back into the symbiotic whole, to restore the memory of indigeneity and love of land and those who exist within it, crafting an alternative language able to provide new contexts to live and dwell within.

As in any home, compassion is a critical ingredient and necessary social arrangement, able to dissolve harmful psychological and physical relationships. New narratives, languages, and political therapies able to reorganize key relationships and ensure more skillful, poetic living within alternative paradigms will be contingent upon the valuing and liking for all those who dwell together within shared spaces, and therefore needs the presence of all to ensure vulnerable communities remain resilient to and inoculated against the allure of accelerationist terror, white supremacy, and violent extremism.

NOTES

1. Swatting is a form of phone-mediated harassment where an individual makes a phone call to emergency services with the aim of having police forces (i.e., SWAT teams) dispatched to a target address. The victim of a swatting incident may have armed police breach their residence for no reason other than the perpetrator placing the false report.

2. Luke Austin Lane, Jacob Kaderli, Michael John Helterbrand

3. Brian Mark Lemley Jr., William Garfield Bilbrough IV, Patrik Jordan Mathews

4. Yousef Barasneh

5. John William Kirby Kelley

6. Cameron Brandon Shea, Kaleb Cole, Taylor Ashley Parker-Dipeppe, Johnny Roman Garza, John Cameron Denton

7. Andrew Jon Thomasberg

8. "Going dark" is a term used by law enforcement to point toward criminal individuals and networks employing encryption, and other anonymity-centric technologies to conceal their communications and avoid intelligence gathering, infiltration, and disruption.

9. Siege-pilling refers to the popular film *The Matrix*, in which the main character takes a pill that wakes him from the dreamworld, appropriated by the alt-right as "red-pilling" (i.e., learning the unpleasant knowledge of daily life) and later "black-pilling" (i.e., acceptance of despair and nihilism), which has been adopted by various subgroups (Men's Rights movements, incels, etc.).

10. Further detail concerning the study's coding framework, values, and the visual coding dictionary will be explored in a future publication. The authors have designed their approach to allow future researchers an opportunity to utilize these instruments to study other fascist, neo-Nazi, and white power video texts.

11. Percentages represent what portion of the total instances fit a particular value. In this case, of all of the 24 activity-types identified, 17% of instances were coded as the displaying of flags.

12. For the purpose of comparing the corporea under discussion to "standard" (i.e., non-fascist) English, we employed a keyword analysis using Antcone 3.5.8 and the AmE06 corpus comprised of 1 million American English words developed by linguist Paul Baker at Lancaster University.

13. Doxing is a tactic used by antifascists within a wider strategy of deplatforming, wherein far-right individuals are exposed and named with the aim of exerting pressure for them to disengage through public naming and shaming. For a comprehensive

discussion of deplatforming, one can review Mark Bray's 2017 book, *Antifa: The Anti-Fascist Handbook.*

APPENDIX 1: FURTHER READING

Belew, K. (2018). *Bring the War Home: The White Power Movement and Paramilitary America.* Harvard University Press.
Fielitz, M., & Thurston, N. (Eds.). (2019). *Post-Digital Cultures of the Far Right: Online Actions and Offline Consequences in Europe and the US.* Transcript-Verlag.
Morton, T. (2019). *Humankind: Solidarity with Non-Human People* (Reprint edition). Verso.
Nagle, A. (2017). *Kill All Normies: Online Culture Wars From 4Chan and Tumblr to Trump and the Alt-Right.* Zero Books.
Schirch, L. (Ed.). (2018). *The Ecology of Violent Extremism: Perspectives on Peacebuilding and Human Security.* Rowman & Littlefield Publishers.
Tenold, V. (2018). *Everything You Love Will Burn: Inside the Rebirth of White Nationalism in America.* Bold Type Books.

REFERENCES

AFP. (2020, February 14). German police arrest 12 over far-right plot to spark "civil-war-like situation." *The Guardian.* https://www.theguardian.com/world/2020/feb/14/german-police-arrest-12-men-on-far-right-terrorism-charges
Anti-Defamation League. (2019). *"OK" and other alt right memes and slogans added to ADL's hate symbols database* (Extremism, Terrorism & Bigotry) [Press Release/Statements]. Anti-Defamation League. https://www.adl.org/news/press-releases/ok-and-other-alt-right-memes-and-slogans-added-to-adls-hate-symbols-database
Atomwaffen Division Videos. (2019, November 9). *Atomwaffen Division Videos.* https://t.me/awdarchive
Beauchamp, Z. (2019, November 11). Accelerationism: The obscure idea inspiring white supremacist killers around the world. *Vox.* https://www.vox.com/the-highlight/2019/11/11/20882005/accelerationism-white-supremacy-christchurch
Belew, K. (2018). *Bring the war home: The white power movement and paramilitary America.* Harvard University Press.
Berger, J. M. (2018). *Extremism.* The MIT Press.
/BMW/ - The Bureau of Memetic Warfare. (2019, October 14). *By associating the IP of multinationals with the HK protests.* https://t.me/economichitlist
Brenton Tarrant's Lads. (2019, September 22). "Will you make it onto the leadeboard" [Image]. *Telegram.* Retrieved from https://t.me/tarrants_lads
Burke, J. (2019, August 11). Norway mosque attack suspect "inspired by Christchurch and El Paso shootings." *The Guardian.* https://www.theguardian.com/world/2019

/aug/11/norway-mosque-attack-suspect-may-have-been-inspired-by-christchurch
-and-el-paso-shootings

Catloaf News. (2020). *Telegram-канал catloafnews—Catloaf News* [Telegram Channel]. Telegram Channel. https://en.tgchannels.org/channel/catloafnews?start =5041&lang=all

Davies, G. (2019, November 20). British neo-Nazi, 16, listed places in his home city "worth attacking" in manual as he is convicted of terrorism. *The Telegraph.* https://www.telegraph.co.uk/news/2019/11/20/british-neo-nazi-16-listed-places -home-city-worth-attacking/

Davis, D. W. (2010). *The Phinehas priesthood: Violent vanguard of the Christian Identity movement.* Praeger.

Death Kvlt Archive. (2019, November 16). Bowlcast: "The distance in time between happenings is shrinking . . ." [Image]. *Telegram.* Retrieved from https://t.me/ deathcultpostingarchive

Durov, P. (2018, March 22). *200,000,000 monthly active users.* Telegram. https:// telegram.org/blog/200-million

Eco Gang. (2020, February 1). *Eco gang.* https://t.me/ecofascist

Eco-Fascist Central. (2020, February 1). *Eco-fascist central.* https://t.me/ecofascistcentral

Esoteric Ecology. (2020, February 1). *Esoteric ecology.* https://t.me/bloodandsoil88

Feuerkrieg Division. (2019, November 16). "Turn your sadness into rage" [Image]. *Bitchute.* Retrieved from https://t.me/fk_divisionofficial

Glaser, A. (2019, August 8). *Telegram was built for democracy activists. White nationalists love it.* Slate Magazine. https://slate.com/technology/2019/08/telegram -white-nationalists-el-paso-shooting-facebook.html

Goldenberg, A., & Finkelstein, J. (2020). *Cyber swarming, memetic warfare and viral insurgency: How domestic militants organize on memes to incite violent insurrection and terror against government and law enforcement* (p. 11) [NCRI White Paper Memetic Warfare]. The Network Contagion Research Institute. https://ncri .io/reports/cyber-swarming-memetic-warfare-and-viral-insurgency-how-domestic -militants-organize-on-memes-to-incite-violent-insurrection-and-terror-against -government-and-law-enforcement/

Green, J. (2020, January 19). The lost boys of Ukraine: How the war abroad beckoned American white supremacists. *Triad City Beat.* https://triad-city-beat.com/the-lost -boys-of-ukraine/

Gurman, J. K., Dan Frosch and Sadie. (2020, January 18). Men discussed opening fire at pro-gun rally in Richmond, officials say. *Wall Street Journal.* https://www.wsj .com/articles/men-discussed-opening-fire-at-pro-gun-rally-in-richmond-officials -say-11579291691

Hughes, B. (2019). "Pine tree" Twitter and the shifting ideological foundations of eco-extremism. *Interventionen, 14,* 18–25.

Jackson, P. (2020). *Transnational neo-Nazism in the USA, United Kingdom and Australia* (p. 36). George Washington Program on Extremism. https://extrem-ism.gwu.edu/sites/g/files/zaxdzs2191/f/Jackson%20-%20Transnational%20neo %20Nazism%20in%20the%20USA%2C%20United%20Kingdom%20and %20Australia.pdf

Jensen, D., McBay, A., & Keith, L. (2011). *Deep Green Resistance: Strategy to save the planet*. Seven Stories Press.

Lamoureux, M., & Makuch, B. (2019, January 29). Online neo-Nazis are increasingly embracing terror tactics. *Vice*. https://www.vice.com/en_us/article/8xynq4/online-neo-nazis-are-increasingly-embracing-terror-tactics

Loadenthal, M. (2017). *The politics of attack: Communiqués and insurrectionary violence*. Manchester University Press.

Ma, M. (2019). *Harassment architecture*. Independently published.

Makuch, B., & Lamoureux, M. (2018, November 20). Neo-Nazis are organizing secretive paramilitary training across America. *Vice*. https://www.vice.com/en_us/article/a3mexp/neo-nazis-are-organizing-secretive-paramilitary-training-across-america

Mason, J. (2003). *Siege* (2nd ed.). Ironmarch.

Mason, J. (2019, October). *Doppelgangers*. Atomwaffen Division. http://www.atom-yn4lngoqw5it.onion/doppelgangers

Misanthropik Mayhem. (2020, January 24). "You turn west and stand in front of mosque entrance . . ." [Image]. *Telegram*. Retrieved https://t.me/misanthropikmayhem

Misanthropik Mayhem. (2020, February 19). "Save your race, join the base" [Image]. *Telegram*. Retrieved from https://t.me/misanthropikmayhem

Nagle, A. (2017). *Kill all Normies: Online culture wars from 4Chan and Tumblr to Trump and the alt-right*. Zero Books.

Owen, T. (2019, October 7). How telegram became white nationalists' go-to messaging platform. *Vice*. https://www.vice.com/en_us/article/59nk3a/how-telegram-became-white-nationalists-go-to-messaging-platform

Paxton, R. O. (2005). *The anatomy of fascism*. Vintage.

Pronk, D. (2019). *The return of political warfare*. Strategic Monitor 2018-2019. https://www.clingendael.org/pub/2018/strategic-monitor-2018-2019/the-return-of-political-warfare/

Ross, A. R., & Bevensee, E. (2019, December 19). *Transnational white terror: Exposing Atomwaffen and the Iron March networks*. Bellingcat. https://www.bellingcat.com/news/2019/12/19/transnational-white-terror-exposing-atomwaffen-and-the-iron-march-networks/

Sadlark. (2019). The present is a foreign country. [Streaming video]. *Bitchute*. Retrieved from https://www.bitchute.com/video/So50g4L5W7E8/

Scrimshaw Saga. (2020, January 1). *Kang versus Kike has potential to wreck havoc on the system*. https://t.me/scrimshawsaga

Slovak's Siege Relief Shack. (2019, October 9). *...Destroy industrial society and...* https://t.me/slovaksiege

Slovak's Siege Relief Shack. (2020, January 1). *2019 has been a great year for us on Telegram*. https://t.me/slovaksiege

Survive Now! (2020, March 16). Embrace collapse [Image]. *Telegram*. Retrieved from https://t.me/survivenow

Tarrant, B. H. (2019). *The great replacement*. Self-published (distributed by Twitter and 8chan).

Terrorwave Refined. (2019, October 16). *As for the Atomwaffen Division.* https://t.me/terrorwaverefined

Terrorwave Revived. (2019, June 20). Please note: Do not do any of these things [Image]. *Telegram.* Retrieved from https:/t.me/terrorwaverevived

Thayer, N. (2019a, February 8). *U.S. law enforcement: Leader of U.S. Nazi terror group is a Russian spy.* Nate Thayer - Journalist. https://www.nate-thayer.com/u-s-law-enforcement-leader-of-u-s-nazi-terror-group-is-a-russian-spy/

Thayer, N. (2019b, April 12). *U.S. soldiers uncovered in Atomwaffen Division: Satanic Nazi death cult terror group.* Nate Thayer - Journalist. http://www.nate-thayer.com/u-s-soldiers-uncovered-in-atomwaffen-division-satanic-nazi-death-cult-terror-group/

The Atomwaffen Division. (2017a). *#OperationRockwell* [Streaming video hosted on .onion site]. http://www.....onion/

The Atomwaffen Division. (2017b, August). *The lesson of Charlottesville* [Streaming video hosted on .onion site]. http://www.....onion/

The Atomwaffen Division. (2019, October 10). *Fission—A reckoning of modernity* [Streaming video].

The Base Official. (n.d.). *Accelerationism.* https://t.me/thebaseofficial

The Base Official. (2020, January 1). *The Base.* https://t.me/thebaseofficial

The Green Brigade. (2019, November 7). *The Green Brigade is.* https://t.me/thegreenbrigade

The Green Brigade. (2020, February 1). *The Green Brigade.* https://t.me/thegreenbrigade

The Watering Hole. (n.d.a). *A user by the name of Catload (Peace be upon him).* https://t.me/the_watering_hole

The Watering Hole. (n.d.b). *If this really becomes a point of contention.* https://t.me/the_watering_hole

The Watering Hole. (n.d.c). *It's pretty night and day on what is the divide.* https://t.me/the_watering_hole

The Watering Hole. (n.d.d). *We got 20 channels to change into a spawn of Catloaf in 12 hours.* https://t.me/the_watering_hole

There Is No Political Solution. (2019, December 8). *To be honest, you have to have a very high IQ to understand SIEGE.* https://t.me/tinps

Chapter 6

When Cyberhate Turns to Violence

White Nationalism to the Manosphere

Kevin Borgeson and James Bacigalupo

The social media landscape, dominated by Facebook and Twitter, is often accused of being operated by advocates of the political left. The consequence of this, according to many on the right and certainly on the far right, is that the speech of right-wing users is disproportionately identified as "violating terms of service," resulting in censorship, account suspensions, and bans. This alleged ideological discrimination is what motivated Andrew Torba, a young tech advertising CEO from Scranton, Pennsylvania, to create Gab, an alternative social media platform with the mission "to defend free expression and individual liberty online for all people" (Coaston, 2018). The only content banned on this platform are threats of terror, direct threats of violence, illegal pornography (e.g., child porn), and doxing (Zannettou et al., 2018). In August 2017, one year after the creation of Gab, a violent rally "Unite the Right" took place in Charlottesville, Virginia, leaving one counter-demonstrator and two responding police officers dead, with many more injured. In the wake of this deadly rally, tech companies such as Internet domain registrars that were servicing white supremacist websites and crowdfunding organizations that collected donations for far-right figures began cracking down on extremist content and its funding mechanisms (Guynn, 2018). Gab became a reliable platform to disseminate controversial content as the company made no adjustments to their content policies. One user who took advantage of these lenient parameters was Robert Bowers, a white supremacist terrorist who killed 11 and wounded 6 at a Pittsburgh area synagogue. Bowers posted a final message on Gab before he carried out the deadly attack: "HIAS likes to bring invaders in that kill our people. I can't stand by and watch my people get slaughtered. Screw your optics, I'm going in" (Amend, 2018).

Is Bowers representative of the type of person that uses Gab? Are his hateful posts representative of what is commonly disseminated on the platform?

To better understand the content and user base of Gab, Zannettou et al. (2018) analyzed 22 million posts on the platform produced by 336K users between August 2016 and January 2018. The findings suggest that Gab is mainly used for discussing news and world events. They found hate speech to be present in 5.4% of posts, positioning Gab between Twitter and 4Chan with regard to hate speech prevalence—Gab being 2.4 times higher than Twitter but 2.2 times lower than 4Chan's Politically Incorrect board. The presence of hate speech was rampant enough for both Google and Apple to pull the Gab mobile app from their stores (Brandt & Dean, 2021). Zannettou et al. note that there is a presence of alt-right users, as well as accounts that make coordinated efforts toward recruiting millennials to the group. Lima et al. (2018) conducted a similar analysis and found Gab to be a platform that hosts users from other social networks that were banned due to hate speech infractions and that among the top 10 most followed users, four are considered extremist users by both the Anti-Defamation League (ADL) and the Southern Poverty Law Center (SPLC).

WHITE GENOCIDE: THE IMAGINED
WAR ON THE WHITE RACE

In Bowers's final Gab post, he referenced HIAS, which is the Hebrew Immigrant Aid Society—an agency that services refugee populations around the world (Amend, 2018). The post claims that they "like to bring invaders in that kill our people" (Amend, 2018). This notion, that Jews are actively orchestrating and carrying out the demise of white people, is commonly referred to as "white genocide." This is the overarching theory that many, if not all, white identity extremists adhere to and is often the impetus of their violence. Far-right extremists do not always agree on the specifics of this conspiracy or which group represents the biggest threat, but they all share the belief that there is some coordinated effort to displace, dispossess, and even eradicate the white race. The manifestos and subsequent attacks of recent white nationalists provide some insight as to the perceived threat that various minority groups pose and how they factor into the white genocide plot.

On June 17, 2015, at 8:16 p.m., Dylann Roof entered one of the nation's oldest black churches, the Emanuel AME Church in downtown Charleston, South Carolina. He spent an hour in the company of African American parishioners before opening fire on them, killing nine (Alcindor & Stanglin, 2015). Roof later told authorities that he wanted to start a race war (Mosendz, 2015). Roof's manifesto, which he posted on his now defunct website last-rhodesian.com, provides deeper insight into the beliefs that motivated this deadly attack. Unlike many white supremacists, Roof considered Jews to be white. In fact, the small section of his manifesto that discusses Jews is short and generally dismissive. It is clear that he found African Americans to be the biggest threat to whites. Roof came to this conclusion after googling "black on white crime," which led him to the website of the Council of Conservative Citizens, a group that according to the SPLC refers to African Americans as "a retrograde species of humanity" (Potok, 2015a). According to Roof, the site provided pages upon pages of cases where whites were the victims of black perpetrated murders. He identified this to be a global issue by noting that it was widespread all over Europe. Roof was incensed that the Trayvon Martin shooting case, which involved an unarmed black teen being shot dead by a neighborhood watch coordinator, George Zimmerman, was getting so much attention while these killings of whites at the hands of blacks were being ignored. The manifesto argues that whites subconsciously view blacks sympathetically, and as "lower beings," in part due to "historical lies, exaggerations, and myths" regarding black and white relations in America (Potok, 2015b).

On March 15, 2019, in Christchurch, New Zealand, a white nationalist terrorist targeted a different group thought to be posing a threat to the livelihood of whites. Twenty-eight-year-old Brenton Tarrant of Australia was arrested for shooting and killing 51 Muslim worshippers in two different mosques in the worst mass shooting by a lone gunman in New Zealand's history (Lyons, 2019). Before the heinous attack, which was livestreamed on Facebook, the killer posted a 74-page manifesto on 8Chan, an image board site considered even more hardcore than 4Chan that was frequented by extremists. This document made clear that like Dylann Roof, Tarrant does not see Jews as the primary threat to whites. Tarrant noted that he read the writings of Roof, as well as other extremists, including Norwegian terrorist Anders Breivik. This demonstrates the global threat of this ideology and the influence of those who carry out violence on its behalf. Tarrant was most concerned about changing demographics in white majority nations and the consequences of it. In fact, he titled the manifesto "The Great Replacement," a concept recently popularized by French writer Renaud Camus. In 2012, Camus came out with *Le Grand Remplacement* (*The Great Replacement*), a book that argues Europeans are being reverse-colonized by immigrants from civilizations that are uninterested in assimilating (Williams, 2017). After linking a Wikipedia page of country population predictions for the year 2100, Tarrant noted that even as the birthrates among whites are decreasing, the populations for white nations are predicted to stay the same or increase. He writes, "All through immigration. This is ethnic replacement. This is cultural replacement. This is racial replacement. This is WHITE GENOCIDE" (Tarrant, n.d.).

Like Bowers, Tarrant refers to nonwhite immigrants as "invaders." The manifesto answers the question as to why he chose to kill Muslims: "They were an obvious, visible and large group of invaders, from a culture of higher fertility rates, higher social trust and strong, robust traditions that seek to occupy my peoples [*sic*] lands and ethnically replace my own people" (Tarrant, n.d). He was also clearly troubled by violence perpetrated by Middle Eastern immigrants in European countries. The incident that appeared to have the most impact was the tragic murder of Ebba Akerlund, an 11-year-old girl from Sweden who was walking down the street in Stockholm when she was run over by a truck in a terrorist attack committed by a 39-year-old Uzebek asylum seeker (Pai, 2019). Tarrant noted that "Ebba [*sic*] death at the hands of the invaders, the indignity of her violent demise and my inability to stop it broke through my own jaded cynicism like a sledgehammer" (Tarrant, n.d.). Akerlund's mother has since condemned Tarrant's attack ("Mum of Swedish girl," 2019).

Armed with an AR-15-style rifle and dressed in a tactical vest with five additional magazines, a white nationalist attacker opened fire inside the Chabad of Poway synagogue in Poway, California, fatally striking a 60-year-old women and wounding three more on April 27, 2019 (Hanna & Simon, 2019). Nineteen-year-old John Earnest, a nursing student at Cal State University, was detained and charged with the crime. Unlike Roof and Tarrant, Earnest certainly viewed Jews as the masterminds behind the supposed demise of the white race. Like the other two killers, Earnest posted a manifesto online shortly before the attack. It notes that he has a loving family, friends, and a promising future, but asks, "Is it worth it for me to live a comfortable life at the cost of international Jewry sealing the doom of my race?" (Earnest, n.d.). He then answers his own question, "No," and claimed "Every Jew is responsible for the meticulously planned genocide of the European race" (Earnest, n.d.). He praised Robert Bowers and claimed the Christchurch massacre was a catalyst for his own attack. Earnest certainly didn't receive the same amount of respect from the radical online message boards as Tarrant for his attack; one anonymous 8Chan poster wrote: "if you want copy [*sic*] Tarrant and your killcount [*sic*] is 1, you should stay home. I am ashamed" (Anonymous, 2019).

For the third time in five months, a white nationalist posted a manifesto on 8Chan before carrying out a deadly attack. On August 3, 2019, a gunman entered a Walmart store armed with an AK-47 and began firing at shoppers, leaving 23 dead and 25 injured—making it into the top 10 deadliest mass shootings in modern American history (Helsel & Rosenblatt, 2019). Patrick Crusius, 21, of Allen Texas was arrested for the mass shooting and subsequently indicted for capital murder (Bleiberg & Attanasio, 2019). This attack represents yet another distinct group recognized as being a threat to the white race—Hispanics. It is clear from the manifesto that the killer was influenced by the Christchurch shooter. This attack again demonstrates how these terrorists are instrumental in activating other like-minded extremists to act. Just as Tarrant's manifesto lamented a demographic transformation in Europe and other Western nations driven by Muslims, the El Paso shooter applied this same "great replacement" logic to America and then determined Hispanics to be the primary demographic threat. His manifesto used very similar language, even mentioning Tarrant in the first sentence: "In general, I support the Christchurch shooter and his manifesto" (Crusius, n.d.). He goes on to claim that "This attack is a response to the Hispanic invasion of Texas" and continues, "I am simply defending my country from cultural and ethnic replacement brought on by an invasion" (Crusius, n.d.). He only considered Hispanics as a target after reading Tarrant's manifesto: "Actually the Hispanic community was not my target before I read The Great Replacement" (Crusius, n.d.).

Scrutiny was directed at 8Chan, the self-described "darkest reaches of the internet." The website became a hotbed for extremists because like 4Chan, it provided anonymity, but unlike 4Chan, users could create and operate their own boards. Less than 24 hours after the shooting, Cloudflare, the website's network provider, announced that they were going to terminate the site's network security provision (Perryer, 2020). This effectively shut down the imageboard site; however, it came back in late 2019, with a new name, 8kun, but it can only be accessed through the dark web (Glaser, 2019).

The White Genocide Manifesto

The myth of white genocide goes back to the early roots of Nazism in the nineteenth- and early twentieth-century Germany, but emerged in America in a 1972 issue of *White Power*, the official newspaper of the National Socialist White People's Party (Feshami, 2017). The phrase was further popularized by white supremacist David Lane, a member of the terrorist organization, the Order. Lane wrote the "White Genocide Manifesto" sometime in the 1980s while imprisoned. It is currently published on davidlane1488.com, a website dedicated to the ideas and writings of Lane and other prominent white supremacists. The manifesto has 14 points describing the process of white genocide, which, in his view, was well underway. For example, Lane argued that "All Western nations are ruled by a Zionist conspiracy to mix, overrun and exterminate the White race" (Lane, n.d.) He touched on other topics, such as forced integration, affirmative action, multiracial sports, and abortion. The 14 points serve as a descriptor of the alleged genocide, but it is in the paragraph after the final point, where Lane put forth a call to action: "We must secure the existence of our people and a future for White children" (Lane, n.d.). This battle cry, known as "fourteen words," is just as influential a phrase to the white supremacist movement as "white genocide."

Both sayings, "white genocide" and "fourteen words," have global reach as evidenced by Brenton Tarrant's manifesto, which included both. Lane concluded his manifesto with a threat to those who fail to act: "Let those who commit treason with the Zionist destroyer, or sit on the fence be aware. If we are successful in our goal, expressed in the FOURTEEN WORDS then your treachery will be appropriately rewarded" (Lane, n.d.).

THE MANOSPHERE

The "manosphere" is an umbrella term used to describe online content, communities, and subcultures that focus on male interests, particularly male–female relations, often from a misogynistic perspective. The topics most often covered in the manosphere include, but are not limited to, independence from women, marriage, divorce, picking up women for sex, and gender politics. On one end of the spectrum the content may focus on seemingly legitimate issues such as male-specific health concerns or inequities in divorce courts, while on the other end, the content is most accurately described as hatred for women. The manosphere's explanations for male discontent related to women range from theories found in evolutionary psychology to political movements such as feminism. Because the ideas propagated in these online spaces leave little hope for some men who are in pursuit of love, a small minority of these aggrieved individuals have carried out deadly violence.

There is a glossary of terms and phrases that are commonly used in the manosphere; some are more mainstream than others such as "Chad," "AWALT," "beta male," "alpha male," "taking the red pill," and "hypergamy." "Chad" refers to the guy that women want. They are essentially the polar opposites of the type of men that seek out content in the manosphere. Chads are not desirable because they worked on themselves and made changes, but because they naturally meet the criteria that women crave. The manosphere, generally speaking, does not see average men as able to transform into a Chad; their ability to attract women is seen as fixed and unable to be improved. This prevents followers from being optimistic about their dating prospects if they do not meet certain standards. Along these lines is another term "AWALT," which is an acronym for "all women are like that." This ingrains the notion that one should never believe that a particular woman is somehow different; they all have the same motivations and instincts. The learning and accepting of these harsh "realities" are often referred to as "taking the red pill." This is a reference from the movie *The Matrix* and refers to being enlightened to reality, which is perceived to be in conflict with mainstream depictions. One of the most important distinctions among men according to those in the manosphere is between "beta males" and "alpha males."

These traits are generally seen as permanent; however, there are some that attempt to guide men to a more alpha mindset. YouTube dating coaches, for example, sometimes produce content instructing alpha behavior, but they are sometimes ridiculed in the manosphere as being "confidence hustlers." The alphas are considered as being predisposed to attracting women and making them feel feminine. The betas are less lucky according to this binary model. Their options consist of being single or using gifts/financial support to buy women. Betas are always at risk of having their women leave them or cheat on them with an alpha. In fact, according to the manosphere, hypergamy drives women to men of higher status, which makes no man safe from being left or cheated on.

One of the staples of the manosphere is the pickup artist (PUA) community. Many pickup artists post videos and blogs that include techniques to use when approaching women in various social situations. Some of this material is best described as giving confidence and advice to men who struggle with talking to women. Then there are the content creators who focus on strategies for getting women to have sex, often with various pseudo-psychological techniques. Going down that path further is a man named Roosh V. He represents the extreme misogyny that exists in the PUA community. His hatred is apparent in his blogs and books, where he describes many of his sexual experiences as "hate fucks" ("Misogyny: The Sites," 2012). He argued that some of his most controversial content is meant to be satirical, such as a blog titled *How to Stop Rape*, where he suggests that making rape legal would result in women being more cautious about their safety, effectively eliminating it (Nagle, 2016). Another notable manosphere movement is called "Men Going Their Own Way," or MGTOW. This movement advocates for male independence from women and even suggests separating from them in all aspects of life if possible. There are many different movements and ideologies that sometimes contradict each other in the manosphere; it is certainly not a monolithic community. In fact, according to Nagle, Roosh V labeled those in the MGTOW movement as "sexual losers and bitter virgins" (p. 89–90). While there are certainly disagreements among the disparate groups, one of the common points of agreement is disdain for feminism. Author of *Manosphere: A New Hope for Masculinity*, Ian Ironwood (2013) claims "To us . . . well, in the manosphere, there are two types of feminists: bad and worse."

Incels

The standards that are required for attracting women as outlined in the manosphere exclude a certain percentage of individuals. These men are sometimes referred to as "TFLers," TFL being an acronym for "true forced loneliness."

Another more popular label has also reemerged from the manosphere, "incel," short for involuntarily celibate. This term is said to have actually originated from a Toronto woman in her 40s known only by her first name "Alana," who started an online forum in the late 1990s for people who had difficulty forming intimate relationships (Laidlaw, 2019). Today, the term "incel" refers to unattractive and/or socially challenged males, who desire having sexual relations with women but due to factors outside of their control, believe they will never acquire a sexual partner. The "red pill" content that these individuals adhere to forecasts a bleak future for the prospects of finding a woman. It is likely that some of the content has comforted these lonely men by providing explanations that act as excuses, relieving them of the pressure of having to make an effort or work on personal shortcomings. It is also true that some of the content so harshly criticizes women that these men feel like they may even be lucky to never have to deal with the hardships of a relationship. It is evident, however, that for some, the realization, real or perceived, that they will never experience relations with a woman invokes a deep anger that is expressed in places like message boards and comment sections. This includes the promotion of extreme sexual violence and fantasies of killing. This spiteful subset of incels has a hero who carried out deadly violence as revenge against a society perceived to have denied him a sexual relationship with a woman; his name was Elliot Rodger.

Incel Violence

On May 23, 2014, in Isla Vista California near the UC Santa Barbara campus, 22-year-old Elliot Rodger used knives, handguns, and his car to murder six people and injure 13 before killing himself (Springer, n.d.). Hours before the attack, Rodger posted a video on YouTube that explained the motivation for his rampage.

> Tomorrow is the day of retribution, the day in which I will have my revenge against humanity, against all of you. For the last eight years of my life, ever since I hit puberty, I've been forced to endure an existence of loneliness, rejection and unfulfilled desires all because girls have never been attracted to me. Girls gave their affection, and sex and love to other men but never to me. ("Transcript of Video," 2014)

He was extremely jealous of his college peers, holding hatred mostly for the women but also the sexually active men. Elliot's killing spree didn't go as planned; he attempted to enter a sorority house but the door was locked. He then embarked on a killing spree of shooting and running people over after stabbing to death three people in his apartment. Rodger also wrote a

141-page single spaced manifesto that provides a deeper understanding of the motivations and lead-up to the deadly attack. The manifesto, which is a detailed autobiography, reveals Elliot Rodger as being a deeply troubled individual who became obsessed with finding a sexual partner and increasingly distraught over failing to do so. It got to the point that he would lash out at couples in public and even had to drop college courses because he couldn't stand to see couples in the classroom. He would sometimes scream and cry in his room, and had a difficult time learning that others, such as his roommates, had experienced sex while he had never even kissed a girl. Eventually Rodger determined that he "had nothing to live for but revenge" (Rodger, n.d.).

Elliot Rodger became a hero to the incel community. "The Incel Rebellion has already begun! We will overthrow all of the Chads and Stacys! All hail the Supreme Gentleman Elliot Rodger!" was posted on Alek Minassian's Facebook page on April 23, 2018, just before he drove a van down a busy sidewalk in Toronto killing 10 and injuring 15 (Janik, 2018). "Stacy," another manosphere term, basically refers to desirable women who are only interested in "Chads." Laidlaw (2019) notes that Minassian was bullied growing up and was diagnosed with autism. He suffered from physical tics and was extremely awkward in social settings. He did, however, excel in the area of computer science. After a short-lived attempt in the army, Minassian finished a computer programming degree at York University. Apparently, he was also frequenting incel message boards. Three years after Elliot Rodger's killing spree, incel-themed message boards grew exponentially, including Reddit's incel forum which grew to 40,000 active members (Laidlaw, 2019). The sites that Minassian visited often discussed vile topics such as selling women as slaves. Janik (2018) reported that after Minassian's deadly van attack, he, like Rodger, was celebrated on these very forums: "I hope this guy wrote a manifesto because he could be our next new saint."

Elliot Rodger is connected to other incel violence as well, including an attack at a yoga studio in Tallahassee, Florida. On November 2, 2018, 40-year-old Scott Paul Beierle posed as a customer upon entering Hot Yoga Tallahassee and began shooting, killing two women and wounding five others. He then turned the handgun on himself (Burlew, 2018). Beierle was a self-described misogynist and had a history of grabbing women at the Florida State University campus. In a video posted online, Beierle said:

> I'd like to send a message now to the adolescent males that are in the position, the situation, the disposition of Elliot Rodger, of not getting any, no love, no nothing. This endless wasteland that breeds this longing and this frustration. That was me, certainly, as an adolescent. (Mack, Jamieson, & Reinstein, 2018)

Overlapping Ideologies

According to Nagle (2016), antifeminist manosphere subcultures constantly cross-pollinate with far-right online movements and even use a similar glossary of online dialect; terms such as "red pill" are common in both incel and alt-right forums. Both the alt-right and the incels are misogynistic, whereas other far-right movements, such as neo-Nazis and militias, are better described as patriarchal (Vysotsky, 2021). Many of those who feel society has turned on whites also feel the same way about males. Together, these ideologies make up a broader framework that sees straight white men as up against a tide of social engineering bent on trying to decrease their power and influence in the world.

While there is certainly significant overlap between these ideologies, there are some important differences in the role that the ideologies play in constructing the grievance. For incels, the strong desire for romantic involvement, and the subsequent grief of never obtaining it, is a prerequisite to the ideology. It is less clear which specific life experiences and inadequacies drive people toward white nationalism. The grievances in the incel community seem to be on behalf of themselves more often, where the white nationalist types seem to employ their grievances at the group level (the white race). For example, John Earnest, the alleged synagogue shooter, appeared to have a good family and was a good student. He had every reason to be optimistic about his future. Unfortunately, Earnest was, and likely still is, possessed by an ideology that believes the white race is currently being eradicated in a plan orchestrated by Jews. While he may be able to see himself being personally successful, he sees his in-group, the white race, as being existentially threatened. This is much different than Elliot Rodger, who was aggrieved due to his personal perceived rejection from women.

EXPLANATIONS FOR VIOLENCE

As the quotes from the previous manifestos demonstrate, frustration has come as a result of seeing the world become a place that has become hostile to whites and in some cases men. The gains of women and nonwhite races are seen to have come at the expense of white males. Recognizing this to be an organized effort, they resort to scapegoating the "other" as the source of both personal and societal problems. Relevant theories will be explored that can help explain this phenomenon.

Frustration-Aggression Hypothesis

In 1939, John Dollard, Neal Miller, Leonard Doob, Orval Mowrer, and Robert Sears developed a theory known as the frustration-aggression hypothesis. In its early stages, the hypothesis theorized that all acts of aggression are a direct result of frustration driven by individuals being prevented from attaining what they deem important. This notion was challenged by Gregory Bateson (1941), as well as Neal Miller (1948), who argued that it was an individual choice if violence would be used in response to frustration. Bateson was not convinced that it was a psychological response that explained aggression. He argued that there was a sociological aspect that determined if an individual would turn to aggression. He believed that culture has an important role; if a person is socialized in a culture that supports aggression as a means to end, they see it as more satisfying behavior and are more likely to engage in it. Researchers (Blee, 1991; Borgeson & Valeri, 2017) have shown that individuals learn to hate when they join hate groups or when they begin to associate with like-minded individuals who have prejudicial attitudes. Borgeson and Valeri (2017) demonstrated in their research that indoctrination to ideas that demonize out-groups such as Jewish conspiracy theories can be learned through peer groups and potentially lead to violence toward others.

Revisions to the frustration-aggression hypothesis found that when the source of frustration cannot be targeted, one will seek alternative outlets to let out one's aggression. When interviewing gay skinheads, Borgeson and Valeri (2015) discovered that some gay skinheads actually committed acts of aggression toward other gays within the community. These acts were a direct result of frustration developed in their childhood into adulthood. While they were unable to act out against their parents or bosses, they found other targets to unleash their aggression on. The gay skinheads chose to attack effeminate gays because they didn't project an image of masculinity, which in the skinhead culture is extremely important.

For those researching the frustration-aggression link it wasn't until Pastore (1952) looked at justified and unjustified frustration to detect whether or not blocked goals played a role in frustration leading to aggression. In his study, he presented individuals with complex scenarios that could be categorized as either a justified or unjustified frustration. He found that those who felt their frustration was justified had lower levels of aggression than those who felt their frustration was unjustified. In research pertaining to attribution theory, Weiner (1985) and Weiner et al. (1982) found a potential explanation for the differences in aggression for justified and unjustified frustrations: the level of control that a person has over the situation and allowing it to occur. If the frustration is perceived to be controlled by someone, and they allow it to occur, aggression is a more likely outcome.

When examining the biographies of the shooters examined in this chapter, most appear to be unsuccessful in achieving common life goals. Far-right ideologies are appealing to those experiencing failure as they provide an explanation that identifies the "other" as the source of their lack of success.

For example, Kathleen Parker (2017) described Dylann Roof as a physically underdeveloped high school dropout in an article titled "Dylann Roof is a loser," published in the *Washington Post*. The El Paso Walmart shooter was apparently an "extreme loner," who was picked on for the way he spoke and dressed (Elmahre et al., 2019). He hated work and was not motivated to do anything more than was necessary to get by according to his personal LinkedIn profile. All of the grievance-fueled attackers highlighted in this chapter, with the exception of John Earnest, could be described as under-achieving and unsuccessful. Their shortcomings were the likely source of frustration that resulted in aggression toward individuals who represented demographic groups that they came to believe were blocking their goals.

Conspiracy Theories

Conspiracy theories play an integral role in extreme ideologies and are the driving force behind most of the actions of white nationalists. An overarching theme in these conspiracies is that Jews control social institutions and that laws are passed to forward the "Jewish agenda." Since they believe that Jews control the government, and that there is nothing that can be done about this, it creates aggravation. As a result, some of them act out on their bigoted beliefs on those that they believe are the source. This is demonstrated most noticeably in white genocide theories. If the "Jewish government" controls immigration they must be doing it for a bigger endgame—the destruction of the white race.

Conspiracy theories have become so synonymous with extremist violence that an FBI bulletin obtained by Yahoo News warned of the growing threat coming from "conspiracy theory-driven domestic extremists" (Steinbuch, 2019). While conspiracies are a central element to white supremacist ideology, the FBI was referring to a new set of conspiratorial movements that have emerged in some of the same areas of the Internet that other extremist communities exist. "QAnon" is a truly odd online conspiracy movement that believes everyone in power in the U.S. government and media besides President Trump is a pedophile that engages in cannibalism (Nelson, 2019). According to this theory, "Q" who is the anonymous leader of the movement is embedded in the government and is working to bring the criminals to justice. While this movement is the subject of mockery for obvious reasons, it is also tied to deadly violence. After killing mob boss Francesco Cali in the most high-profile mafia killing in decades, the accused gunmen Anthony Comello appeared in court with symbols and phrases associated with the QAnon movement written on his hand (Watkins, 2019). He since has made statements that the victim was a member of the "deep state" and was actively working with democrats to thwart President Trump's agenda.

Known as the "Thomas Theorem," William Isaac Thomas and Dorothy Swaine Thomas (1928) asserted that "If men define situations as real, they are real in their consequences" (p. 572). The extreme acts of violence that have been examined in this chapter can be at least partly explained by the fact that at some point the perpetrators came to believe that these conspiracy theories were a description of reality. It is no wonder that a subset of individuals who believe that that their race is being targeted for extinction by another race or group respond with violence.

Dehumanization

As the events outlined in this chapter demonstrate, there is a direct relationship between bigoted views of immigrants, Muslims, women, and Jews and the reactions by white nationalists around the globe. Most violence against others comes as a direct result of dehumanizing someone that he or she sees as a member of the out-group.

Kteily et al. (2015) introduced a measure to examine blatant dehumanization based on the depiction of evolutionary progress. This "Ascent of Man" measure uses a scale ranging from 0 to 100, with 0 corresponding with an image of a human ancestor resembling an ape-like figure. The silhouette of a fully formed man corresponds with a score of 100. Using a survey, they found individuals were willing to associate members of different demographic groups as being less evolved than those in their own group.

Kteily and Bruneau (2017) employed this scale to understand the role that dehumanization was playing in the 2016 presidential primaries. The concern was due to the focus on Islamist terrorism, as well illegal immigration in the Republican primaries which put Muslims and Mexican immigrants at the center of harsh policies. The findings suggest that those who dehumanize Mexican immigrants and Muslims to a greater extent were more likely to endorse strict measures such as building a wall on the southern American border and denying Muslims entry into the United States. This was also felt by those on the receiving end of the dehumanization. They found that Latino residents of the United States felt that their group was strongly dehumanized during the 2016 presidential cycle. Muslims responded similarly, reporting that they felt dehumanized by both Donald Trump and non-Muslim Americans (Kteily & Bruneau, 2017).

One of the authors of this chapter encountered an example of dehumanization when interviewing a member of a militia group who would travel to the southern border to engage in border enforcement:

These people that cross the border are scum. They want to cross the border to have a better life. You know what that means? They want to steal, live off our welfare system, and commit crime. That's what that means. I do this (border patrol) in order to prevent these evil hordes of people from crossing into the US and ruining our way of life. ("Mike," personal communication, November 16, 2019)

According to Dave Grossman (2009), dehumanization is effectively implemented in the military for the purposes of killing the enemy. Grossman, who is a retired lieutenant colonel in the U.S. Army, points out that in order for soldiers to commit acts of violence against the enemy, they must first be dehumanized. The military puts recruits through a rigorous routine of desensitizing by creating war scenarios in which the enemy is reduced to the role of "other" and must be eliminated. Recruits are put through endless scenarios where they must kill under a range of conditions. Grossman shows that over the years kill ratios increased as the military perfected how to dehumanize the enemy.

In Robert Lifton's (1986) book *The Nazi Doctors*, he demonstrates how medical doctors during World War II could engage in heinous experiments with Jews, gays, and other minorities. Lifton was curious how doctors, who take a Hippocratic oath to preserve life, could turn against that promise and do the opposite. The first thing Lifton discovered was that not all the doctors who committed these acts were actually enjoying this work. Most had to rationalize what they did by convincing themselves that these acts needed to be carried out for the greater good of medicine and science. In other words, they engaged in a combination of desensitization, dehumanization, and compartmentalization in order to carry out their daily routines. It was through the combination of these three elements that these physicians were able to emotionally disassociate from their acts.

A common theme that runs through both Grossman and Lifton's work is that violence toward others can be done if the right conditions are in place: desensitization to violence and the creation of an out-group which must be eradicated. These two examples are drawn from the context of war, which is not unlike the attackers highlighted in this chapter, who believed that they were in a type of war as well. These imagined wars are constructed by extreme ideologies, and unfortunately lead to real-world violence.

REFERENCES

Amend, A. (2018, October, 28). Analyzing a terrorist's social media manifesto: The Pittsburgh synagogue shooter's posts on Gab. *Southern Poverty Law Center.* Retrieved from https://www.splcenter.org/hatewatch/2018/10/28/analyzing-terrorists-social-media-manifesto-pittsburgh-synagogue-shooters-posts-gab

Anonymous. (2019, April, 28). [Online forum comment]. Message posted to 8ch.net

Bateson, G. (1941). The frustration-aggression hypothesis and culture. *Psychological Review, 48*(4), 350–355.

Blee, K. M. (1991). *Women of the Klan: Racism and gender in the 1920s*. Berkeley, CA: University of California Press.

Borgeson, K., & Valeri, R. (2015). Gay skinheads: Negotiating a gay identity in a culture of traditional masculinity. *Journal of Men's Studies*, *23*(1), 44–62.

Borgeson, K., & Valeri, R. (2017). *Skinheads: History, identity and culture*. New York, USA: Routledge.

Brandt, L., & Dean. G. (2021, January 11). Gab, a social-networking site popular among the far right, seems to be capitalizing on Twitter bans and Parler being forced offline. It says it's gaining 10,000 new users an hour. *Business Insider*. Retrieved from https:/news.yahoo.com/gab-social-networking-popular-among -201845314.html

Burlew, J. (2018, November 3). Scott Beierle, gunman in Tallahassee yoga studio shooting, remembered as "really creepy." *Tallahassee Democrat*. Retrieved from https://www.tallahassee.com/story/news/2018/11/03/gunman-had-history -arrests- grabbing-women/1871941002/

Coaston, J. (2018, October 29). Gab, the social media platform favored by the alleged Pittsburgh shooter, explained. *Vox*. Retrieved from https://www.vox.com/policy -and-politics/2018/10/29/18033006/gab-social-media-anti-semitism-neo-nazis -twitter-facebook

Crusius, P. (n.d.). *The inconvenient truth*. Retrieved from https://randallpacker.com/ wp-content/uploads/2019/08/The-Inconvenient-Truth.pdf

Dollard, J., Miller, N. E., Doob, L. W., Mowrer, O. H., & Sears, R. R. (1939). Frustration and aggression. Yale University Press

Earnest, J. (n.d.). *An open letter*. Retrieved from https://bcsh.bard.edu/files/2019/06/ Earnest-Manifesto-042719.pdf

Elmahrek, A., Etehad, M., & Ormseth, M. (2019, August 4). Suspect in El Paso massacre "didn't hold anything back" in police interrogation. *Los Angeles Times*. Retrieved from https://www.latimes.com/world-nation/story/2019-08-03/what-we -know-about-patrick-crusius-el-paso-rampage

Feshami, K. A. (2017, September 6). Fear of white genocide: Tracing the history of a myth from Germany to Charlottesville. *Lapham's Quarterly*. Retrieved from https://www.laphamsquarterly.org/roundtable/fear-white-genocide

Glaser, A. (2019, November 11). Where 8channers went after 8chan. *Slate*. Retrieved from https://slate.com/technology/2019/11/8chan-8kun-white-supremacists-tele- gram-discord-facebook.html

Grossman, D. (2009). *On killing: The psychological cost of learning to kill in war and society*. New York: Back Bay Books.

Guynn, J. (2018, February 21). Alt-right escalates war against Silicon Valley, pledges to expose bias against conservatives. *USA Today*. Retrieved from https://www.usa- today.com/story/tech/2018/01/18/alt-right-escalates-war-against-silicon-valley-ple dges-expose-bias-against-conservatives/1037524001/

Hanna, J., & Simon, D. (2019, April 30). The suspect in Poway synagogue shooting used an assault rifle and had extra magazines, prosecutors said. *CNN*. Retrieved from https://www.cnn.com/2019/04/30/us/california-synagogue-shooting-investi- gation/index.html

Ironwood, I. (2013). *The manosphere: A new hope for masculinity.* Red Pill Press.

Janik, R. (2018, April 24). "I laugh at the death of normies": How incels are celebrating the Toronto mass killing. *Southern Poverty Law Center.* Retrieved from https://www.splcenter.org/hatewatch/2018/04/24/i-laugh-death-normies-how-incels-are-celebrating-toronto-mass-killing

Kteily, N., & Bruneau, E. (2017). Backlash: The politics and real-world consequences of minority group dehumanization. *Personality and Social Psychology Bulletin, 43*(1), 87–104.

Kteily, N., Bruneau, E., Waytz, A., & Cotterill, S. (2015). The ascent of man: Theoretical and empirical evidence for blatant dehumanization. *Journal of Personality and Social Psychology, 109,* 901–931.

Laidlaw, K. (2019, April 22). The man behind the Yonge street van attack. *Toronto Life.* Retrieved from https://torontolife.com/city/man-behind-yonge-street-van-attack/

Lane, D. (n.d.). *White Genocide Manifesto.* Retrieved from http://www.david-lane1488.com/whitegenocide.html

Levin, J., & Levin, W. (1982) *Functions of discrimination and prejudice.* 2nd ed. New York: Harper & Row.

Lifton, R. (1986). *The Nazi doctors: Medical killing and the psychology of genocide.* New York: Basic Books.

Lima, L., Reis, J., Melo, O., Murai, F., Araujo, L., Vikatos, P., & Benevenuto, F. (2018). Inside the right-leaning echo chambers: Characterizing gab, an unmoderated social system. *Proceedings of the 2018 IEEE/ACM International Conference on Advances in Social Networks Analysis and Mining (ASONAM '18),* August 18, 515–522.

Lyons, K. (2019, May 21). Christchurch mosque attacks: Suspect charged with "terrorist act." *The Guardian.* Retrieved from https://www.theguardian.com/world/2019/may/21/christchurch-mosque-attacks-suspect-charged-with-terrorist-act

Mack, D., Jamieson, A., & Reinstein, J. (2018, November 5). The Tallahassee yoga shooter was far-right misogynist who railed against women and minorities online. *Buzzfeed News.* Retrieved from https://www.buzzfeednews.com/article/davidmack/tallahassee-yoga- shooter-incel-far-right-misogyny-video?ref=bfnsplash&utm_term=4ldqpho

Miller, N. E. (1948). Theory and experiment relating psychoanalytic displacement to stimulus-response generalization. *The Journal of Abnormal and Social Psychology, 43*(2), 155–178.

Misogyny: The Sites. (2012, March 1). *Southern Poverty Law Center.* Retrieved from https://www.splcenter.org/fighting-hate/intelligence-report/2012/misogyny-sites

Mosendz, P. (2015, June 19). Dylann roof confesses: Says he wanted to start "race war." *Newsweek.* Retrieved from https://www.newsweek.com/dylann-roof-confesses-church-shooting-says-he-wanted-start-race-war-344797

Mum of Swedish girl named in NZ killer's manifesto condemns attacks. (2019, March 15). *France24.* Retrieved from https://www.france24.com/en/20190315-mum-swedish-girl- named-nz-killers-manifesto-condemns-attacks

Nagle, A. (2017). *Kill all Normies: Online culture wars from 4Chan and Tumbler to Trump and the alt-right.* Winchester, UK: Zero Books.

Nelson, K. T. (2019, January 22). What I learned inside the lonely, sad world of QAnon Facebook groups. *Vice*. Retrieved from https://www.vice.com/en_us /article/gyapg7/what-i-learned-inside-the-lonely-sad-world-of-qanon-facebook -groups

Pai, A. (2019, March 15). New Zealand mosque shootings: Who is Ebba Akerlund? Story of 11-yr-old girl mentioned on shooter's manifesto revealed. *Meaww*. Retrieved from https://meaww.com/to-take-revenge-ebba-akerlund-who-is-the-11 -year-old-schoolgirl-new-zealand-mass-shooter-manifesto

Parker, K. (2017, January 3). Dylann Roof is a loser. *The Washington Post*. Retrieved from https://www.washingtonpost.com/opinions/dylann-roof-is-a-loser/2017/01 /03/b5ed2f9a-d1f6-11e6-945a-76f69a399dd5_story.html

Pastore, N. (1952). The role of arbitrariness in the frustration-aggression hypothesis. *The Journal of Abnormal and Social Psychology*, *47*(3), 728.

Perryer, S. (2020, January 15). A sorry site: 8chan gets the axe, raising questions about internet censorship. *The New Economy*. Retrieved from https://www.the-neweconomy.com/technology/a-sorry-site-8chan-gets-the-axe-raising-questions -about-internet-censorship

Potok, M. (2015a, October 27). The council of conservative citizens: What is it? *Southern Poverty Law Center*. Retrieved from https://www.splcenter.org/fighting -hate/intelligence-report/2015/council-conservative-citizens-what-it

Potok, M. (2015b, October 27). Carnage in Charleston. *Southern Poverty Law Center*. Retrieved from https://www.splcenter.org/fighting-hate/intelligence-report/2015/ carnage-charleston

Rodger, E. (n.d.). *My twisted world: The story of Elliot Rodger*. Retrieved from https://www.documentcloud.org/documents/1173808-elliot-rodger-manifesto.html

Springer, A. (n.d.). The secret life of Elliot Rodger. *ABC News*. Retrieved from https://abcnews.go.com/US/fullpage/secret-life-elliot-rodger-24322227

Steinbuch, Y. (2019, August 1). FBI: Conspiracy theory "extremists" are a terror threat. *New York Post*. Retrieved from https://nypost.com/2019/08/01/fbi-con-spiracy-theory-extremists-are-a-terror-threat/

Tarrant, B. (n.d.). *The great replacement*. Retrieved from https://wikispooks.com/ wiki/File:The_Great_Replacement.pdf

Thomas, W. I., & Thomas, D. S. (1928). *The child in America: Behavior problems and programs*. New York: Alfred A. Knopf.

Transcript of video linked to Santa Barbara mass shooting. (2014, May 27). *CNN*. Retrieved from https://www.cnn.com/2014/05/24/us/elliot-rodger-video-transcript

Vysotsky, S. (2021). *American antifa: The tactics, culture, and practice of militant antifacism*. New York: Routledge.

Watkins, A. (2019, December 6). Accused of killing a Gambino mob boss, he's pre-senting a novel defense. *The New York Times*. Retrieved from https://www.nytimes .com/2019/12/06/nyregion/gambino-shooting-anthony-comello-qanon.html

Weiner, B., Graham, S., & Chandler, C. (1982). Pity, anger, and guilt: An attribu-tional analysis. *Personality and Social Psychology Bulletin*. 8, 226–232.

Weiner, B. (1985). An attributional theory of achievement motivation and emotion. *Psychological Review.* 92(4), 548–573.

Williams, T. C. (2017, Nov 27). The French origins of "you will not replace us." The New Yorker. Retrieved from https://www.newyorker.com/magazine/2017/12/04/the-french-origins-of-you-will-not-replace-us

Zannettou, S., Kwak, H., Bradlyn, B., Sirivianos, M., Blackburn, J., De Cristofaro, E., & Stringhini, G. (2018). What is gab? A bastion of free speech or an alt-right echo chamber? *The 2018 Web Conference Companion.*

Chapter 7

The Alt-Right

Breaking into the Mainstream

James Bacigalupo and Kevin Borgeson

The "alt-right," short for "alternative right," is a tech-savvy amorphous white nationalist movement known for its online tactics, and animus for both the mainstream political left and right alike. The movement is largely anonymous and exists primarily online. The Internet headquarters of the alt-right are imageboard sites like 4Chan, where followers share memes and develop their glossary of racial terms and phrases, often with an ironic or sarcastic theme. Unlike other online political subcultures, the alt-right is not relegated to the obscure corners of the Internet; they successfully make use of mainstream platforms such as Twitter where they harass political enemies and nonwhites, as well as disseminate their ideology. They also have been able to penetrate the mainstream political news cycle. This was undoubtedly due to successfully associating themselves with Donald Trump, who in June of 2015 embarked on a presidential campaign, a contest that he eventually won in 2016. His Democratic opponent, Secretary Hillary Clinton, further established a link between Trump and the alt-right in a press conference in August of 2016. She attacked Trump's rhetoric and his policies as being racist and connected his candidacy to the emergence of the alt-right, and even discussed the ideas that make up the group's ideology. Clinton denounced the movement but doing so in a highly viewed press conference provided them with peak exposure. The alt-right stands alone in comparison to recent radical right-wing political movements with regard to being both culturally and politically relevant in the modern era. The movement surprisingly became a political player in one the most highly covered and contentious presidential election cycles in recent memory.

STRUCTURE OF THE MOVEMENT

It is best to think of the alt-right as a movement made up of three main components: the online activists, the intellectuals, and the content creators. These are not strict categories; for example, many of the intellectuals also produce content; however, those that make up this movement fall into one of these three groups as their primary role. The online activists shape the culture of the movement, producing memes and trolling adversaries. They are the ones that turned Pepe the Frog into a hate symbol. While the thought leaders take themselves and their ideas very seriously, the online activists do not. Because the alt-right is primarily an online movement, they provide the character of the group, doing so through digital content that suggests that they are just as interested in humor as they are in politics. The intellectuals, in a sense, are polar opposites of the online activists. They do not care about the alt-right as a subculture. These alt-righters are very serious about their ideas and see the alt-right as the newest vehicle to get their views disseminated. The intellectuals provide the ideological foundation for the movement. The third faction of the movement are the content creators. These are the most well-known figures in the alt-right, producing podcasts, blogs, YouTube channels, and websites. This category of alt-righters are concerned with both the culture and the intellectual substance.

Online Activists (Trolls)

Alt-right trolls are typically anonymous. Anonymity is an important aspect of the movement; adherents can participate without the stigma of being associated with the group. Doxing, or the broadcasting of identifying information about a person, a tactic often used by the alt-right, has also been used against white nationalists, leading to many losing their jobs (LaChance, 2017). While most people considered trolls in the movement are unknown, there are exceptions. One example is a man named Andrew Aurenheimer, better known as "Weev," who in 2012 was convicted of fraud for his role in a hack that harvested the personal data of more than 100,000 customers of AT&T (Johnson, 2016). Since then, Weev's political views appear to have gone much further right. In 2016, he hacked printers at universities across the country and directed them to print messages such as "WHITE MAN are you sick and tired of THE JEWS destroying your country through mass immigration and degeneracy?" (Johnson, 2016). The messages included swastikas and an advertisement for *The Daily Stormer* website, where he was working at the time. Weev's views are extreme, even for the alt-right's standards. After the deadly El Paso mass shooting that left 22 dead, he claimed that "Random violence is not detrimental to the cause" and that "There's no way to remove a hundred million people without a massive element of violence" (Miller, 2019).

The Intellectuals

The intellectuals partake in what scholar George Hawley (2017) describes as "highbrow white nationalism" (p. 26). Those who make up this wing of the alt-right often have extensive academic credentials and some once held prestigious academic positions, providing a bit of legitimacy to the movement. Kevin McDonald, the emeritus professor of psychology at California State University, Long Beach, meets this criteria. While most mainstream academics in his field have ignored his work, which has a focus on Jews, often employing anti-Semitic conspiracy theories, the alt-right has embraced it (Schulson, 2018). Jared Taylor is another figure who fits into this category. He could also be placed in the "content creator" category based on his website Amren.com (further detail on this website is provided in chapter 2) and the vast content that he has produced on other platforms ranging from popular far-right YouTube channels and podcasts to mainstream news media. He is known for his promotion of race realism (more on this later in the chapter) and is a bit controversial within the white nationalist movement for not being anti-Semitic. The ADL notes how Taylor's background and intellectual style has been used by adherents:

> Taylor's portrayal of his racist views as intellectual inquiry enables him to maintain a position as a respectable academic source for racists, many of whom frequently cite his work. He and his admirers often cite his educational background, including a Yale undergraduate degree and mastery of Japanese and French, in order to grant his and their ideas a veneer of credibility. (Jared Taylor/American Renaissance, 2013)

The Content Creators

The content creators are the most important members of the alt-right, bridging the gap between the young online activists and the much older intellectuals (King, 2016). They are the public face of the movement, charged with expositing both alt-right culture and intellect. Credited with coining the term "alternative right" (later shortened to "alt-right"), the de facto leader of the movement is Richard Spencer. After dropping out of a Ph.D. program at Duke University, Spencer took a position at *The American Conservative*. From there his politics kept moving further right, and he eventually took a leadership role in the National Policy Institute, a white nationalist think tank. He founded the *Radix Journal*, which, according to its website, publishes books, essay collections, and online content focused on "culture, man-kind, geo-politics, meta-politics, and critical theory" (Radix: About, n.d.) and also created the website altright.com in 2017. Most of Spencer's fame and exposure did not come way of his own media sources; he has appeared on just about every mainstream news media outlet and has been the focus in popular documentaries, where he explains and defends the movement.

Another content creator who is extremely important to the alt-right is Michael "Enoch" Peinovich. He founded the website *The Right Stuff* (*TRS*) in 2012 and is the cohost of "The Daily Shoah," which is the most popular of the over two dozen podcasts that his website is home to (Marantz, 2017). According to Hawley (2017), *TRS* is probably the most influential website to the movement. In the promotion of the deadly 2017 Unite the Right march in Charlottesville, Virginia, names of figures that would be in attendance were listed on a digital flyer that was circulated around the web. Richard Spencer and Michael Enoch were the first two names on that list. The image also included an army of cartoon Pepe the frogs holding a confederate flag.

ALT-RIGHT POLITICS

When they broke into the mainstream in 2015, the alt-right's positions on two issues overlapped with the preferences of a majority of conservatives—immigration and political correctness. This was at a time when there was a wave of Islamist terror attacks in European countries, leading to a record number of fatalities from jihadist violence from 2014 to 2016 (Nesser et al., 2016). This was a reality that many Americans feared could happen if the lax immigration policies, which were blamed for these attacks, were to be implemented in the United States (Reynolds, 2016). It wasn't just immigration from overseas that was a concern; in Donald Trump's presidential announcement speech, he characterized the people who were entering the United States from Mexico as "rapists" (Phillips, 2016). In the eyes of Republican voters, Trump established himself as not just someone who would be tough on immigration but also someone who did not cow to the demands of political correctness. Some even thought that his fierce opposition to political correctness was the reason he was ultimately elected president. Robby Soave (2016) of *Reason* argued, "Trump won because of a cultural issue that flies under the radar and remains stubbornly difficult to define, but is nevertheless hugely important to a great number of Americans: political correctness."

It is in this extremely polarized political context that the alt-right was able to rise. Right-wingers were looking to be liberated from the constraints of political correctness and were in no mood to begin policing activists on their side of the isle. The alt-right made it easy for them by obfuscating their white nationalist positions—often going back and forth sometimes discussing mainstream political issues from a relatively rational perspective and other times discussing radical political positions such as advocating for a white ethno-state. Much of their political agenda looks similar to paleoconservatism, but then again, they also have positions that are well beyond the pale by modern political standards. Alt-right thought leader Richard Spencer acknowledged this political back and forth in an interview with podcaster Dave Smith: "We gotta have one foot in the world right now, and one foot in that fantasy world" (Alt-Media, 2019).

Paleoconservative Influence

When analyzing the alt-right as a traditional right-wing movement, paleoconservatism is what it most closely resembles. While this movement has not been relevant for decades, it had a major voice in the Republican Party at one point, such as when paleocon Pat Buchanan won four states including New Hampshire in the 1996 Republican presidential primary (Mathews, 2016a). Paleocons have called for restrictions of legal immigration and have proposed drastic measures in preventing illegal immigration, including deploying the military to the southern border (Drolet & Williams, 2020). While conservatives often rely on economic concerns for their motivations for or against immigration, paleos have been much more direct in their belief that non-Western people may not be able to assimilate into the European culture of the United States (Drolet & Williams, 2020).

Paleoconservatism stands in opposition to globalization. In comparison to mainstream conservatives, paleocons are isolationists in terms of both foreign and economic policy (Mathews, 2016b). Overwhelmingly against the war in Iraq, paleos have a nonintervention approach to foreign policy, which has led them to become consistent critics of the United States' relationship with Israel. Moreover, they are against free-market trade and support protectionist measures, such as tariffs on imports, putting them at odds with mainstream conservatives.

The degree that paleoconservatism can explain the alt-right's politics has its limitations. For example, paleocon intellectual Paul Gottfried is credited with coining the term "alternative right" along with Richard Spencer sometime around 2010; however, he has distanced himself from the movement. In responding to an article where he is described as "the godfather of the alt-right" (Fulford, 2018), Gottfried (2018) responded "I am a Jew, whose cousins were killed by the Nazis. Thus any suggestion that I might be associated with what is depicted as a neo-Nazi movement is especially offensive." Paleoconservatives are not openly racist in the way the alt-right is, although their positions seem to align on many issues. Hartzell (2018) notes "paleoconservatives take hard isolationist positions on American economic and foreign policy and by adopting anti-immigration and anti-multiculturalist positions that, by implication, are oriented toward maintaining a majority white United States" (p. 17).

Beyond the Pale

The political views of the alt-right are not controversial because of their association to paleoconservatism; it is because of their white nationalist agenda. Because the movement includes right-wingers who subscribe to a number of different ideologies, there is a wide range of views on some political questions, as well as how to go about achieving their goals. The alt-right seems to welcome everyone from the far right and included in this coalition are hardcore neo-Nazis. This radical fringe is not necessarily representative of the movement overall, but the fact that they are included at all is telling. The alt-right is not militant or thuggish in their presentation. They style themselves as intellectuals and attempt to persuade through reason, rather than with theological concepts. While the ideology that they espouse is inherently violent and would require government force, the tactics that they use to further their agenda are not openly violent such as the use of terrorism. The movement has hopes of achieving their political goals through the democratic system, as evidenced by their infatuation with Trump.

"Race realism," or biological racism, is a widely held belief system that alt-righters use to explain the differences in social outcomes between races. Jared Taylor describes it as "the recognition that race is a biological phenomenon, that human races are not identical or interchangeable, and that race is an important part of individual and group identity" (Taylor, 2018, p. 115). Ignoring these differences leads to conclusions that have political consequences:

> In the United States, compared to whites, blacks and Hispanics do worse in school, and are more likely to be poor and in jail. If we accept the principle of biological equality, this can only be because blacks and Hispanics are being exploited and oppressed by whites. If we accept this proposition, it becomes the responsibility of whites to transform themselves and restructure society so that less successful groups can achieve at the same level as whites. (Taylor, 2018, p. 118)

Adhering to the idea that there are important biological distinctions between ethnicities that are responsible for social outcomes often comes with radical solutions. For example, alt-righter Bill Matheson (2018) argues, "the only realistic solution is not just the current cultural separation, but a political and territorial separation" (p. 145).

Alt-right intellectual Greg Johnson seems to agree. In a piece published on counter-curerents.com, the website for the white nationalist publishing company that he cofounded, Johnson claims:

> If the relationship between whites and blacks in America today were a marriage, we would have divorced long ago. The same is true of whites and Jews, and any other non-white group. White Nationalists are simply proposing a policy of racial divorce. (Johnson, 2015)

Alt-righters definitely put in effort to make their positions sound less extreme than they are. A "racial divorce" sounds a bit more reasonable than advocating for a white ethno-state, but when asked directly, they do not run from the label. In fact, Richard Spencer is very hopeful that it could someday become a reality: "But history presents opportunities, and it becomes possible. So, the ethnostate's not going to happen next week. It's most likely not going to happen through Donald Trump. What the ethnostate is, is an ideal" (Leston, 2016).

NOT ALT-RIGHT

"Alt-right" was on the short list of being *Oxford Dictionaries'* 2016 international word of the year; however, it was ultimately beaten out by "post-truth" (Schuessler, 2016). This is certainly a testament to the popularity of the movement, but a contributing factor is that the term "alt-right" evolved into a broader meaning. For many journalists, columnists, bloggers, content creators, and even academics, "alt-right" transformed from referring to a specific group (albeit amorphous) to a synonym for "racist." For this reason, it has become important to identify not just what the alt-right is but what it is not. The broadening out of the term "alt-right," and its intentional misuse, contributes to an overall confusion about the group and what it believes.

There is a wide range of individuals—pundits, scientists, comedians, and even movie characters—being labeled or associated with the alt-right. *The Guardian* published an article by Graeme Virtue (2017) asking if the Bruce Willis remake of the film *Death Wish*, a vigilante action thriller, was an "alt right fantasy." Nick Schager (2018) of *The Daily Beast* describes Willis's character in the film as "an alt-right wet dream." Steven Pinker, a world-renowned scientist and Harvard psychology professor, was linked to the group as well. PZ Myers (2018), a biologist and associate professor, wrote a blog about Pinker titled "If you ever doubted that Steven Pinker's sympathies lie with the alt-right." Comedians are not safe from the alt-right association either. Christian Blauvelt (2018) of *IndieWire* accused disgraced comedian

Louis C.K. of "courting the alt-right as a new audience." Ben Shapiro, a popular conservative podcaster, author, and columnist, was interviewed for a story in *The Economist*. The original title that they ran for the article was "Inside the mind of Ben Shapiro, the alt-right sage without the rage." The problem with this is that Shapiro, an Orthodox Jew, has been one of the most consistent critics, as well as a frequent target of the alt-right. In fact, in June of 2016 an ADL task force examined 2.6 million anti-Semitic tweets and found that a small number of journalists took the brunt of the online abuse—Shapiro topped that list (ADL Task Force, n.d.).

When the mainstream media uses "alt-right" to describe someone who may have done something that they perceive as racist or even just controversial, it provides the movement with free advertising. When they label people, especially popular figures, as being alt-right without cause, it works in the service of softening the image of the group. George Hawley (2017) interviewed students at the University of Alabama who were waiting to see a talk by provocateur Milo Yiannopoulos. Out of the students that Hawley talked to, a consistent finding was that the alt-right didn't have anything to do with race. The students saw the group as an anti-political correctness movement. Without question, the alt-right is not always clear about their politics; however, the confusion of what the group is, and what it believes, is likely contributed by inaccurate labeling on behalf of the media.

ALT-RIGHT WEBSITE ANALYSIS

The present research looks at the complexities of the alt-right movement, as it exists on the Internet. The media has portrayed the alt-right as white nationalists searching for an updated image to replace that of the robed Klansmen of the past. If this is the case, then new cultural elements are going to develop which separate them from previous radical right movements. The media and social scientists have had a tendency to make statements that the alt-right is solely based on hate. While this is the case for some white nationalist movements, identities, and the cultural elements which make up their everyday existence, are complex and go beyond hate. Borgeson and Valeri (2005) have shown in their research on web-based skinhead sites and social media (2017) that culture depicted in these virtual communities is complex, consisting of many identities and vast cultural themes to make up their virtual culture.

Presentation of Self in the Internet Era

The work of Erving Goffman (1959) has been used by many sociologists and social psychologists to interpret how individuals, groups, and movements present an image to the general public. Goffman believed an individual's presentation of self could be looked at through a theatrical perspective with individuals putting on a performance showing others a sanitized version of representation in what he referred to as the front stage, while the real representation is hidden backstage from the view of the general public. For hate groups this front stage performance has a wider range than that depicted by the general public. In Borgeson and Valeri's (2004, 2005, 2017) work they have shown the presentation of self that hate groups depict online, and in person, is complex in nature and does not represent one solid front (front stage). For them, the hate they project can be divided into three projected selves, which they want others to see. These "faces of hate" that they choose to show to the public are "in your face, subtle, and misleading" presentations (2004). Borgeson and Valeri's (2005, 2017) work also demonstrates the multilayered complexity of the presentation. While the Internet does not allow us to see the backstage self, that which is depicted allows us to see how they shape the representation of self.

Since the alt-right is a relatively new movement on the radical right, we want to explore shared identities among the movement, what members self-identify as, and cultural elements they deem significant. In order to do this the authors decided to construct a coding sheet for a content analysis to help determine what presentation of self they wish to put forward to the general public via the web.

METHODS

For each search engine, "alt-right" was entered as the search term. Given the large number of hits, and the impossibility of examining all the sites to determine the proper number of sites, the researchers decided to count the number of alt-right sites within the first 250 listings, which were generated by each of the three search engines. Most of the results were sites condemning the movement and were disqualified from being in the dataset collected by the authors. Only those sites associated with being alt-right were used.

From each search engine, twenty sites were randomly selected using a random number generator. Once sites were chosen, the URL was recorded and made available for future coding. When the researchers began coding, a significant number of sites were no longer available. A large number of sites were taken down as a result of the aftermath of the deadly Charlottesville rally. This left us with a small number of sites to code. Since the numbers were low, the researchers turned to a different method of collecting sites for analysis.

Because one of the researchers was conducting interviews with alt-right members, obtained via snowball sampling techniques, they decided to ask members for the top five sites they believed best represented the movement. With ten members, this gave the researchers 50 sites to gather data from. Each member was asked to rank-order from 1 to 5 based on what they believed was most representative of the alt-right. Fifty sites were gathered, and the URLs were recorded for future use in the content analysis. From the 50 sites that were obtained, via the members, only 17 were still live on the Internet. The other 33 had been taken down because the web server believed the content was too prejudicial in nature. Due to the websites going down, the researchers asked the members to pick the number one overall site for representation. This allowed the researchers to get ten active sites for coding purposes.

From interviews with members, themes began to emerge. Members also expressed themes they believed the media held about their culture. In order to see which themes dominated, the researchers included both beliefs to see which image was projected—that of the alt-right or that of the public. Themes from both were represented among the six variables analyzed. The variables explored were identity, hate ideology, culture, audience, functionality, and presentation of self.

VARIABLES AND RESULTS

Identity

Identity was defined as the uniqueness of the group associated with the website or social network page and was coded as having one of five themes. They are:

Alt-Right: Site may be presented as a news site, think tank, or information source. Racist in nature. Savvy about presentation. Use of science and social science to prove whites are superior.
Racist/Nationalist Skinhead: Endorses racism and racial purity and promotes patriotism and nationalism. These groups will identify the target(s) of their hate, often use terms such as "White Power" and "White Pride," as well as infuse the identity with Nazi or fascist symbols, dress, and ideology.
Militia: These sites are patriotic with the main focus centering on gun rights and constitutional issues in the United States. An example of this may be rhetoric surrounding the government's infringement on citizens' right to bear arms.
Religious: The site may claim that whites are the chosen people of God and superior to other races or religions. Examples are Christian Identity or other pseudo-religions which claim superiority.
White Nationalist: Thread of nationalism which is expressed in their desire to have a separate country for races. Overall theme is that they do not feel they are superior to other groups; they just want to separate the races

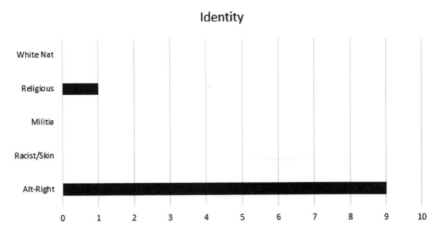

Figure 7.1   Alt-Right Websites Coded for Identity. Figure created by authors based on data collected by authors' analysis.

As depicted in figure 7.1, 90% of websites self-identified as being part of the alt-right movement. On the other hand, only one website was coded as being religious for its identity. No alt-right members identified as militia, white nationalists, or racist/nationalist skinheads which some media have suggested make up the ranks of the movement. These results are not that surprising when we take into effect that over the past decade or two, those that see their white heritage as being the most important identifier have steered away from negative labels that have become synonymous with the radical right. Most of this shift began with David Duke who changed his image from the Klan robe to the suit. Duke won office and future movements learned that if they soften their rhetoric and image, they become more attractive to other like-minded individuals who agree with their ideology, but do not want to become a card-carrying member of a group. This can also be seen in the work by Borgeson and Valeri (2004), in which they show that the image seen on the Internet has softened over the years and that more white nationalists are going with a subtle approach to bringing people around to their way of thinking. This will be explored deeper in the later section on faces of hate.

Hate Ideology

To better understand ideology as it pertains to out-group targets promoted by the websites, each site was coded regarding statements of the group's philosophy on Islamophobia, homophobia, racism, anti-Semitism, anti-immigrant, or hatred toward another group. These ideologies were defined as:

Islamophobia: Any sign of anti-Muslim sentiment. These could be explicit statements, jokes, or cartoons.

Homophobia: Any signifier of anti-homosexuality sentiment. These could be explicit statements, jokes, or cartoons.

Racism: Any display of prejudicial attitudes about particular racial minority groups (e.g., African Americans, Asians, or Hispanic).

Anti-Semitism: Any signifier of anti-Jewish sentiment. These could be explicit statements, jokes, or cartoons.

Anti-Immigrant: Any sign of anti-Immigrant sentiment. These could be explicit statements, jokes, or cartoons.

Other: Any other form of identity-based hate (e.g., women).

As the graph depicted in figure 7.2 indicates, hate ideology toward out-groups were prominently represented on the websites. Anti-immigrant was the largest category with 50% of all sites believing that the nation is becoming worse because of the existence of immigrants in the United States. Anti-Islamic sentiment was represented on 40% of all websites. Homophobic and racism were tied for third appearing on 30% of sites. The category with the least representation (excluding the "other' category") was anti-Semitism with only 10% of webpages depicting such language or imagery.

The stats show significant changes in the targets of hate. For instance, in most reported hate crimes in the United States, race is usually the largest motivator leading to victimization. In most years, religion comes in second and gays third

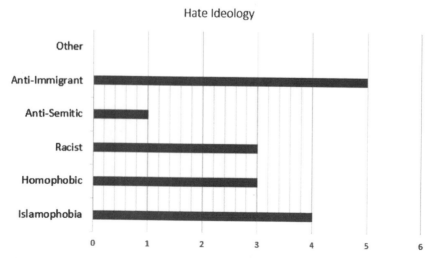

**Figure 7.2	Alt-Right Websites Coded for Hate Ideology.** Figure created by authors based on data collected by authors' analysis.

for groups that fall prey to some form of discrimination. Some Americans are using the influx of immigrants as a scapegoat for the loss of jobs and decrease in wages of the average American. This can be seen in a study done by the Southern Poverty Law Center (SPLC) (2016) following the 2016 election of Donald Trump. Victimization was measured by calculating incidents which were reported to their agency as well as reports in the media. Starting on November 8, 2016, an overwhelming amount of incident reports began flooding their agency. Once the tally was done, they determined that 867 hate incidents occurred over a ten-day period. These were only the incidents reported. Considering roughly 50% of all hate crimes are not reported in the United States, we can assume that the number of victims during this time is far greater than the data suggests.

The SPLC study corresponds to what was found in our analysis. Their findings suggest that of the 867 acts reported, 280 of them were directed toward immigrants. Other beliefs about minorities were in line with previous hate crimes research, not ours. For instance, black was the second largest category with 187 incidents and anti-Semitic attitudes came in third with 100 incidents. Our research had some similar results and some different. Our findings are more reflective of the changes in prevailing attitudes toward minorities which is embodied by the alt-right. The future may see a swing in victimization that is more representative of the ones we found.

Culture

Eight themes were defined which both the media and alt-right members believe are part of this new right-wing belief system emerging in America. They include:

Violence: Because hate groups have been associated with traditional masculinity, the attributes of aggression and violence were coded. Any violent material including threats to certain groups and pictures of physical violence would be an indicator of this theme.

Politics: Espousing a political ideology, pros and cons of the Democratic or Republican agenda, any commentary of government (local, state, or federal) would be an indicator of this theme.

Religion: Having religious overtones. This could be expressed in values, criticisms of mainstream religion, or the benefits of pseudo-Christianity, Christian Identity, or Odinism.

Constitution: Any focus on the U.S. Constitution. Examples may include the mentioning of gun rights and freedom of speech or other constitutional rights that are guaranteed or being threatened.

Patriotism: Content surrounding the founding fathers and/or the founding of the United States and its unique ideals.

Nationalism: Extreme loyalty or devotion to home country or the expression of feeling superior to other countries.

Anti-Drug/Alcohol: A focus on the negatives of drugs and alcohol use, often blaming them for destroying the moral fabric of society.

Bio/Scientific Discrimination: Any information that suggests the superiority of whites based on a biological claim.

Seven out of eight themes were found in the websites. According the results (figure 7.3), the largest category represented on their sites was politics (80%). This is not surprising considering that during the interviews, ten out of ten members stated "political correctness" is the most important thing to change in America. They claim that one of the primary reasons that the movement began was to counteract the Left's assaults on freedom of speech. This is supported by the second largest category—constitutional issues. Forty percent of all sites had constitutional issues discussed on their site. The movement is not as concerned with gun rights and other far-right themes as the media claims. The current movement should not be confused with conservatism—they disagree on a wide range of issues. The primary concerns for these adherents are freedom of speech and the right to be able to get out the white nationalist word on college campuses.

Four additional themes—patriotism, nationalism, anti-drug, and conspiracy—were each represented on 20% of sites. These are also strong beliefs of the conservative right and as one would expect did not have a large presence

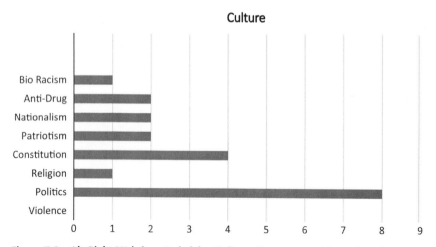

Figure 7.3   Alt-Right Websites Coded for Culture. Figure created by authors based on data collected by authors' analysis.

on alt-right sites. Two themes—religion and biological racism—appeared on 10% of pages. The last category, violence, did not appear on any of the sites which were part of the study. This finding was not surprising to the researchers since hate group members in other organizations have been trying to change the radical right image over the past two decades (for an exception to this trend, see Atomwaffen Division in chapter 5). Those in the past have also taken a step back from violent rhetoric being depicted on their material. One of the biggest contributors to this change has been the lawsuits which the SPLC won against hate groups for their actions and rhetoric contributing to some of the most violent hate crimes in the United States. People in today's radical movements do not want to be seen as influencing others who may attend rallies and end up committing acts of violence—this is something they can be sued for now. The United States is a very litigious country and just like the general public who are afraid to be sued, so are members of hate groups. These lawsuits garner negative attention, hurting their effectiveness in furthering their political cause. This is also supported with the results below on their presentation of self, and the face of hate they choose to get out their word.

Audience (gender)

The intended audience of the website was determined by examining whether the content on the website was gender-specific. For each website, we coded either men, women, or both. They were defined as follows:

Male: A webpage was coded as male if it contained male-exclusive content or if it explicitly stated that it was intended only for males.
Female: A webpage was coded as female if it contained female-exclusive content or if it explicitly stated that it was intended only for females.
Both: A webpage was coded as appealing to men and women if the content appeared to be intended for both sexes.

Not one of the alt-right websites examined were gender specific. This differs from research on movements in the past (Blee, 1991). In the late twentieth century, most groups were divided along patriarchal lines with men and women and having a clear division in each of their duties. To the alt-right, gender is not considered a barrier—spreading the message is more important than excluding women. Not all members feel that way, though. Some define themselves as incels (see chapter 6 for a further discussion) and have a vile hatred for women—blaming them for all the misery in their lives.

Functionality

Functionality was coded into six main themes: recruitment, sell, podcasts, blogs, rallies, and links to other sites. These themes have been used by previous researchers (Borgeson and Valeri, 2004) to look at the ways of communicating with other like-minded people and to get the word out to those who may be curious about what the movement stands for. We defined the themes in this way:

Recruitment: Any information on how to join the group, a membership application, or links to material for individuals interested in becoming members
Sell. Selling any items, such as books or clothing
Podcasts: Hosting or providing links to podcasts
Blog: Including a blog
Rally: An advertisement for an upcoming rally
Links to Social Media: Including a link to other like-minded groups or individual's social media accounts

The findings of this section are particularly of interest since most media outlets depict the alt-right's use of the net as a recruitment tool. This is misleading since it is a movement—a way of thinking—not an organization that one can join like the Ku Klux Klan or the Aryan Nations. Zero percent of sites had anything to do with recruiting others to join. None of the sites were used to promote rallies either. This does not mean that they do not use the Internet for getting other like-minded people to go to rallies. The alt-right has become aware that their public activities are being monitored by watch dog agencies like the SPLC, law enforcement, and militant antifascists. A large percentage of sites used the Internet as a way to share information with others via blogs (40%) and links (70%). In other words, websites are not used as a tool for recruitment but as a tool to disseminate the "proper" way to "correctly" read the mainstream media's news with an antipolitically correct lens (figure 7.4).

Presentation of Self and the Multiple Faces of Hate

As seen in the previous sections, the alt-right is not using the rhetoric of the past. Derogatory tones have been softened and a new face is emerging. In order to measure this change, we used the faces of hate concepts outlined by Borgeson and Valeri (2004) in their work on cyberhate. The concepts are defined as follows:

In Your Face: Message is blatant and straightforward with its views on race, gender identity, homosexuality, or immigration status. The message is

Functionality

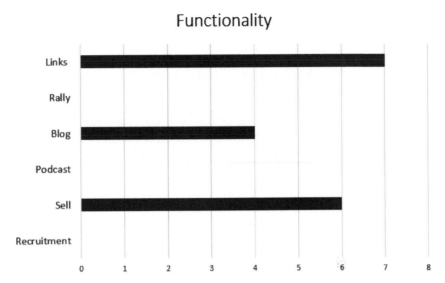

Figure 7.4   The Functionality of Alt-Right Websites. Figure created by authors based on data collected by authors' analysis.

demeaning and meant to be informative about the true nature of the groups they express bias for.

Misleading: The sites' message on race, religion, homosexuality, gender identity, or immigration status creates a rational and newsworthy tone and presents information as if it were unbiased and factual

Soft-Sell: The overall presentation of their message is subtle and use mild rhetoric to get the reader to believe that what they are stating is true and that mainstream media is false.

As figure 7.5 demonstrates, zero percent of webpages have an "in your face" style with their presentation of self. This is the old way of doing things—a new one has emerged. Six out of ten (60%) sites were misleading in their presentation and four out of ten (40%) used a soft-sell approach in order to get their message across to those who land on their page.

THE CURRENT STATE OF THE ALT-RIGHT

As an Online Movement

Internet subcultures come and go. The language, the memes, and even the political positions constantly evolve, giving them a relatively short shelf life. In some ways, the success of the alt-right and its ability to become a

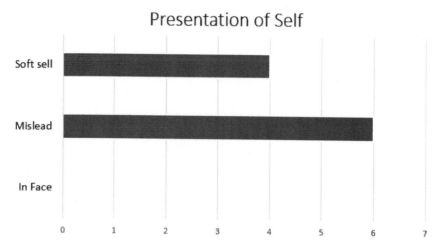

Figure 7.5   Presentation Style of Alt-Right Websites. Figure created by authors based on data collected by authors' analysis.

household name hurt its status as an online subculture. These groups thrive off being obscure; once the mainstream media is privy to their ways, the movement loses its veneer. Elements of the alt-right can be spotted in more recent movements. An offshoot of the alt-right is the Groyper movement. "Groyper" refers to another frog mascot like Pepe but bigger. This group appears to be a bit more religious, as well as homophobic, than the alt-right. They made a name for themselves by confronting mainstream conservatives such as Charlie Kirk, Ben Shapiro, Matt Walsh, Jonah Goldberg, Congressman Dan Crenshaw, and even Don Trump Jr. at public speaking events, mostly on college campuses (Coaston, 2019). Key members of this movement have since created the America First Political Action Conference, which has garnered support from former and current elected officials.

Boogaloo Bois, an antigovernment gun enthusiast movement, is another group with alt-right elements. They seem to have adopted their humor as a central theme, as evidenced by their memes and even their clothing choice. One of the more popular Boogaloo images, which is sometimes worn by their members as a patch, is Pepe the Frog outfitted with a rifle, tactical gear, and their signature Hawaiian shirts. This movement is more openly violent than the alt-right, calling for a civil war with the state, and members have allegedly targeted law enforcement with deadly attacks (Mooney, 2021).

As a Political Movement

The alt-right as a political movement died out relatively soon after Trump's election. Key members of the movement including Richard Spencer expected their policy preferences to be pursued by Trump, and when that didn't occur to their liking, alt-righters were public in their refutation. These were the figures who cared less about rhetoric and fighting culture wars and more about the white nationalist agenda. While their association to President Trump propelled them into the mainstream conscious, it was also his presidency that pulled it back down by not adhering to their agenda. One of the first public spats was when Trump approved airstrikes in Syria. Richard Spencer led a protest outside the White House where he chanted, "we want walls, not war!" (Hernandez, 2018). By the time of Trump's reelection bid, many alt-righters were open about not supporting him. The same cannot be said for other right-wing groups, such as QAnon, the Proud Boys, and the Oath Keepers, who's support for President Trump grew throughout his presidency and was on full display during the June 6, 2021, Capitol riots, where many of them were involved in attempting to overturn his defeat. While the alt-right as a political force seems to have come and gone, the movement will likely have a lasting impact by their ability to change the image of white nationalism to something more appealing to the mainstream.

REFERENCES

ADL task force issues report detailing widespread anti-Semitic harassment of journalist on Twitter during 2016 campaign. (n.d.). *ADL*. Retrieved from https://www.adl.org/news/press-releases/adl-task-force-issues-report-detailing-widespread-anti-semitic-harassment-of

Alt-Media. (2019, August 17). Richard spencer on the white ethnostate [Video]. *YouTube*. Retrieved from https://www.youtube.com/watch?v=h8RRM1-6J9I

Blee, K. M. (1991). *Women of the Klan: Racism and gender in the 1920s*. University of California Press.

Borgeson, K., & Valeri, R. (2004). Faces of hate. *Journal of Applied Sociology, 22,* 91–104.

Borgeson, K., & Valeri, R. (2005). Examining differences in skinhead ideology and culture through an analysis of skinhead websites. *Michigan Sociological Review, 19,* 45–62.

Borgeson, K., & Valeri, R. (2017). *Skinheads: History, identity and culture*. Routledge.

Coaston, J. (2019, November 11). Why alt-right trolls shouted down Donald Trump jr. *Vox*. Retrieved from https://www.vox.com/policy-and-politics/2019/11/11/20948317/alt-right-donald-trump-jr-conservative-tpusa-yaf-racism-antisemitism

Drolet, J., & Willams, M. (2020). America first: Paleoconservatism and the ideological struggle for the American right. *Journal of Political Ideologies, 25*(1), 28–50.

Fulford, R. (2018, March 29). Robert Fulford: How the alt-right's godfather transformed our world. *National Post*. Retrieved from https://nationalpost.com/opinion

/robert-fulford-how-the-alt-rights-godfather-transformed-our-world-not-in-a-good
-way

Goffman, E. (1959). *The presentation of self in everyday life*. Bantam Doubleday Dell Publishing Group.

Gottfried, P. (2018, April 17). Paul Gottfried: Don't call me the "godfather" of these alt-right neo-Nazis. I'm Jewish. *National Post*. Retrieved from https://national-post.com/opinion/paul-gottfried-dont-call-me-the-godfather-of-those-alt-right-neo -nazis-im-jewish

Hartzell, S. L. (2018). Alt-white: Conceptualizing the "alt-right" as a rhetorical bridge between white nationalism and mainstream public discourse. *Journal of Contemporary Rhetoric*. 8(1/2), 6–25.

Hawley, G. (2017). *Making sense of the alt-right*. Columbia University Press.

Hernandez, S. (2017, April 8). Alt-right and white nationalist supporters led tense protests against trump's airstrikes on Syria. *Buzzfeed News*. Retrieved from https://www.buzzfeednews.com/article/salvadorhernandez/spencer-protests-trump -on-syria

Jared Taylor/American Renaissance. (2013). *Anti-Defamation League*. Retrieved from https://www.adl.org/sites/default/files/documents/assets/pdf/combating-hate/ jared-taylor-extremism-in-america.pdf

Johnson, A. (2016, March 28). Infamous hacker "weev" says he blasted college print-ers with antisemitic message. *NBC News*. Retrieved from https://www.nbcnews .com/news/us-news/infamous-hacker-weev-says-he-blasted-college-printers-anti- semitic-message-n547001

Johnson, G. (2015, March 13). Irreconcilable differences: The case for racial divorce. *Counter-Currents*. Retrieved from https://counter-currents.com/2015/03/irrecon- cilable-differences/

King, J. (2016, November 22). Cucks & kek: Racism's old guard reaches out to an online generation. *Vocativ*. Retrieved from https://www.vocativ.com/377958/alt -right-richard-spencer/index.html

LaChance, N. (2017, August 16). More Nazis are getting identified and fired after Charlottesville. *Huffpost*. Retrieved from https://www.huffpost.com/entry/more -nazis-are-getting-identified-and-fired-after-charlottesville_b_599477dbe4b0eef 7ad2c0318

Leston, A. (2016, November 10). A frank conversation with a white nationalist. *Reveal News*. Retrieved from https://revealnews.org/podcast/a-frank-conversation -with-a-white-nationalist/

Marantz, A. (2017, October 9). Birth of a white supremacist. *The New Yorker*. Retrieved from https://www.newyorker.com/magazine/2017/10/16/birth-of-a -white-supremacist

Matheson, B. (2018). Irreconcilable differences. In G. T. Shaw (Ed.), *A fair hearing: The alt-right in the words of its members and leaders* (pp. 136–145). Arktos.

Mathews, D. (2016a, May 6). Paleoconservatism, the movement that explains Donald Trump, explained. *Vox*. Retrieved from https://www.vox.com/2016/5/6/11592604/ donald-trump-paleoconservative-buchanan

Mathews, D. (2016b, August 25). The alt-right is more than warmed-over white supremacy. It's that, but way way weirder. *Vox*. Retrieved from https://www.vox.com/2016/4/18/11434098/alt-right-explained

Miller, C. (2019, August 5). El Paso massacre galvanizes accelerationists. *Southern Poverty Law Center*. Retrieved from https://www.splcenter.org/hatewatch/2019/08/05/el-paso-massacre-galvanizes-accelerationists

Mooney, M. J. (2021, January 15). The Boogaloo Bois prepare for civil war. *The Atlantic*. Retrieved from https://www.theatlantic.com/politics/archive/2021/01/boogaloo-prepare-civil-war/617683/

Myers, P. Z. (2018, January 9). If you ever doubted that Steven Pinker's sympathies lie with the alt-right. *Freethought Blogs*. Retrieved from https://freethoughtblogs.com/pharyngula/2018/01/09/if-you-ever-doubted-that-steven-pinkers-sympathies-lie-with-the-alt-right/

Nesser, P., Stenersen, A., & Oftedal, E. (2016). Jihadi terrorism in Europe: The IS-effect. *Perspectives on Terrorism*, *10*(6), 3–24.

Phillips, A. (2017, June 16). "They're rapists." President Trump's campaign launch speech two years later, annotated. *The Washington Post*. Retrieved from https://www.washingtonpost.com/news/the-fix/wp/2017/06/16/theyre-rapists-presidents-trump-campaign-launch-speech-two-years-later-annotated/

Radix: About. (n.d.). *Radix Journal*. Retrieved from https://radixjournal.com/about/

Reynolds, A. (2016, July 23). Don't blame immigration for homegrown terrorism. *Cato Institute*. Retrieved from https://www.cato.org/publications/commentary/dont-blame-immigration-homegrown-terrorism

Schager, N. (2018, March 2). Bruce Willis' "death wish" vigilante is batman for the Breitbart crowd. *The Daily Beast*. Retrieved from https://www.thedailybeast.com/bruce-willis-death-wish-vigilante-is-batman-for-the-breitbart-crowd

Schuessler, J. (2016, November 15). "Post-truth" defeats "alt-right" as Oxford's word of the year. *The New York Times*. Retrieved from https://www.nytimes.com/2016/11/16/arts/post-truth-defeats-alt-right-as-oxfords-word-of-the-year.html

Schulson, M. (2018, June 27). Kevin MacDonald and the elevation of anti-Semitic pseudoscience. *Undark*. Retrieved from https://undark.org/2018/06/27/kevin-mac-donald-anti-semitism-psychology/

Soave, R. (2016, November 9). Trump won because leftist political correctness inspired a terrifying backlash. *Reason*. Retrieved from https://reason.com/2016/11/09/trump-won-because-leftist-political-corr/

SPL Center. (2016). Ten days after: Harassment and intimidation in the aftermath of the election. *Southern Poverty Law Center*. Received from https://www.splcenter.org/sites/default/files/com_hate_incidents_report_final.pdf

Taylor, J. (2018). Race realism. In G. T. Shaw (Ed.), *A fair hearing: The alt-right in the words of its members and leaders* (pp. 115–125). Arktos.

Virtue, G. (2017, August 8). Death wish: Is the Bruce Willis remake an alt-right fantasy? *The Guardian*. Retrieved from https://www.theguardian.com/film/filmblog/2017/aug/08/eli-roth-death-wish-remake-alt-right-film-bruce-willis

Chapter 8

Responding to Cyberhate

James Bacigalupo

When contemplating solutions to the issue of cyberhate, censorship is a common instinct. While it is certainly the legal right of companies like Twitter and YouTube to ban users on their platform, there are some important things worth considering. First, the vocabulary used by individuals on mainstream platforms is often coded to avoid censorship. In his book *The New Right*, Michael Malice (2019) noted that in 2016 YouTube began a campaign to suppress hate speech. In response, a user on 4Chan came up with the tactic of substituting racial slurs with common words. This strategy, "Operation Google," resulted in African Americans being referred to as "Googles" and Jews as "Skypes" (Malice, 2019). As the ADL notes, the constantly evolving terminology plays a huge role for members of these online subcultures:

> From the incel movement to the alt-right, many subcultures are born online, and members use the internet as their primary method of contact and radicalization. This means group "belonging" is demarcated by language and nomenclature rather than the uniforms and marches that defined earlier extremist groups. Earlier groups—and most subcultures in general—maintained their own language to establish and solidify a sense of group belonging, but for some of these more recently established groups, coded language is vital. It's used for everything from explaining how far one might be willing to go in the name of an extremist cause to weeding out interlopers and spies. ("The extremist medicine cabinet," 2019)

It is certainly important that the communications of far-right extremists can be understood. Keeping up with the lingo may be instrumental in determining if a person is on the verge of committing an act of violence. With that being said, the world does not need to be made aware of each new development in the far-right online lexicon. Taking these phrases out of obscure Internet forums and into the mainstream for the purpose of "awareness" only assists in expanding its reach. For example, holding up three fingers while touching the index and thumb is commonly known as the "OK" symbol. In 2017, 4Chan users began what they called "Operation O-KKK," to trick the mainstream media into believing that the "OK" symbol is a white supremacist gesture (Swales, 2019). Instead of pushing back against this ruse and continuing to use the hand symbol as it has been used for centuries, some people began policing its use and accusing those making "OK" symbols as signaling their affinity with white supremacy. In the latest example, Kelly Donohue, a *Jeopardy* contestant, was introduced as having won three games. He then flashed three fingers with his hand in an "OK" symbol. This resulted in an open letter posted by 467 purported former participants denouncing Donohue for the "white power hand gesture" (Hibberd, 2021). The 4Channers' plan worked masterfully as their prediction of a massive overreaction to the fake hate symbol came to fruition, but why did we let it? Not only did this give online trolls the power to dictate our use of a gesture that has existed for centuries; it encourages them to continue.

When users get banned from a platform, do they stop using social media altogether? We cannot say for sure, but it is unlikely they do. The most egregious examples of cyberhate are found on platforms that allow it. While this could be used as evidence of the effectiveness of censorship, it also demonstrates that cyberhate will always have a home. We shouldn't want to lead people down that path. While banning individuals is sometimes a necessity, being too strict could lead users to the online communities that are replete with extremism and linked to some of the violence highlighted throughout this book. Allowing people to block and mute users engaged in forms of online abuse should be encouraged, but banning people altogether should be seen as a last resort.

LAW ENFORCEMENT'S ROLE

The federal government has a history of infiltrating, prosecuting, and ultimately dismantling radical violent political organizations. What has changed is that far-right extremists who commit deadly violence are less likely to be members of formal organizations. Radical message boards have become the new meeting places for hate. These lone actors operate in an ideological community that they attend virtually rather than in-person. It is more straightforward to infiltrate or conduct surveillance on a location such as an Aryan compound or a KKK chapter than it is to monitor website posts and attempt to decipher who is actually likely to operationalize. The fact that three terrorists in a relatively short time span used the same website (8Chan) to post their manifesto is indicative of the individuals who frequent the site and their propensity to carry out violence. Understanding the patterns of individuals likely to attack is essential to prevent further acts of violence.

In the wake of the El Paso massacre, law enforcement took a more proactive approach in preventing mass shootings. In the four weeks following the attack, police arrested over 40 people as potential mass shooters (Mathias & Reilly, 2019). The problem of mass shootings in the United States is not limited to white nationalists; however, approximately one dozen of the arrestees were influenced by a far-right ideology. Some suspects even made threats that included attacking a Walmart, mimicking the El Paso shooting. Richard Clayton was arrested by authorities in Florida after posting "3 more days of probation left then I get my AR-15 back" and "Don't go to Walmart next week" (Mathias & Reilly, 2019). Clayton reportedly asked the arresting officer if he was Hispanic and added, "They come in and are ruining everything" (Mathias & Reilly, 2019).

Recent legislation has allowed law enforcement to take preventative steps in reducing mass shootings. Usually referred to as "Red-Flag" laws, these state laws give law enforcement and family members the ability to petition a state court to temporarily confiscate firearms from a person who has indicated that they may be a danger to themselves or others. While these laws were not enacted to tackle domestic political extremism solely, they have been used to combat this growing threat. In December of 2019 in Washington State, a suspected leader of the neo-Nazi extremist group Atomwaffen Division (see chapter 5 for further analysis on this group) was charged with unlawful possession of a firearm after violating a court order that barred him from possessing firearms for a year (Fields, 2019). Kaleb James Cole was considered an extreme risk and was alleged to have participated in "hate camps," where group members engage in military-style training exercises. This case emphasizes the importance of these laws considering it was the only legal mechanism preventing an individual leading a domestic terrorist organization from legally stockpiling weapons.

In response to the U.S. Capitol riots, the Department of Homeland Security plans to ramp up social media tracking in an effort to tackle violent extremism (Merchant, 2021). DHS announced that it is in its early stages of creating a new office in its intelligence branch that aims to better identify people, who are likely to engage in extremist-related violence. The agency is seeking contracts with tech companies, universities, and nonprofit groups for the office (Merchant, 2021). This could prove to be a tricky strategy for the DHS, both politically and legally. While the government is bound by the constitution, tech companies are not, and their collaboration could be seen as a way to get around these protections.

Polarization

In what he calls the "law of group polarization," Sunstein (1999) argues:

> [D]eliberation tends to move groups, and the individuals who compose them,
> toward a more extreme point in the direction indicated by their own predelib-
> eration judgments. For example, people who are opposed to the minimum wage
> are likely, after talking to each other, to be still more opposed; people who tend
> to support gun control are likely, after discussion, to support gun control with
> considerable enthusiasm; people who believe that global warming is a serious
> problem are likely, after discussion, to insist on severe measures to prevent
> global warming. (p. 1)

When this principle is applied to the online political landscape, it is no wonder that we continue to drift further apart, as the Internet, and especially social
media, play a larger role in our lives. Sunstein (2018) has since commented
on how his law of polarization relates to modern online echo chambers
describing them as "information cocoons" and that they lead to an "increase
in fragmentation, polarization and extremism."

While online political discourse is a reflection of our polarization, it also
reinforces it. Online media caters to our specific belief systems with curated
news stories that provide us with "evidence" of the biases we hold. Cross-
group interactions between the left and right are limited and often devolve
into toxic exchanges. Partisan media depicts those with opposing politics as
not just having a different perspective but having less moral standing and the
worst possible motives for their positions. This type of journalism is unfortunately incentivized by the fact that "going viral" on Twitter and Facebook
can be predicted by the mention of political opponents, meaning out-group
animosity drives traffic to stories (Rathje et al., 2021). We seem to be losing
our shared values, leaving us with more in common with the radicals on our
respective side than the moderates across the aisle. It is no wonder that people
are open to extreme movements when their media diet is constantly reiterat-
ing the threat posed by their ideological adversaries. It is in this climate that
extremist movements thrive. A way forward is to recalibrate our political
rhetoric away from the "us versus them" model that has come to define our
political discourse.

REFERENCES

Fields, A. (2019, December 17). Suspected Washington leader of neo-Nazi
group charged with violating gun ban under state's red-flag law. *The Seattle
Times*. Retrieved from https://www.seattletimes.com/seattle-news/crime/suspected

-washington-leader-of-neo-nazi-group-charged-with-violating-gun-ban-under
-states-red-flag-law/

Hibberd, J. (2021, April 21). "Jeopardy!" slammed for winner's alleged white power
hand gesture. *The Hollywood Reporter.* Retrieved from https://www.hollywoodre-
porter.com/tv/tv-news/jeopardy-slammed-winner-alleged-white-power-hand-ges-
ture-4175660/

Malice, M. (2019). *The new right: A journey to the fringe of american politics.* New
York: All Points Books.

Mathias, C., & Reilly, R. J. (2019, August 31). Over 40 people have been arrested as
potential mass shooters since El Paso. *Huffington Post.* Retrieved from https://m
.huffpost.com/us/entry/us_5d66d1eae4b063c341f9f2da

Merchant, N. (2021, May 20). U.S. to ramp up tracking of domestic extremism on
social media. *PBS.* Retrieved from https://www.pbs.org/newshour/nation/u-s-to
-ramp-up-tracking-of-domestic-extremism-on-social-media

Rathje, S., Van Bavel, J. J., & van der Linden, S. (2021). Out-group animosity drives
engagement on social media. *Proceedings of the National Academy of Sciences of
the United States of America, 118*(26), e2024292118.

Sunstein, C. R. (1999). The law of group polarization. John M. Olin Program in L. &
Econ. Working Paper No. 91, 1999.

Sunstein, C. R. (2018, January 22). Cass R Sunstein: Is social media good or bad
for democracy? *Facebook.* Retrieved from https://about.fb.com/news/2018/01/
sunstein-democracy/

Swales, V. (2019, December 17). How did the ok sign become a symbol of white
supremacy? *Independent.* Retrieved from https://www.independent.co.uk/news
/world/americas/ok-sign-white-power-supremacy-alt-right-4chan-trolling-hoax
-a9249846.html

The extremist medicine cabinet: A guide to online "pills" (2019, November 6). *Anti-
Defamation League.* Retrieved from https://www.adl.org/blog/the-extremist-medi-
cine-cabinet-a-guide-to-online-pills

Index

Note: Page locators in italics refer to figures.

privacy, 3, 9, 11, 45, 61n2, 67, 69
professional appearances, with websites and credibility, 34
prosecution, of white supremacists, 50–53, 108, 161
Proud Boys, 155
psychological harm, 55, 56
psychology of persuasion, 19–22, 33
PUA (pickup artist) community, 125

QAnon, 130, 155
qualitative coding, 91, 97
Quant, T., 1

race, 35, 53, 139, 142, 144
racial minorities, 29
racism, 17, 43–44, 73, 132, 147–48, 150–51, 159
racist/nationalist skinhead, alt-right websites, 146, 147
Racketeer Influenced and Corrupt Organizations (RICO) Act, 50–51, 61n6
Radix Journal, 139–40
Randazza, Marc, 75
ransomware attacks, 10, 72
Reason (magazine), 140
reasonable doubt, 47
rebranding, of white supremacist groups, 22, 35, 84
recruitment, *88*, 97–98, 120, 152
Reddit, incel forum, 127
"Red-Flag" laws, 161
Redice.tv, 68
"red pill," 114n9, 124, 126, 128
religion, 53, 146, 149, 151
religious minorities, 29
Republican Party, 141
RICO Act. *See* Racketeer Influenced and Corrupt Organizations (RICO) Act
rifles, 43, 49, 89, 122, 154
The Right Stuff (website), 77, 78, 80, 82, 84, 140
Rise Above Movement, 113

Rockwell, George Lincoln, 92–93, 95
Rodger, Elliot, 126–27
Roman law, 43
Roof, Dylann, 120–22, 130
Roosh V., 125
Rosen, L. D., 8
Ross, Alexander Reid, 113
Russel, Brandon, 89
Russia, 7, 9, 113
Rye Brook Dam systems, 11

Sandy Hook Elementary School, 57
Satanism, 25, 98, 108
Schager, Nick, 143
Schneider, Robert A., 18
scientific racism, 17, 73, 132
search engines, 5, 6, 28, 145–46
Sears, Robert, 128–29
Second Amendment, 87, 92
security, 9, 11–12, 65
self presentation, alt-right with, 144–45, 152–53, *154*
separation of powers, 45
sex crimes, against children, 51
sextortion attacks, 72–73
Shapiro, Ben, 144, 154
Shenma, 5
shootings, 126–27; mass, 29, 49, 57, 87–89, 102–3, *103–4*, 113, 119–23, 130, 138, 161
Siege (Mason), 91, 93–96, 98, 102, 110, 114n12
siege-pilled, 91, 114n9; alt-right and, 90, 96–99; community, 99–109; memes, 100, 103, 105–6, 108
Silk Road, 79
skinheads, 22, 35–38, 92, 129, 144, 146–47
Skype, 4, 7, 159
"Skypes," Jews as, 159
Slavros, Alexander, 113
smartphones, 4, 28
Smith, Dave, 141
Snapchat, 7
Soave, Robby, 140

University of Mississippi, 43
users, 7–8, 76, 160

Valeri, R., 22, 31, 129, 144, 145, 147, 152
value, bitcoin, 67, 69, *70*
value-relevant (ego) involvement, 20–21
vandalizing, of monuments, 43–44
victimization, hate crimes, 149
video communiqués, 90, 91, 112
videos, 23, 91–93, 100–101, *111*
violence, 1, 51, 88, 140, 149; Capitol
    riots, 155, 161; explanations for,
    128–32; with imagined war on white
    race, 120–24; manosphere and, 124–
    28; Unite the Right rally, 65, 69, 75,
    78, 84, 89, 93, 100–101, 119. *See
    also* neo-Nazi terrorist groups
Virtue, Graeme, 143
visual analysis, 91, 97
VK (VKontakte), 7

Wakabayashi, D., 9
Wall, D. S., 9
wallets: cryptocurrency, 66, 68, 69,
    71–73; finances of cyberhate groups,
    71–80, *81–82*, *83*. *See also* bitcoin,
    white supremacists and
Walmart shooting, 122, 130, 161
Walsh, Matt, 154
warnings, on hate websites, 28–29
Watering Hole, 102–3
wearable technology, 4, 5
webpages, 2, *37*, 37–38
websites, alt-right: analysis of, 144–53,
    154; audience, 151; culture, 138–39,
    144, 149–51, *150*; functionality of,
    152, *153*; hate ideology, 147–49,
    148; with identity, 144, 146–47, *147*;
    methods, 145–46; presentation style

of, 153, *154*; *The Right Stuff*, 77, 78,
    80, 82, 84, 140; variables and results,
    146–53
websites, hate: *The Daily Stormer*, 6,
    57, 58, 68, 74–77, 138; headers on,
    28, 33; with professional appearances
    and credibility, 34; recognizing, 28–
    38, *32*, *37*; warnings on, 28–29
WeChat, 7
Weiner, Bernard, 129
WhatsApp, 7
White, William, 52
White Aryan Resistance, 92, 99, 100
white genocide, myth of, 2, 112,
    120–24
white jihad, 108
White Knights, 51
white nationalists, 6, 22, 139, 142–43,
    146
White Power (newspaper), 123
white supremacists, 2, 6, 10, 17–19, 34,
    36–38, 58; donors to, 71–80, *81–82*,
    83; doxing of, 138; ideology, 130;
    language and terminology of, 124,
    159–60; prosecution of, 50–53, 108,
    161; rebranding of, 22, 35, 84. *See
    also* bitcoin, white supremacists and;
    neo-Nazi terrorist groups
Wolters, Raymond, 17–19
World Wide Web, 1, 3–5
Wu, Brianna, 62n14

Yahoo, 5, 130
Yiannopoulos, Milo, 144
YouTube, 7, 55, 68, 71–73, 79, 125,
    138–39, 159

Zannettou, Savvas, 120
Zimmerman, George, 121
Zuckerberg, Mark, 7, 60

About the Contributors

James Bacigalupo is a doctoral student in the Criminology and Justice Studies program at the University of Massachusetts, Lowell. His research interests include political extremism, institutional corrections, gangs, and media representations of crime. He works full time as a correctional officer in Boston, MA, where he has been since 2011. James received his B.S. in criminal justice in 2010 and M.S. in criminal justice in 2018, earning both degrees from Salem State University.

Kevin Borgeson is an associate professor of criminal justice at Salem State University and former research fellow for the Center for Holocaust and Genocide Studies. He has published several articles on female skinheads, gay skinheads, and skinheads on the Internet. He is coeditor with Robin Valeri of the book *Hate Crimes: Typology, Motivations, and Victims.* Professor Borgeson has appeared on various national and international media outlets on the topic of hate, hate groups, white nationalists, cyberhate, and hate crimes.

Robin Maria Valeri is a professor of psychology and the director of the Center for Nonviolence, St. Bonaventure University. She graduated with a B.A., cum laude, in psychology from Cornell University and an M.A. and Ph.D. in psychology from Syracuse University. Valeri's current research focuses on hate, hate groups, and terrorist organizations.

John Bambenek is the president of Bambenek Labs, a global cybersecurity threat intelligence firm, and has been working in cybersecurity and investigations for over 20 years. He has led large international investigations into ransomware, election manipulation, and other high profile cybersecurity threats. He currently tracks extremist cryptocurrency fundraising by neo-Nazi and other hard-right groups in the United States and abroad. He has served as a pro bono expert witness for litigation against those groups to help recover damages for victims of those groups. He is currently finishing his Ph.D. at the University of Illinois in informatics studying cybersecurity machine learning.

Samantha Hausserman is a senior comparative religion and social justice studies double major at Miami University (Oxford, Ohio), with a concentration in crime, law, and social justice. In her undergraduate career, she has done research on radically controversial religious groups, such as fundamentalist Christian and Islamist groups, and on immigration policy, as well as working at nonprofit organizations, which focus on systemic issues including affordable housing, food security, and immigration justice. She currently works as a fellow for an on-campus interfaith initiative, doing community organizing and event planning around interfaith collaboration. After graduation, Sami plans to continue her education in a Master of Social Work program, focusing on community organizing and systemic injustice.

Janine Fodor is an attorney who works as in-house counsel for Iroquois Group, Inc. She is an instructor at St. Bonaventure University, where she teaches courses including cybersecurity law and policy, business law, and business ethics. Janine received a B.A. in philosophy from the University of Michigan, earned an M.Phil. in history and philosophy of science from Cambridge University, and received her J.D. from Yale Law School.

Dr. Michael Hoffman received his doctorate in higher education administration from Northeastern University, where he received the Dean's Medal Award. He also holds an M.B.A. from St. Bonaventure and a bachelor's in computer science from the University of Pittsburgh at Bradford. He serves as an associate provost, dean of Graduate Studies, and the chief information officer at St. Bonaventure University. Hoffman is also a part-time instructor in St. Bonaventure's School of Communications, in which he regularly teaches a graduate course in change leadership. He has published numerous peer-reviewed papers, presented at conferences, and serves as a co-chair of St. Bonaventure's strategic planning committee. Hoffman serves as chair of the Board of Directors of Universal Primary Care, a federally qualified health center headquartered in Olean, New York.

Dr. Michael Loadenthal is a researcher, consultant, and professor working at the intersections of political violence, protest, security, and the law. He has organized with grassroots, direct action movements on four continents and regularly serves as a strategist for emergent networks, often providing digital and operational security training for antifascist and other social movement researchers. Michael serves as the founder and executive director of the Prosecution Project, the executive director of the Peace and Justice Studies Association, and a postdoctoral research fellow for the University of Cincinnati's Center for Cyber Strategy and Policy. He has previously worked as a professor of sociology, terrorism studies, and research methods for Georgetown University, Miami University, the University of Cincinnati, George Mason University, the University of Malta's Mediterranean Academy of Diplomatic Studies, and Jessup Correctional Institutions' Prison Scholars Program.

Michael holds a Ph.D. from the School for Conflict Analysis and Resolution at George Mason University and a master's degree in terrorism studies from the Centre for the Study of Terrorism and Political Violence at the University of St Andrews. He has published frequently in venues including *Critical Studies on Terrorism, Perspectives on Terrorism, Journal of Applied Security Research, Radical Criminology, Global Society*, and the *Journal for the Study of Radicalism*, which described his work as "the cutting edge of movement Studies" (2016, 10:2; 5). His most recent single-authored book, *The Politics of Attack* (Manchester University Press, 2017), investigates contemporary, clandestine networks of insurrectionary anarchists and the development of the *communique*. He has also recently published three edited volumes, focused on peace history (Routledge, 2020), environmental resistance movements (University of Massachusetts Press, 2020), and research methods for investigating political violence (Routledge, 2021).

Matthew Thierry, M.A., is a doctoral student in the Philosophy and Religion Department at the California Institute of Integral Studies, with a background in world literature and cultural studies. An educator, organizer, and writer, Matthew currently works as a middle school social studies department chair in the San Francisco Bay Area. His work focuses on the intersection of ecology, spirituality, political activism, violent extremism, and peacebuilding and has been presented in diverse forums including the American Society for Esotericism, the International Big History Association, the International Society for the Study of Information, and the British Society for Criminology, as well as journals for bioregionalism, community organizing, and green anarchy. When he is not doing research or writing stories, he can usually be found playing with his puppy at the shoreline.